"Ralph Parsons is one service comes to be w of the Fur Trade."

"[Ralph Parsons] was an intrepid pioneer, a courageous explorer, a lovable personality and a man who served this company with selfless devotion."
—Robert H. Chesshire

"Mr. Parsons was a very honest man and a strong HBC man. He would always put the HBC interests ahead of his own...he knew his work, he did it well, and he looked for no other recognition than the one he awarded another faithful servant, 'He was a ... good man'."
—Leonard Budgell

"Parsons ruled over an immense empire with the righteousness of a latter day Cromwell. The company was everything to him, not just his job but his religion."
—Peter C. Newman

"[Ralph Parsons] was a legend in his time and in 1992 was probably better known among the people of the north than in Newfoundland."
—John Parsons

"Ralph Parsons was a figure of national importance."
—Anne Morton

"Arctic travel held no terrors for him for he went where few white people had ventured before his time."
—Frank G. Mercer

"Mr. Parsons was admired by all. A kinder-hearted man, you never met, with a heart the size of an ox and a great sense of dry humour."
—William O. Douglas

"A tall, good-looking man, with a pleasant if rather abstracted manner, he is one of the ablest executives I have ever met...the great Company is Parsons' god. He thinks of it, and works tirelessly day and night for it."
—Henry T. Munn

"Parsons had established an excellent record in the company's Fur Trade Department by the time the Canadian Committee chose him to direct it."
—Arthur J. Ray

The King of Baffin Land

The Story of William Ralph Parsons
Last Fur Trade Commissioner
of the Hudson's Bay Company

John Parsons and Burton K. Janes

Ralph Parsons (about 1930).

The King of Baffin Land

The Story of William Ralph Parsons
Last Fur Trade Commissioner
of the Hudson's Bay Company

John Parsons and Burton K. Janes

Creative Publishers
St. John's, Newfoundland
1996

© 1996, John Parsons and Burton K. Janes

Appreciation is expressed to *The Canada Council* for publication assistance.

All rights reserved. No part of this work covered by the copyrights hereon may be reproduced or used in any form or by any means—graphic, electronic or mechanical—without the prior written permission of the publisher. Any requests for photocopying, recording, taping or information storage and retrieval systems of any part of this book shall be directed in writing to the Canadian Reprography Collective, 214 King Street West, Suite 312, Toronto, Ontario M5H 2S6.

All Biblical selections quoted herein are from the King James Version.

∝ Printed on acid-free paper

Cover art: Helen Parsons Shepherd, R.C.A., L.LD.
Cover design: David Peckford

Published by
CREATIVE BOOK PUBLISHING
a division of 10366 Newfoundland Limited
a Robinson-Blackmore Printing & Publishing associated company
P.O. Box 8660, St. John's, Newfoundland A1B 3T7

Printed in Canada by:
ROBINSON-BLACKMORE PRINTING & PUBLISHING

Canadian Cataloguing in Publication Data

Parsons, John, 1939-
    The king of Baffin land
    Includes bibliographical references and index.
    ISBN 1-895387-65-5

1. Parsons, William Ralph, 1881-1956.   2. Hudson's Bay Company — History.   3. Hudson's Bay Company — Biography.   4. Fur traders — Canada — Biography.   I. Janes, Burton K., 1957-   II. Title.

FC2173.1.P37P37   1996   971.9'02'092   C96-950068-8

*Dedicated to the
memory of
Flora May (House) Parsons
1887 – 1920,
Dorcas Catherine (Mosdell) Parsons
1856 – 1940,
and
Rachel Fannie ("Datie") Parsons, O.B.E.
1878 – 1966
and for
three lovely ladies
Betty, Elsie and Sherry*

Official Hudson's Bay Company Coat of Arms

Table of Contents

Foreword ix

Preface xi

Introduction xvii

Prologue 1

Chapter 1 — The Man and His Background 7

Chapter 2 — First Years With the Company 27

Chapter 3 — Adventure in the North 43

Chapter 4 — Years of Joy and Years of Sorrow 57

Chapter 5 — Expanding the Fur Trade in the North 69

Chapter 6 — North to Adventure—The Odyssey of 1934 93

Chapter 7 — Conflict and Resignation 111

Chapter 8 — Retirement Years 129

Chapter 9 — A Date With Destiny 149

Chapter 10 — The Last Voyage 163

Epilogue 175

Appendices 183

Bibliography 217

Index 227

FOREWORD

oon after the death of my father, William Ralph Parsons, I, along with friends and other family members, felt that a biography should be written about him, relating his adventures and accomplishments during his four decades with the Hudson's Bay Company, from which he retired as the youngest and last Fur Trade Commissioner in May 1940.

For almost forty years, I have kept my father's official papers and I have tried on many occasions to get someone to use them to research and write a book about him.

At long last in August 1993 my search was rewarded when John Parsons and Burton K. Janes, two Newfoundland scholars and writers, agreed to undertake the project. They estimated they would have the biography written and published in less than three years.

I loaned them my father's papers and since they began their research and writing I have cooperated with them to the best of my ability as I tried to recall and record for them stories about family relationships and anecdotes about my father.

From the beginning two men who knew my father, my cousin, Jack Hambling, who lives in South River, Newfoundland (himself a writer), and Frank G. Mercer of Bay Roberts, who spent many years as a policeman in the North, have helped in every way they could. I appreciate their efforts. Undoubtedly, Parsons and Janes feel the same way.

Both biographers have shared the research and writing and have kept in close contact with me from the start. They have asked me to recall events in my life long past, right up to the day my father died.

A trip was made to the Hudson's Bay Company Archives in Winnipeg, where most of the documents pertaining to my father's career with the great Company are kept. Trips have also been made to the National Archives in Ottawa, the Anglican Church Archives and the Hudson's Bay Company corporate offices, both in Toronto. These trips were necessary since there were many documents relating to my father's life and work with the Company which he himself did not possess.

I have read the manuscript, and it is easy to see that the authors have worked long and hard to produce a book which is both factual and interesting and which grips the reader's interest from start to finish. For my part, I have learned many things about my father that were previously unknown to me.

It is my opinion that the biographers have done justice to their subject, this native of Bay Roberts, Newfoundland, who in 1900 joined the Hudson's Bay Company as an apprentice clerk in Cartwright, Labrador, and forty years later retired from the top position in its Fur Trade Department.

My father died in 1956, and although I feel that his modesty would not have permitted him to relate many of the incidents included in this biography, I also feel that he would be very pleased—as I am myself—with this very interesting account of his colourful, exciting, and fulfilling life.

—*David R. Parsons*
Hantsport, Nova Scotia
August 31, 1995

David R. Parsons, Hantsport, Nova Scotia, 1995.

David R. Parsons (b. 1919) is the only son of William Ralph Parsons of Hudson's Bay Company fame. He grew up in Bay Roberts and Winnipeg. During the Second World War, he served overseas with the Royal Canadian Air Force. After the War, he earned a degree in Mechanical Engineering and has worked in that capacity in Nova Scotia for most of his life. Now retired, he lives with his wife, Betty (née Christian), in Hantsport, Nova Scotia.

PREFACE

hrough the years, Bay Roberts and area have produced certain outstanding men and women. Some have made good by remaining in Newfoundland, indeed, a few in their own communities; while others have made a name for themselves outside their communities or outside Newfoundland, and a few outside Canada.

Ralph Parsons was a great Newfoundlander and a true Bay Roberts man, although he spent a large part of his life "up in Canada," the expression that was used in pre-Confederation days. He retired to Newfoundland in 1940 and died there sixteen years later.

Generally, people who occupy important positions in life leave behind them a collection of letters, reports, memos, and other documents, which are then referred to as "papers." Ralph Parsons' personal papers were stored in two filing cabinets in his son's house at Hantsport, Nova Scotia, from 1956 — the year of Parsons' death —until they were brought to Newfoundland by one of the co-authors and his wife in August 1993.

David R. Parsons, Ralph Parsons' only son and official owner of his father's papers, has always believed that his father, because of his important positions with the Hudson's Bay Company, deserved to have his story written and published, but until the summer of 1993 nobody came forward to take on the project. On August 7, 1993, we, along with Jack Hambling, Ralph Parsons' nephew, and Frank G. Mercer, a retired policeman who spent most of his life in the North and a friend of the Parsons family, discussed the project. In the end, we decided to take on the job. We then telephoned David Parsons in Hantsport and relayed our decision to him. He was pleased with our decision. So this book is a fully-authorized biography. The only restriction was that David wanted the right to read each chapter and make suggestions and changes, if he felt they were necessary. This right was granted to a limited degree. Jack Hambling and Frank Mercer agreed to be our main constructive critics, and both men have assisted considerably throughout the project. Our tentative deadline to have the manuscript in the hands of the publisher was set for August 31, 1995.

In late August 1993, John Parsons and his wife, Elsie, drove to Hantsport, and brought back to Newfoundland Ralph Parsons' papers, along with several books and photographs from David Parsons' collection. Jack Hambling and Frank Mercer loaned us a number of books, as well. We have spent two years researching and writing this biography.

In August 1994, John and Elsie Parsons spent almost two weeks in the Hudson's Bay Company Archives in Winnipeg, Manitoba. Since that visit, photocopies of many documents from the Archives have been sent to us. Judith Beattie and Anne Morton and staff at the Archives have made every effort to accommodate us, assisting us in so many ways. It is doubtful that this biography could have been written without the help of Anne Morton, who has become John Parsons' favourite penpal! To her we express our sincere thanks and appreciation.

In addition, we express our appreciation to all those who have replied to our letters and helped us by sending us material relating to Ralph Parsons, the Hudson's Bay Company, and the fur trade in the North. Our thanks are due to the following individuals from outside Newfoundland and Labrador: Peter Nichols, Len Budgell, Reuben Ploughman, Farley Mowat, Peter C. Newman, Arthur J. Ray, John E. Foster, Robert H. Chesshire, Chris K. Koskie, Pam Cormack, Gerald Parsons, Harold Horwood, Victor Parsons, Isaac Butler, Brian Grose, Dorothy Kealey, Tom Lindley, Paul Lemieux, Louise Bertrand, Bev Sherman, Marie Reidke and Dorothy Bosma. In Newfoundland and Labrador we wish to thank Eric N. Dawe, James Y. Parsons, Eric M. Gosse, Llewellyn Bradbury, Nigel Rusted, Newton Morgan, Edward H. Vokey, Michael Harrington, Harry D.Roach,* George Pinkston, Stephen Dawe, Guy Fowlow, Cyril Goodyear, Leonard Coates, Greta French, Helen Bowering, Eileen (Dawe) Elms, Doris J. Saunders, Augustus H. Flowers, Norma (Cave) Sparkes, Margaret Knott and Cecil E. Bradbury.**

As a background to our study, we have read most of the secondary source material available. It was easy to become hooked on books dealing with the North, whether or not they related directly to our project. The following are useful books: Ray Price's *The Howling Arctic*, J.W. Anderson's *Fur Trader's Story*, Arthur J. Ray's *The Canadian Fur Trade in the Industrial Age*, and Peter C. Newman's *Merchant Princes*. These books,

---

* Harry D. Roach (Sept. 24, 1913 - May 16, 1996) passed away while this book was in the process of publication.
** Cecil E. Bradbury (Feb. 6, 1901 -Jan. 13, 1996) also passed away while this book was in the process of publication.

along with the others listed in our bibliography, have helped to put everything into proper perspective.

We will admit that we have conducted very few interviews, because most of the people who knew Ralph Parsons on a personal basis are long since dead. The two most notable exceptions are Len Budgell and Robert H. Chesshire. For firsthand information we have had to return time and again to our constructive critics, Jack Hambling and Frank Mercer, and especially David Parsons. We have "forced" David to write more essays, letters and mini-reports about his father than he ever thought possible. However, we feel that David has enjoyed every minute of it. Frank Mercer wrote an excellent article about our project when we began. A synopsis of this article was published, thanks to editor Heather May, in *The Compass*,* a local newspaper. Jack Hambling has written the Introduction to the book.

We have included in our Appendices items which we feel add something to the biography, and we have chosen a selection of photographs to illustrate our work. Reference notes are included, since we believe the proper way to write a historical biography is to document all sources of information. We have included a Prologue and Epilogue, because we wanted to say a few things about Ralph Parsons that would probably not fit well in the ten chapters.

John C.W. Parsons, the co-author's son, and Barbara Derkson, a professional typist, have helped with the typing. Karen Janes, the co-author's sister, has assisted on countless occasions by helping her brother become more computer literate. John C.W. Parsons has, over the past two years, checked out many books relevant to our project from the library at Memorial University of Newfoundland. Jessie Parsons, the co-author's mother, and Ada Mercer, Frank Mercer's wife, have read the manuscript and have offered suggestions for improvement. Our families have been helpful at all times and have learned to put up with us during the time we have been "obsessed" with Ralph Parsons.

We apologize to anyone we have forgotten to mention. If such is the case, then it certainly has not been intentional. All those individuals who have assisted us have, of course, helped to improve this biography immensely. Their collective input has been invaluable and most encourag-

---

* *The Compass*, Carbonear Newfoundland, Vol. 26, No. 45, November 9, 1993, Section B.

ing. Of course, we take full responsibility for any shortcomings this book may have. *Errare humanum est*. It is human to err.

Finally, we wish to thank Don Morgan, our publisher, for his professional help and guidance, the people at the Hudson's Bay Company corporate offices in Toronto, particularly Brian C. Grose and Hélène Yaremko-Jarvis, for their help and assistance, both tangible and intangible, the staff of the National Archives in Ottawa, Dorothy Kealey and the staff of the Anglican Church Archives in Toronto, Robert Richard of the Canada Council in Ottawa for a grant towards our travel and research, Catherine R. Parsons, for providing the co-author, her father, with a place to stay during two research trips to Toronto, Constance R. Parsons who helped with the chapter on the genealogy of the Parsons' clan, Helen Parsons Shepherd, who did the artwork for the cover, and David Peckford, who designed the cover of the book.

We are especially grateful to David R. Parsons for his invaluable help and assistance and particularly his steadfast commitment to our project. We thank him most sincerely for entrusting his father's valuable papers to us. It was David's commitment that launched the project in the first place. We thank Jack Hambling and Frank G. Mercer for their help and especially their confidence in us. As well, we wish to thank the following individuals, each of whom made a small financial contribution towards our travel and research: Don and Della Parsons, Eric N. Dawe, Allan M. Ogilvie, Clyde H. Parsons, Alice M. Butler and Jessie Parsons. Last, but by no means least, we thank the two most important people in our lives, our wives, Elsie and Sherry, the most loving and devoted critics of all.

—*John Parsons*
Burton K. Janes
Shearstown, Bay Roberts, and St. John's, Newfoundland
August 31, 1993 - August 31, 1995.

* * *

Part of the royalties from this project will be donated to the Grace General Hospital, Health Sciences Centre, St. Clare's Mercy Hospital, Janeway Children's Hospital, St. John's, and the Carbonear General Hospital, in memory of Ralph Parsons (1881-1956), David's father, George W. Parsons (1911-73), John's father, and Eva H. Janes (1914-80), Burton's mother.

J.P.
B.K.J.

Arctic Mood

For those who have been to the Arctic
I do not need to declaim.
You are forever gathered to its beauty;
to its long winter of night days with their swift
crackling phenomena of Northern Lights;
to its bright beautiful summer with the never setting
sun and far frozen distances with pageant of incredible
color; to its bewildering bird and animal life filled
with strange interest;
forever holding in admiration the little people who
have made the Arctic their own, the Eskimo, who have
by their nimble wit wrested from its desolate wastes
all things for happy living.
All of these will no more let you go than that the Pole
Star should fall from its place in the vault of heaven.

—Eva Alvey Richards, *Arctic Mood,*
A Narrative of Arctic Adventures, 1949, p. 9.

From the great days of the fur trade until the Company was reorganized in the 1970s, the Hudson's Bay Company conducted its far-flung business and trading activities under its own distinctive Company flag, the familiar red ensign with the HBC initials in the fly.

INTRODUCTION
Jack Hambling

In those halcyon days of long ago when I was still young enough to believe, unequivocally, in the magic of Christmas, men of "great do and dare" were, for the most part, of the fictitious variety as portrayed in the writings of Jack London, James Fenimore Cooper, or Zane Grey. Then, in 1940, when I was thirteen, I got to know firsthand a man whose exploits equalled, and, in many cases, surpassed those of storybook legend. That man was Ralph Parsons, my mother's eldest brother. The reason why prior to 1940 our relationship was, to say the least, tenuous was simply because his visits home were so few and far between that he had very little time to spend with his parents, much less a teenaged nephew.

Here, at last, is a long-overdue portrait of that remarkable individual who, at sixteen, in true Horatio Alger fashion, left home and from humble beginnings—that of apprentice clerk with the Hudson's Bay Company at Cartwright, Labrador—retired forty years later as Fur Trade Commissioner. En route to that important position, he established no less than twenty-eight trading posts on Baffin Island and along the coast of Hudson Bay, every one a lasting memorial to his exceptional vision and determination, no small accomplishment for a man from outport Newfoundland, or from any other place, for that matter.

A veritable legend in his time, he became known throughout the Arctic as the "King of Baffin Land." Of this king without a throne, Archibald Lang Fleming, first Anglican Bishop of the Arctic, has written:

> He was naturally reserved, independent, self-controlled. He also had amazing powers of detachment and never appeared to be surprised no matter how unexpected or absurd a report or incident might be. These qualities enabled him to rise step by step in the Company's service until he became Fur Trade Commissioner in charge of the whole extensive and complicated transportation system. There can be little doubt that the fur trade in Canada owes more to Ralph Parsons than to any other individual during the first half of the twentieth century. I do not make this statement because he established more fur trading posts than any four of his predecessors as commissioners, but because he raised the whole tone of the fur trade. He was ruthless in his determination to stop drunkenness and immorality, not perhaps because of any deep religious conviction,

but because he knew that these spelled ruin to both trapper and trader.

Writing any biography, even under the most favourable conditions, is, by its very nature, a demanding job. Portraying Ralph Parsons is exceptionally so. A man of quiet dignity and uncompromising honesty, "R.P.," as he was known by his contemporaries, was not predisposed to speaking about his many accomplishments. Neither, unfortunately for his biographers, did he record all that much, nor, with few exceptions, did those who were close to him, apart from his brother, Richard Augustus who, in 1958, wrote a poetic tribute to him, entitled "To 'R.P.'." Perhaps the following excerpt will further enhance this Introduction:

> *But yet old Hudson's Bay men now remain,*
> *Who shared his trek from Baffin Bay to Nain,*
> *And still with kindliness do yet recall,*
> *How he would let his conduct answer all*
> *Its consequence, reluctant to complain*
> *Of other's faults and thus transpose the blame;*
> *How lonely lands and seas, beyond the reach*
> *Of subterfuge, so disciplined his speech*
> *In ways of truth, that men became as fond*
> *Of his own spoken word, as of his bond.*
> *They too, are wont to note he rose to place;*
> *But let no eminence of his efface*
> *The memory of loyalties of those,*
> *Who travelled times agone the Arctic snows;*
> *That igloo, tilt, that lodged an early friend,*
> *Was his to hearten still, to nourish, fend....*
> *To speak of his achievements, I refrain.*
> *His way of life alone, I but maintain,*
> *And you my masters will not hold me rude,*
> *If I, in circumstance of love, conclude:*
> *He loved his friends, deserved of them their trust,*
> *And feared his God, and was in mercy just.*

I have no difficulty in recommending this biography to the reading public, if for no other reason than that it is but a just and lasting tribute to a distinguished Newfoundlander and a decent human being. Frank G. Mercer, former Staff Sergeant with the Royal Canadian Mounted Police and himself a veteran of the North, wrote in a letter to the editor of *The Evening Telegram* (St. John's, Newfoundland) on March 21, 1991: "His name was synonymous with integrity; an outstanding personality, one of whom Newfoundland can be justifiably proud." As I am to be his nephew.

Born in Bay Roberts in 1927, Jack Hambling now makes his home in South River, Conception Bay. A dedicated outdoorsman, he has written two books, *Stage Heads and Warm Dandelions* (1985) and *The Second Time Around: Growing Up in Bay Roberts* (1992).

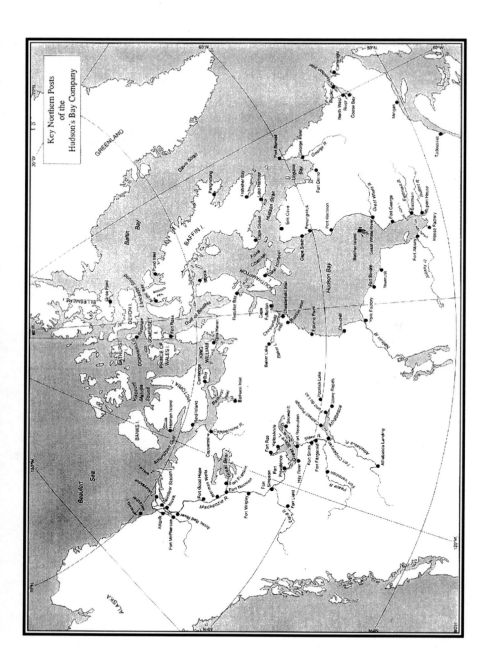

Prologue

Two roads diverged in a wood, and I—
I took the one less travelled by,
And that has made all the difference.
    —From *The Road Not Taken* by Robert Frost

Between 1900 and 1940 and even a few years beyond, Ralph Parsons of Bay Roberts, Newfoundland, had an outstanding career with the Hudson's Bay Company. He began as an apprentice in Cartwright, on the Labrador coast, and retired as Fur Trade Commissioner, the senior executive position in the Fur Trade Department in Winnipeg, Manitoba. As Fur Trade Commissioner he headed an organizational staff of some fifteen executive personnel. Based in Winnipeg from 1931 to 1940, he had full responsibility for the Fur Trade Department, as well as the extensive transportation system of the Hudson's Bay Company right across Canada's northern frontier from the Labrador coast to the coast of British Columbia.

Up until his taking over as Fur Trade Commissioner on January 1, 1931, Parsons had a very successful career as a Post—and later District—Manager in the Eastern Arctic. His senior executive position in Winnipeg during the 1930s was not an easy one to hold, given the economic climate of the times. In terms of training and experience, he appeared to be the ideal man to take over from Charles H. French at the end of 1930, and he worked hard to build up and reorganize the Fur Trade Department in his first five years as Fur Trade Commissioner, but by early 1935 the Canadian Committee, the Winnipeg-based Board which was a "sub-board" of the London Board in England, had come to the conclusion that Parsons was no longer the man to do the job they wanted done.

As far back as 1918 the then Fur Trade Commissioner, Norman Bacon, resigned because he could not get along with the Canadian Committee.[1] The Committee members believed they could make the Fur Trade Department more efficient by "applying modern business procedures."[2] However, it failed to work, at least the way the Committee envisaged. In 1930 the Committee, now exercising its new authority, granted by the London Board, to make appointments, effectively forced the then Fur Trade Commissioner out and replaced him by Ralph Parsons. By 1935 they were ready to get rid of Parsons as well, but it took five years to do it, during which time the Fur Trade Department of the Hudson's Bay Company suffered, not because of a lack of hard work or enthusiasm on the part of Ralph Parsons, but because of the insistence of the Canadian Committee and the General Manager that the Fur Trade Department be organized differently. The process of organization took time. The Committee seems to have lost faith in Parsons because of his strong resistance to delegation of authority.[3] Robert H. Chesshire, who worked closely with the Fur Trade Commissioner, says that Parsons' difficulties came about because of "his refusal to recognize that considerable changes had to be made in the administrative management of the Department."[4] For his part, Parsons felt that the Fur Trade Department was his domain, and he felt fully competent to run it the way he wanted to. His competence was not brought into question, but even with his expertise in the fur trade, it seems that he could not do enough to satisfy George Allan, head of the Canadian Committee, and Philip Chester, the General Manager.

The implementation of the new organizational and business procedures, to which Parsons could not become reconciled, caused him considerable stress, and eventually he felt, in the words of his son, David, that "It would be better for all concerned, including himself, if he retired and handed over the reins to newer blood."[5] Parsons admired his young assistant, Robert H. Chesshire for his organizational ability, and it was Chesshire who was his choice to become the next head of the Fur Trade Department. Thus, Chesshire during the 1940s became responsible for the wholesale changes within the Fur Trade Department that the Canadian Committee wanted implemented.

Arthur J. Ray believes "that the increasingly complex nature of the fur trade itself caused particularly serious management problems for a large organization like the Hudson's Bay Company."[6] By the beginning of the twentieth century, two particular types of fur trade had developed—the traditional trade which operated as a credit-barter system, and the newer line post business which operated on the basis of cash trading. Ray claims that to operate both types of trade,

...the company needed to have skilled managers, appropriate policies, and an administrative structure that provided both enough central control and enough flexibility at the district level to deal with local circumstances in a coherent fashion. The company largely failed to achieve this objective.[7]

In the three decades before Ralph Parsons became Fur Trade Commissioner, Company officials had given their attention to other aspects of the total business operations, particularly real estate interests and retail merchandising, and effectively had neglected the fur trade. Thus Ralph Parsons in 1931 inherited a vitally important division of the Hudson's Bay Company that had suffered long years of organizational neglect. The Canadian Committee wanted organizational changes to come about overnight but, given the economic conditions of the 1930s, this proved to be rather difficult, even for a fur trade expert like Ralph Parsons.

With Parsons' excellent record with the Company, it seems that he was the ideal man to get the Fur Trade Department back on track, but time was to prove that even he could not fulfil the expectations of George Allan and Philip Chester. Historians will probably argue about this for decades to come, but to date Arthur J. Ray's analytical assessment of the situation seems reasonable and is consistent with our own research:

> It was not until the 1930s that the Canadian Committee undertook a series of detailed studies of the problems of the Fur Trade Department, with the intention of rejuvenating this ailing division. But, by that time the administration of the department had broken down entirely, and the various district managers were conducting their affairs generally as they pleased.
>
> Once the Canadian Committee was ready to take action, it clashed with Fur Trade Commissioner Ralph Parsons and the London board because of differences in basic management philosophies. The Canadian Committee members believed the fur trade should be conducted along 'modern management' lines which involved having the commissioner establish broad policy guidelines, while he delegated operational authority to his assistants, who were experts in the fields of accounting, merchandising, transportation and communications, and fur buying. The trouble was that Parsons was an old-style manager, who had worked his way up through the service in the days when the company expected good post managers to be generalists who had a grasp of all aspects of the business. Reflecting his background, Parsons steadfastly refused to delegate authority. Board members, particularly Governor Cooper, were more sympa-

thetic to Parsons and to the older traditions he represented. As far as the board was concerned, the fur trade was unlike any other business and therefore it had to be managed differently.[8]

By mid-1939, since matters appeared to be going from bad to worse, Ralph Parsons felt that there was only one way he could extricate himself from the administrative quagmire in which he then found himself. Resignation was the only option open to him. A move to another division within the Company would have been a demotion, and further, his expertise was in the fur trade. He set his retirement date for May 31, 1940.

Whether or not the situation that led to his retirement can be attributed to a lack of ability or understanding on his part, or whether or not the Canadian Committee and Philip Chester expected too much too fast from him is open to sustained debate; but Parsons, being the independent-minded individual that he was, made his own decision which, in retrospect, was the best one for all concerned, including himself.

Early in June 1940 Ralph Parsons left Winnipeg, purchased a new car in Ontario, and headed back to Newfoundland, his forty-year career as a Hudson's Bay Company man behind him. The circumstances under which he left the Company stayed with him for the rest of his life, and he probably always believed that, given a fair chance, he could have done what was expected of him. There is no doubt that he felt that Philip Chester and the Canadian Committee could have been more cooperative and considerate. The situation that led to his resignation probably affected him more than he admitted, as he indicated in a prepared speech to a gathering of friends in Montreal a short time after his resignation.[9]

During the 1940s Parsons worked out of the St. John's office and inspected the Hudson's Bay Company trading posts along the Labrador coast, but eventually he severed virtually all connections with the Company, other than carrying on correspondence with certain Company personnel—some still with the Company, others, retired—whom he considered his friends.

His official papers, which he accumulated himself, his personnel file in the Hudson's Bay Company Archives in Winnipeg and his extensive correspondence file in the National Archives in Ottawa, indicate clearly that he was a real gentleman, a diplomat, and a thoroughly fine man to the very end of his life.

Anne Morton of the Hudson's Bay Company Archives in Winnipeg says that "Ralph Parsons was a figure of national importance."[10] Peter C. Newman has referred to him as "the wonderful Ralph Parsons."[11] Michael Harrington of St. John's, in his "Offbeat History" columns in *The Evening Telegram*, has on many occasions written about Ralph Parsons, praising him as an outstanding Newfoundlander.[12] Arthur J. Ray writes that "Parsons had established an excellent record in the company's Fur Trade Department by the time the Canadian Committee chose him to direct it."[13] The authors of this biography concur with these assessments; furthermore, we feel that he was one of the very few truly significant individuals in the Hudson's Bay Company in this century.

When we began this study, one of the first Hudson's Bay Company men we talked with was Len Budgell from Rigolet and North West River, Labrador, who now lives in retirement in St. Boniface, Manitoba. During the course of our discussion in the Battery Hotel in St. John's, at which Ralph Parsons' only son, David, was present, Budgell said several times that he hoped our biography of Ralph Parsons would "do him justice." At one point, Budgell even said, "If you don't do him justice, then don't write a book about him at all." In subsequent letters to us, Budgell made the same or similar comments.[14]

It is our belief that Len Budgell was and is fully aware of the difficulties that Ralph Parsons encountered in his job as Fur Trade Commissioner in his last years with the Hudson's Bay Company. Budgell, who worked in the field in the Fur Trade Department in both Western Canada and the Eastern Arctic, was a good friend of Parsons and may have been a confidant of his during the late 1930s. Of course, Budgell sided with Parsons, and we believe he feels that Parsons did not get a fair deal from George W. Allan and Philip A. Chester. Budgell has probably always been concerned about the position we would take. This might be the explanation for his concern that justice be done to Ralph Parsons.

Historians study documents and, particularly where conflict is involved, take and then justify a position. Hence, history is based on the interpretation of documents by historians. Usually biographers are biased towards their subject matter, take a middle-of-the-road position or, on rare occasions, come out against their subject, justifying everything by a particular interpretation of the evidence. We are both historians, as well as biographers, so we too have had to interpret the documents and come to our own conclusions about Ralph Parsons and his difficulties with George Allan and Philip Chester.

We hope we have done Ralph Parsons justice. Our readers, especially Parsons' relatives, his close friends like Len Budgell and Robert H. Chesshire and others, will have to be the judges of that. *Audi alteram partem et fiat justitia, ruat coelum.*[15]

Notes to Prologue

1. Arthur J. Ray, *The Canadian Fur Trade in the Industrial Age* (Toronto: University of Toronto Press, 1990), p. 172.
2. *Ibid.*, p. 171.
3. *Ibid.*, p. 177.
4. Robert H. Chesshire to John Parsons, May 25, 1995.
5. David R. Parsons to John Parsons and Burton K. Janes, June 3, 1995.
6. Ray, *The Canadian Fur Trade in the Industrial Age*, p. 225.
7. *Ibid.*
8. *Loc. cit.*
9. Ralph Parsons, "Farewell Speech," p. 7.
10. Anne Morton to John Parsons, February 17, 1995.
11. Peter C. Newman to John Parsons, January 19, 1995. See also Peter C. Newman to John Parsons, February 6, 1995.
12. Michael Harrington, "Offbeat History," *The Evening Telegram*, January 29, 1990, p. 5 ("The last of the Factors"), March 4, 1991, p. 5 ("The last of the Factors: memories of the early days"), August 14, 1993, p. 5A ("Captain's daughter remembers"), and September 25, 1993, p. 2A ("Correspondents help fill blanks").
13. Ray, *The Canadian Fur Trade in the Industrial Age*, p. 173.
14. Interview by John Parsons with Len Budgell and David R. Parsons, Battery Hotel, St. John's, October 13, 1993. See also Len Budgell to John Parsons, November 8, 1993.
15. A Latin expression for "Hear both sides, and let justice be done."

Chapter 1

The Man and His Background

"The virtues by which decent men live are not just goody-goody ways; they are not merely Puritanical prejudices; they are abiding spiritual good which speak to the heart of man, which give rewards by themselves, whether or not they bring success, wealth, or power."
—Robert I. Kahn, *Lessons for Life*, 1963, p. 66

n Thursday, December 1, 1881, a child was born to Dorcas and William Parsons of Bay Roberts, Newfoundland. The couple named their son William Ralph. His death seventy-five years later would be the culmination to a life of adventure and achievement. In his distinguished career, "R.P.," as he became known among people in the Hudson's Bay Company, gave his very best to that company, establishing twenty-eight of its new posts, serving as its last Fur Trade Commissioner, and seeing the completion of the Northwest Passage as a commercial reality. In a tribute to him, published in 1940, the year of his retirement, the author observed with obvious pride that Ralph Parsons had "left the imprint of his rugged personality on the North of fact and fiction."[1]

Bay Roberts, one of Newfoundland's oldest communities, is located on the west side of Conception Bay about eighty-nine kilometres (fifty-five miles) by road from St. John's, the island's capital city. At the time of Parsons' birth, Bay Roberts was a thriving, seafaring town with a history going back more than 200 years.

Until the 1930s, the fishery was the prime source of wealth in Bay Roberts. The early settler-fishermen pursued the inshore fishery. In addition, there was the Labrador fishery, which involved sending as many as sixty to seventy ships to the Labrador coast each summer. In the late 1800s, foreign ships called at Bay Roberts for fish. In conjunction with the cod fishery, the seal fishery formed the mainstay of Bay Roberts' economy in the nineteenth and the early twentieth centuries. In 1837 alone, the towns of Bay Roberts and Port de Grave together sent out eighty-three vessels. In the winters the harbour was blocked with fifty or more vessels laid up for the season, frozen into the ice.[2]

Bay Roberts received its share of disasters in the seal hunt. On April 28, 1872, the *Huntsman* was lost off Cape St. Charles near Battle Harbour, Labrador, with forty-three men, all from Bay Roberts. On April 2, 1875, there was a boiler explosion on the *Tigress*; twenty-one men, again most from Bay Roberts, were killed.[3]

By the late 1800s, Bay Roberts was the site of considerable boat-building. A shipyard, which operated between 1865 and 1910 by C. and A. Dawe, produced about twenty large schooners. For many years, the firm of E. and J. Bowering operated a boat-building factory which produced about fifty boats a year.

Bay Roberts has for some time been an important business and commercial centre for Conception Bay. Since the establishment of the first firm there in 1810, there have been important business families and names, none being more important than the Dawes. In 1864, Charles and Azariah Dawe formed a business in Port de Grave that was moved to Bay Roberts shortly thereafter because of better business opportunities. Under Captain Azariah Dawe, this firm became an important fishery supply firm exporting 300,000 quintals (a quintal is a weight of 100 or 112 pounds) of fish a year, building an average of two vessels a year, and owning more than thirty at one time.[4]

The child, William Ralph, was the product of a cultured and fairly prosperous Bay Roberts family, Parsons being one of the oldest family names in the area. E.R. Seary in his book, *Family Names of the Island of Newfoundland*, refers to James and William Parsons who resided in Bay Roberts in 1769. Those men owned land in the area which, they claimed, had been in their family for 102 years.

Seary also refers to a Samuel Parsons who about 1825 arrived from Devon, England, and settled at Running Brook, Bay Roberts. Family tradition maintains that he was the paternal ancestor of most of the Parsonses in and around Mercer's Cove, as well as the Parsonses who presently live in Bay Roberts, Coley's Point, Country Road, and Shearstown, but that he was never close to Devon, having been born in Bay Roberts in either 1788 or 1789.[5]

Parsons' homestead, Bay Roberts, c.1940.

Samuel Parsons married Rachel French of French's Cove. Their first son was John, born in 1812; and their last, William, born in 1825. In between were George, Charles, Elijah, Jonathan, Abraham, Stephen, and Isaac; their sisters were Emma, Selina, Mary and Rachel. The birth records for all of these individuals are in church books or family Bibles. Marriage records can be found for most of them, since with the exception of two or three all were married in the St. Matthew's Anglican Church in Bay Roberts.

Rachel and Samuel Parsons died about mid-century. Their eldest son, John, married Susannah Russell on December 8, 1842 and became the ancestors of the Shearstown Parsonses who settled at Grassy Pond in 1886. Dying on June 7, 1887, John was one of the first, if not the first, to be buried in the Anglican cemetery in Shearstown. Charles married Francis Bradbury on June 25, 1845, and Isaac married Ann Deare on December 14, 1843.[6]

Jonathan who died in 1907 and Stephen who died in 1913 were the only male members of that family to live into the twentieth century. Emma, who married Thomas Mercer, died in 1902. William, who died in 1894, was the father of Captain Abe Parsons, the well-known mariner who died in the 1960s. William was also the father of Susannah who married George Henry Spencer. These two were the ancestors of most of the

Spencers in the Bay Roberts area. William was also the grandfather of Captain Sam Parsons (1897-1976), captain during the 1940s of Ralph Parsons' inspection boat, the *Fort Amadjuak*.[7]

The early nineteenth century Parsonses were all born in the Running Brook area of Bay Roberts East. There Stephen Parsons was born in 1818. A sea captain who plied the coastal waters of Newfoundland and Labrador in schooners, he was also well-known as a foreign-going captain, sailing to Europe and the Caribbean, during the peak period of Newfoundland's salt fish industry.[8]

Occasionally, Stephen Parsons when in Europe would bring out Englishmen with him to settle in the Bay Roberts area. Some of those young men lived with the Parsons family until they got established on their own. Two notable examples of this were Thomas Copley and William Richards. Copley came out with Captain Stephen in 1856, and Richards came out with Stephen's son, Captain William, in 1880. Copley married Rebecca Kelligrew, a widow from Coley's Point, in 1858, and settled at Country Pond. These two are the ancestors of some of the Snows in Country Road, some of the Parsonses in Country Road and Shearstown, and most of the Seymours in Butlerville. Richards, who came from England on Captain William Parsons' ship, arrived directly from London and in Newfoundland was nicknamed "Billy London." The Richardses in Butlerville and Tilton are direct descendants of this man.[9] Ralph Parsons' brother, Gus, wrote a poem about this unusual character and entitled it "The Ballad of Billy London." A portion reads:

> *He often reminisced, as men will do*
> *And dealt then in the fabulous and true*
> *And there were those, who would his tales pursue,*
> *That out of these, they might his past construe... .*[10]

Stephen married Rachel Russell, sister to Susannah, John Parsons' wife, on November 25, 1847. Six children were born to the couple: William, Isaac, Stephen, Susan, Naomi, and Rachel. All of Stephen's children married and stayed in the Bay Roberts area, except Stephen, Jr. (b. 1860), who moved to St. John's, married, and became the ancestor of some of the Parsonses in the west end of St. John's. Naomi, known locally even today as "Mother Dawe," married Captain Henry Dawe (1852-1921) and produced a large family. A son, Victor, died on the Western Front in

1916, and a daughter, Daisy, was the mother of well-known Bay Roberts businessman, Victor Dawe.

Ralph Parsons' son, David, remembers stories of his great-grandfather in his dotage years, longing to return to Coley's Point. At such times, there seemed to be no comforting or pacifying the old man. David's Aunt Datie would hitch herself like a horse to Stephen's rocking chair and pretend to trot to Coley's Point. Eventually she would say, "All right, Grandfather, you're *home* now." Of course, by "home" she meant Bay Roberts because, as David is quick to point out, she would *never* lie. The old man would then be satisfied for awhile.

When Stephen Parsons married in 1847, he moved with his wife to Coley's Point and lived on the land of his father-in-law, Abraham Russell. There he lived until the early 1870s when he moved across the harbour and settled in neighbouring Bay Roberts centre.[11] On Water Street he built a large house that boasted five fireplaces. When Stephen and Rachel died, they were buried on Coley's Point in the same plot with Rachel's parents in the old Anglican cemetery.

William (1849-1943) and Isaac (1857-1932) are probably the two children of Rachel and Stephen who are best remembered by a few of the older people in the Bay Roberts area. Isaac married Charlotte Mercer (1864-1958), sister of Samuel Mercer, Sr. He was the father of Samuel A.B. Mercer (1879-1969), the world-famous Egyptologist from Bay Roberts. One of Isaac and Charlotte Parsons' children is still living at the time of this writing; Victor, ninety-three, lives in Montreal; his sister, Emmie died in 1995 at the age of 105.

The eldest child of Rachel and Stephen was William. He was a sea captain who had earned his foreign-going papers by studying at the side of his father and by doing advanced navigation courses in Scotland. Being a foreign-going mariner, he was by no means arrogant or snobbish. Although at times he was a bit gruff outwardly, he was a loving husband to his wife and was tolerant of his grandchildren. He referred to himself as simply Will Parsons. His grandchildren called him "Poppy." Often referred to as "Skipper Bill," he sailed with his father until getting a ship of his own. Frank G. Mercer, an elderly resident of Bay Roberts, remembers William as an austere individual, somewhat short in stature, with a full beard, and seemingly not overly approachable.[12]

Later in life, William returned from the sea and obtained employment as Customs Officer at Rigolet, Labrador, a position he held until well into his seventies. He would leave home for Rigolet after the ice broke up early in the spring, his transportation being the first coastal boat—the *Kyle* or other vessels that carried fishermen and their families to the fishing grounds—and return on the last boat in the fall. The Parsons family remembers their grandfather returning home from Labrador, bringing with him a flour barrel packed tightly with wild geese, bakeapples and smoked salmon, a feast he then shared among family members and a few close friends. On his return trip to Rigolet in the spring, he would take some vegetables and a barrel of cabbage to his friend, George Budgell.[13]

According to David Parsons, one of Skipper William's few favourite stories concerned a Frenchman at his meal on a Newfoundland fishing vessel. Presented with a bowl of Newfoundland salt pork "seasick" soup—complete with bones—he tasted it, then pushed it away from him. In an attempt to speak English, he said, "Non bon." His Newfoundland shipmate looked at him and exclaimed, "No bone! 'Tis *all* bone, you fool!"

In 1877 William married twenty-one-year-old Dorcas Catherine Mosdell (1856-1940), also of Bay Roberts. Daughter of Richard Mosdell, one of Newfoundland's most successful fishermen, and his wife, Frances (née Snow), she was sister to Thomas Mosdell, father of the Newfoundland physician, politician and writer, Dr. Harris M. Mosdell (1883-1944). Dorcas was the exact opposite of William; she was the essence of kindness itself. The two, a blend of extremes, were in the top ranks of Bay Roberts society.

William and Dorcas settled into a bungalow on the back road (Smith Street) on land abutting his father's Water Street property. Ten children—an equal number of sons and daughters—were born to the couple. Their first, Rachel Frances ("Fanny"), named for both grandmothers, was the only one to be born in "the big house," the others being born in the bungalow. Their first son was William Ralph. There followed in quick succession Etta May, Stephen Hayward, Florence Violet, Richard Augustus, Mildred Susie, Winnifred, Wilfred, and Stephen (who died in infancy). Eventually the entire family moved back to the old house, where old Stephen died in the winter of 1913.

A real problem with tracing the Parsons family in Bay Roberts is that the same names for both males and females appear in every generation. One has to be especially careful when dealing with those names since in some cases the youngest child in one generation is very close in terms of dates to the oldest child in the succeeding generation.

The Parsons Family at Bay Roberts. c.1899.
Ralph is the tall boy on the left; Hayward is the boy on the right and Richard Augustus is the boy in the middle. Rachel (Miss Datie) is the girl on the extreme right.

New names gradually crept into the family. One of Ralph's brothers was Richard Augustus Parsons; his middle name was a new one in the family. Another brother, Wilfred, carried a new name in the family. The co-author's father was George Wilfred Parsons (1911-73). There was a George in every generation from the start of the nineteenth century, but Wilfred was a new name. Maybe both boys were named for Sir Wilfred Thomason Grenfell (1865-1940), who was highly regarded in Newfoundland and Labrador from 1892 until his death. John, Isaac, Charles, and William are names in the extended family reaching back beyond 1800. So are the Biblical names of Esau, Jacob, Abraham, and Elijah.

The name Ralph was an entirely new Christian name, not only in the Parsons family, but to others in the area. William Ralph Parsons apparently had no great attachment to his first name, William, for it appears infrequently in written records.[14] In time, he dropped the name William altogether and always signed his name as Ralph Parsons. Maybe he just wanted to avoid confusion with his father, Captain William. In Hudson's Bay Company circles, he was more often than not referred to as simply "R.P." To his family and close friends, he was Ralph, and to everyone else, he was Mr. Parsons. On his headstone in Forest Road Cemetery in St. John's, the name, W. Ralph Parsons, appears.

All of those people were staunch members of the Church of England and were leery of other Christian denominations; the religious animosities among them ran deep. It is said that some of the Parsonses and Mercers in Mercer's Cove were quite distressed when Henry and William Badcock became followers of John Wesley about 1800 and started holding meetings in their houses. The Parsons family held to the family church, but some of the Mercers went over to the Wesleyans.

Anglicans believe that the first step toward salvation is infant baptism. Being received into Christ's Church at that sacrament, infants subsequently grow in grace and are trained in the household of faith. To this day, however, a question mark remains over Ralph Parsons' baptism, readily inviting speculation.

William Ralph Parsons is the last birth recorded for 1881 in the records of St. Matthew's Anglican Church in Bay Roberts. His date of birth—December 1—is given, but there is no date for his baptism. The blank space is puzzling.[15]

The handwriting for the last notation in the church records is conspicuous because it is so different. The handwriting of the Rev. William Charles Shears—invariably signed W.C. Shears—is large and coarse. However, the handwriting record of William Ralph Parsons is a much smaller type and is considerably different. Opposite the name and birthdate, as well as the empty space where the date of baptism should be, is a terse note: "N.B. Entered by me after statement by the mother." One is led to speculate about the meaning of this statement since there is presently nobody alive who can throw any light on this situation.

The Rev. W.C. Shears, who was the Church of England priest in that area from 1868 to 1903, apparently took the opportunity to be away from his parish as much as possible, attending seminaries and conferences, or just on extended holidays. After the *Huntsman* disaster of 1872, for example, he did not turn up for over a year. While he was absent, another priest filled in for him.

The Rev. E.M. Bishop of the Harbour Grace parish was filling in for Shears in the spring of 1882 when Dorcas Parsons brought her baby to St. Matthew's Anglican Church to have him "entered into the faith of Christ crucified and manfully to fight against sin, the world and the devil until his life's end."

The Rev. Bishop received baby Ralph into the Church, and even had the audacity to sign the Rev. W.C. Shears' name on the line opposite. But no date was provided for the entry.

Ralph could have been a weak and sickly child, physically unfit to be outdoors in the winter, although the family has never heard of this. Somebody—most likely a relative—baptized him at home. John Parsons (1858-1925), Captain William Parsons' cousin from Mercer's Cove (later of Shearstown), was noted in the area for baptizing infants who were ill and likely to die. Maybe he did the redeeming task for Ralph, as he did for James Snow, who is presently living in Butlerville.

Assuming that Ralph Parsons was weak and sickly as a child, it cannot be denied that he went a long way: from the warmth and comfort of his mother's arms in the winter of 1881-82 to the cold, dark, uninviting cliffs of Baffin Island half a century later. Certainly any weakness on his part went unnoticed by Frank Ryan in 1940, who characterized Ralph Parsons as "of that breed of men who love ships and the sea. He came...from those deep, rock-bound coves that develop strength and skill in seamanship."[16]

The big house on Water Street was the structure which Ralph's brother, Richard Augustus, or "Gus" as he was better known, immortalized in his poem, "The Tale of a Lonesome House." Late in life, Gus remembered an edifice that had been erected on a slight eminence, in sight of the harbour traffic, and with a curtilage extending to the street. A spacious house that looked out upon a garden, its builder must have loved the light, considering the large number of windows on each side. The details of the building were still fresh in Gus' mind almost half a century later:

The dormer windowed roof and chimneys tall,
The broad low steps so fashioned to provide
The means to reach by even leisured stride
The great front door set in the Southern wall
That inward swung upon a spacious hall.[17]

Apart from the kitchen—a place of romance, dance, and singing—the best of all chambers was the dining room. Sailors sat around the hearth and related lusty tales of the sea, and children gathered around the table to do their homework. There were pictures on the walls and no end of flowers everywhere. The parlour, another special place, was opened infrequently.

The house itself was disposed to hospitality, and Gus considered himself privileged to have enjoyed it.

Frank G. Mercer remembers the large, imposing house, located in central Bay Roberts in what was then the most impressive spot in the town. The house was built on the site with three floors. The attic had several bedrooms. David Parsons recalls an oval-shaped indentation in the dining room ceiling. It had evidently been left there as a "trademark" by the mason, who kicked the ceiling to celebrate the completion of his job, a detail that is borne out by Gus Parsons in his obituary to the house. The story handed down is that the plasterer himself was "plastered!"

The first child, Rachel Frances ["Fanny"] (1878-1966), was the eldest child and the darling of the family. She never married, but everybody loved her. A wonderful character, she might not be given sufficient praise because of her selfless and unassuming ways that hid a devoted, loving and determined person.

The name by which she became known—she did not like her given names—was neither of her Christian names. According to family tradition, the first word she spoke as an infant sounded like "datie." Accordingly, her parents called her Datie; her siblings and cousins, Date; her nieces and nephews, Aunt Datie; and her acquaintances, Miss Parsons. On formal occasions, she was addressed as Miss R.F. Parsons, O.B.E. The Order of the British Empire was an honour she received from King George VI in recognition of her contribution to the Women's Patriotic Association during World War II. This association sent thousands of parcels of cigarettes and various knitted items of clothing to Newfoundland servicemen overseas.

Datie seemed to be always around when anyone needed her. Frank G. Mercer recalls his grandfather, Captain Harry Norman, in his last days wanting a bottle of rum. Frank was sent to ask Miss Datie to oblige, which she did, because she always had extra spirits hidden away for medicinal purposes, if for no other reason. Certainly she could never be accused of bootlegging or anything illegal, for she was too much of a saint for that. Frank got the bottle of black rum for his grandfather, who as always was very grateful.[18]

Jack Hambling, in his first collection of short stories, *Stage Heads and Warm Dandelions*, provides a word portrait of his Aunt Datie. She was gracious and petite, weighing under ninety pounds. However, her size belied her power. David Parsons witnessed her grabbing a piano on one end and moving it to another location. Her breakfast consisted of a single cup of strong, milkless, heavily-sweetened tea and a slice of lightly-buttered toast. Occasionally, she would include a taste of lukewarm porridge. But she did her best to encourage others at her table to eat heartily.[19] She took a special interest in the physical and spiritual well-being of her nieces and nephews. For example, to discourage Jack from using bad words, she would speak up the living room chimney to Santa Claus or give the young boy hot tea to burn the words out of his mouth.[20]

Aunt Datie was always in a frenzy. Wearing a crisp, white, flower-bordered apron and with flour on her hands, she flitted about the kitchen, her mincing, birdlike steps tapping on the linoleum-covered floor. She smelled clean and fresh. Her hair, which was parted slightly in the middle, was carefully combed and held in a bun at the back. She grudgingly took infrequent breaks from household duties, and she was able to survive on catnaps. She played Flinch, but apart from the occasional sip of brandy for medicinal purposes, she never indulged, and though always in the range of smoke from the pipes of the men in her household, she did not like tobacco and never smoked.

A teacher at a one-room school at Tilton, six miles from Bay Roberts, she pedalled to work daily on her bicycle in button-style boots and an ankle-length skirt over a rough gravel road. She boarded there during the winter. Because of the amount of time consumed by her professional career, she was not noted for her cooking expertise, although, Jack Hamling recalls she did make delicious strawberry roly-poly.

A devoted teacher and model Christian, she would probably have stayed teaching for many more years than she did had not fate interfered. On September 7, 1919, her sister, Winnifred Butt, died in childbirth; the child, named Winnifred, survived. Although then in her sixty-fourth year, Dorcas Parsons and her husband, William, took their daughter's child, Winnifred, and Dorcas looked after her as if she were her own. In 1918 Ralph Parsons married, and on September 27, 1919 a son, David, was born to his wife, Flora May. On July 20, 1920, at the age of thirty-three, Ralph's wife died, a few days after giving birth to their second child, leaving ten-month-old David motherless.

David's Aunt Carrie Clench, wife of the Rev. Evelyn Clench, took him to her home—the Church of England rectory at Spaniard's Bay—to care for him, despite the fact that she already had three children, the youngest being a one-year-old daughter.

Ralph, who was very involved in the Hudson's Bay Company at the time, realized that this extra burden should be only a temporary measure. So he wrote his sister, Datie, asking her to resign her teaching job in Tilton and go home to Bay Roberts to look after young David. In return, Ralph promised to look after her for the rest of her life and pay for support of David, which he did. He also sent an allowance to David's grandmother. Thus in June 1921, Miss Datie resigned from the teaching profession and assumed the task of substitute mother to her nephew, while her mother cared for the young girl, Winnifred. Winnifred Butt and David Parsons then, although cousins, grew up in the same household as if they were sister and brother.

Winnifred Butt married Howard Moores, an accountant who enlisted in the Royal Canadian Air Force and, after discharge in 1945, joined a business firm in Bay Roberts, where he and his wife lived for many years. Later they moved to Blackhead, Howard's birthplace, where he retired after working several more years. They are both buried there. Winnifred died in 1991. David Parsons joined the Royal Canadian Air Force in 1940 and served overseas as a navigator/bombaimer from 1941 to 1945. He flew out of the British Isles, Gibralter, and a small detachment from French Morocco, always with a Royal Air Force squadron, even though he was in the Royal Canadian Air Force. Afterwards he finished his engineering degree at Dalhousie University and Nova Scotia Technical College, then settled with his wife, Betty, in Hantsport, Nova Scotia, where they still live. They have three sons — John, Peter, and James — and seven grandchildren.

And so the two women, mother and daughter — Dorcas and Datie — cared for the two small children — Winnifred and David — as well as cared for Captain William, Ralph Parsons when he was home, and the retired teacher and educator, Dr. Arthur Barnes, who boarded with the family. In the late 1920s Barnes moved into "the big

Ralph Parsons and his mother, Dorcas, at Bay Roberts, about 1938.

house," living in a study den and bedroom, and having his meals with the family. He stayed there until after Ralph's retirement in 1940. (Ralph referred to Barnes as "Mother's legacy.") Barnes then moved in with David's cousin, Winnifred and her husband, Howard, and their daughters, Marilyn and Roberta, on the back road (Smith Street) in Bay Roberts, where he lived until his death on November 24, 1956.[21] By a strange coincidence, Dr. Arthur Barnes and Ralph Parsons died on this date; Barnes died at 6:00 A.M., and Parsons, 6:00 P.M.

Etta Mae Parsons, known in the family as "Ettie," left home as a young woman, eventually settling in Toronto and marrying a Mr. Newey. They had six children. Although Ettie never returned to Newfoundland, some of her children did, and the family kept in touch with her through visits and letters, until she died at an advanced age.

Stephen Hayward Parsons (1885-1965) was educated at the Bay Roberts Academy and through private studies. He was a schoolteacher from 1901 to 1903. From 1903 to 1912 he worked as a bookkeeper with F.D. Woody Co., Ltd. In 1912 he became an apprenticed clerk with the Hudson's Bay Company and, three years later, was appointed Post Manager with the Company. In 1918 he was promoted District Manager, the same year in which he married Sybil Oakley (1890-1973), a professional nurse. Five children were born to the couple—Jean, Gerald, Rupert, Flora, and William. Hayward's recreations throughout life were fishing and shooting. His son, Gerald, is also a Hudson's Bay Company retiree and an avid outdoor sportsman like his father. Sybil and Hayward were at Cartwright during the devastating influenza epidemic on the Labrador coast in 1918-19. According to Anglican missionary, Henry Gordon (1887-1971), Sybil especially, with the help of others, did magnificent work in nursing the sick and dying.[22]

Florence Violet Parsons (1890-1985), or "Floss" as she was better known, married John Hambling (1892-1980) of Canso, Nova Scotia. He worked with the Western Union Company in Bay Roberts and adjusted well from the start to both the people of the town and the Parsons family. He was an avid sportsman and a keen trout fisherman, and he held the tennis championship of Newfoundland for many years. Three sons were born—Gus, Don, and Jack—and they inherited their father's sportsman-like qualities. Don served with distinction overseas with the Royal Canadian Air Force Bomber Command during World War II. He then practised law in Ottawa for over thirty years, subsequently becoming city solicitor.

Gus joined the Hudson's Bay Company as an apprentice at an early age and served for many years in the North. He eventually left and went to work with his cousin, Ralph Butt, in Saginaw, Michigan, where he now lives in retirement. After completing high school, Jack (b. 1927) left home and throughout an eventful working career held down a variety of jobs, ranging from an Ottawa-based civil servant to stints as mill operator/truck driver in a northern mining town, to partner in a tourist fishing lodge located in Quebec. A dedicated outdoorsman and avid reader, he now lives in South River, located about midway between Bay Roberts and Brigus. A successful author, he has published two delightful collections of short stories, *Stage Heads and Warm Dandelions* and *The Second Time Around: Growing Up in Bay Roberts*.[23] A cultured gentleman, his speech is totally devoid of any trace of the Devonshire brogue accent so typical of Bay Roberts and Shearstown.

Richard Augustus Parsons (1893-1981), or "Gus" as he was familiarly known, was educated at Bay Roberts Academy, Bishop Feild College in St. John's, and Montreal's McGill University, receiving from the latter institution the degree of Bachelor of Civil Law. In 1910 he became a teacher, a profession he followed for five years. He served with the Royal Newfoundland Regiment in World War I. On February 15, 1921 he married Bessie Ash Somerton, daughter of Magistrate Somerton of Trinity. Four children were born to the couple—Helen, Paul, Austin, and Sheila. Gus served from 1924 to 1932 as Clerk of the Legislative Council of Newfoundland, and later tried unsuccessfully to enter politics. On May 6, 1932 he was appointed King's Council. From 1928 to 1935 he was senior partner of the law firm of Parsons and Walsh. After the firm's dissolution, he became a partner in the firm of Parsons and Morgan which eventually dissolved, but Gus continued to practice law alone from his law office in the Exchange Building on McBride's Hill in St. John's. In 1954 he embarked upon another venture—publishing his poetry in book form. His first volume was *Reflections*.[24] His earlier writings, extending back to the *London Times* in 1919 and Joseph R. Smallwood's *Book of Newfoundland* in the 1930s, had been strictly prose. In the next twenty-six years, he published twelve more books of poetry. Dr. Harry A. Cuff wrote in 1980:

> Dr. Parsons' imagery is strong, precise and concrete, never crude. His tone is reverent without being maudlin. His satire does not deteriorate to invective. His diction is refined rather than grandiose, while his use of the Newfoundland dialect is astute and never

offensive. Although he has dealt with a wide range of subjects there is the sense of a unity of theme—the indomitable human spirit portrayed against a Newfoundland background. Dr. Parsons' fascination with Newfoundland and the qualities that make her unique is revealed in every line. His devotion and attachment to Newfoundland is displayed in every phrase.[25]

In later years, Gus' ability was recognized by Memorial University of Newfoundland which in 1974 conferred on him an honourary D.Litt., by Nova Scotia Teachers' College which in the same year made him an honourary Associate in Education, and by his *alma mater* which in 1979 presented him with McGill's Distinguished Service Award.

Mildred Susie Parsons married an Englishman, Arthur Wilson, who had been brought out to Bay Roberts as an operator with the Western Union Cable Company. They had three daughters: Eileen, Catherine, and Edna. Wilson enjoyed reading to his father-in-law when old Captain William's eyesight and hearing began to fail. Wilson was one of many laid off from Western Union in the Great Depression of the 1930s. Among his other jobs, he sailed as wireless operator aboard the Hudson's Bay Company boat that met the Government ship on the first trip through the Bering Sea. For that historic meeting through the Northwest Passage, one ship had left from the east coast, and another from the west coast.

In 1913 Winnifred Parsons married Charles Butt of Heart's Content, also a Western Union operator in Bay Roberts and a contemporary and friend of John Hambling and Arthur Wilson. They had twin sons, Ralph and George born in 1914. Ralph also served for many years with the Hudson's Bay Company in North West River, Labrador, but resigned to get medical care for his young son. Butt, who was later a comptroller in a hospital in Michigan, died in recent years and is buried in Bay Roberts. George was accidentally killed in 1924 after falling over Jones' Head in Bay Roberts East, while playing with friends. Charles Butt left Bay Roberts with his second wife and moved to Far Rockaway, New York. Winnifred died on September 7, 1919 in childbirth with her daughter, Winnifred. Wilfred Parsons, the youngest son of William and Dorcas, served with the Hudson's Bay Company in Pond Inlet, Baffin Island. Later he married Marguerite Dawe of Port de Grave and worked for an oil company in Portland, Maine, where he died suddenly in 1950 at the age of 51. He is buried in Bay Roberts, alongside his parents, and oldest sister, Datie.

Frank G. Mercer, who spent many years in the North as a policeman, practically grew up next door to the Parsons household. Even as a boy he was constantly aware of the esteem and respect accorded the family, Ralph Parsons in particular. He knew the family by sight and, later in life, on a more personal level. Frank's father kept cows and sold milk as a sideline. Ralph's sister, Mildred, was one of Frank's customers to whom he delivered milk on a daily basis for a year or so. Frank's youth in a way revolved around the Parsonses, and in his working life his path often crossed that of Ralph and his brother, Hayward, who also worked with the Hudson's Bay Company. He knew Gus in legal circles. Frank always had the greatest respect for all three brothers. Over the years he has been an admirer of lawyer Parsons' poetry.

According to David Parsons, there was much fun and laughter in the old house when his aunts and uncles were growing up. When they got together in their adult life, they recalled many comical incidents from their youth. Each of them had a terrific sense of humour. But chief among them were Gus, Floss, Mildred, and Hayward. Nevertheless, the others had their own comical ways and appreciated each others' humour. Aunt Datie would laugh silently until the tears rolled down her face. Examples of the Parsons household humour abound.

Like the time Floss dropped a piece of fat pork in her brother, Gus' mouth, which was wide open as he sat in front of the kitchen stove snoring, exhausted from a hard day of trouting. Or like the time Hayward was making a pot of his favourite "seasick" salt pork soup as his siblings looked on, hoping for a bowl. Observing them watching, he ceremoniously *spat* in the soup, dashing any desire on their part for a tasty sip! Or like the time Wilfred came downstairs from the attic bedroom, crying because his siblings would not allow him to play "shops" as they measured and "sold" the bedclothes. "They said I was a poor man and couldn't buy!" he wailed.

David Parsons remembers his Aunt Mildred entering the dining room where his grandfather would be peacefully smoking his pipe. She would be carrying a bucket of water and swinging it in circular fashion over his head. Centrifugal force kept the water from spilling over him. Nevertheless, the old captain would look up in alarm and say, "What's that fool up to now?!" On other occasions, Mildred would grab one of several walking canes from the hall and proceed to "shoot" the layers off Aunt Datie's pie, which she had so carefully prepared for the usual Sunday evening get-together.

In those days when the Parsons children were growing up, the denominational school system was in effect. The Parsons children attended the Bay Roberts Church of England Academy. The most admired teacher at that institution was Arthur (later Dr.) Barnes (1865-1956). Becoming Minister of Education (1920-24), he laid much of the groundwork for the establishment of Memorial University College in St. John's.[26] Most of the Parsons children, including Ralph, attended school in the Barnes era. Without a doubt Ralph Parsons and his siblings benefited greatly from the good teaching of Arthur Barnes, Henry Mercer, Robert Dawe, and James Norman, popular teachers and tutors in the area at the time, but Barnes being so close to the family was in a way a private tutor to the Parsons children. His teaching abilities were legend. The best recommendation that young people could have was to say that they had "gone to Barnes." Years later in a tribute to Dr. Barnes, Gus Parsons penned the following words:

He sought not fame and asked no other than
To be remembered as the friend of man.

His sympathy, claimed Gus, could

...enfold
All folks of every creed, the young and old.

A person of great knowledge, he denied nobody the privileges of education. Indeed, in Gus' words,

He made the dry bones of the old classics live.[27]

The best phrases to describe him, Gus felt, were "The Teacher"—the only inscription on his headstone—and "The Master." When he retired, Dr. Barnes lived in the Parsons' "lonesome house," where he was Grandmother Parsons' "star boarder" for many years.

Being the eldest son in the family, Ralph was relied on by his mother to help as head of the family while his father was away from home. The young boy was especially loving and helpful to her. She in turn was always full of appreciation for his kindness, a mutual feeling that remained until her death in 1940, the same year he retired. Ralph's devotion to his mother was well-known. In the late 1930s he built a cottage in Shearstown for his parents and himself, which family members referred to as "Mother's Place," but again fate interfered and she died before he could spend much of his retirement with her. Family members say that Ralph was shocked when he realized his mother was dying, even though she was in her eighty-fourth year, and at one point implored the attending physician not to let her die.[28] He held her hand as she passed away—and his life was never the same. She had stood by him and held him twenty years before when his young wife died so unexpectedly. The loss of his wife brought him even closer to his beloved mother. As an epitaph, he had the words, "A Mother in Israel," engraved on her headstone.

Ralph was the first son to leave home. He found a job at sixteen years of age as tutor for two years to the two sons of the Hudson's Bay Company's Factor, James Fraser, who was stationed at Cartwright, Labrador.[29] David Parsons has an early recollection of visiting with his father an elderly gentleman with a full white beard. If memory serves him correctly, he was the man whose sons his father had tutored. He was also the individual who had encouraged Ralph Parsons to join the Company.

A London-based corporation which was granted a Royal Charter to trade (principally in furs) in most of north and west Canada (Rupert's Land) in 1670, the Hudson's Bay Company annexed its main competitors, the North West Company, in 1821, and developed extensive sea-based trade in otter pelts and other species along the coast of British Columbia. Rupert's Land was purchased by the Canadian Government in 1870, but by this time an extensive fur trade was carried on by the Hudson's Bay Company from the Labrador coast to British Columbia. This was the Company that Ralph Parsons, the young man from Bay Roberts, joined as an apprentice clerk at Cartwright, Labrador, in 1900. The decision was a wise one and one that was to radically alter his life and the lives of those close to him. A dedicated worker and a man of his word, Ralph Parsons made a significant contribution to the Hudson's Bay Company in this century. By the 1930s, according to Peter C. Newman in *Merchant Princes*: "Parsons ruled over an immense empire with the righteousness of a latter-day Cromwell. The Company was everything to him, not just his job but his religion."[30]

NOTES TO CHAPTER 1: THE MAN AND HIS BACKGROUND

1. Watson, M.D., "Who's Who in Hudson's Bay House: Ralph Parsons," *The House Detective* (II:1), June 1940, unpaginated. See reprint in *Newfoundland Quarterly* (LXXXVIII:3), April 1994, p. 43.
2. "History: Bay Roberts," *Decks Awash* (XX:1), January-February 1991, p. 6.
3. John Parsons, "Huntsman," *Encyclopedia of Newfoundland and Labrador*, vol. III, eds., Joseph R. Smallwood, Cyril F. Poole and Robert H. Cuff (St. John's, Newfoundland: Harry Cuff Publications Ltd., 1991), p. 11; *idem, Labrador: Land of the North* (New York: Vantage Press, 1970), pp. 34-36; *idem*, "Tigress," *Encyclopedia of Newfoundland and Labrador*, vol. V, eds., Cyril F. Poole and Robert H. Cuff (St. John's, Newfoundland: Harry Cuff Publications Ltd., 1994), p. 385.
4. "History: Bay Roberts," *Decks Awash*, January-February 1991, pp. 8-9.
5. E.R. Seary with Sheila M.P. Lynch, *Family Names of the Island of Newfoundland* (St. John's, Newfoundland: Memorial University of Newfoundland, 1977), pp. 372-373.
6. St. Matthew's Church Records, Bay Roberts.
7. Information from James Y. Parsons.
8. Family Bible record. See also Shannon Ryan, *Fish Out of Water: The Newfoundland Saltfish Trade, 1814-1914* (St. John's, Newfoundland: Breakwater Books Ltd., 1986).
9. Interview with Jessie Parsons, 1993. Family Archives.
10. "The Ballad of Billy London," R.A. Parsons, *The Tale of a Lonesome House* (Don Mills, Ontario: The Ontario Publishing Company Limited, 1971), p. 83.
11. Bay Roberts Family Records, Provincial Archives of Newfoundland and Labrador, St. John's, Newfoundland.
12. Frank G. Mercer (b. 1914) grew up in Bay Roberts, but spent most of his life as a policeman in the North.
13. Information from David R. Parsons and Jack Hambling.
14. Letters and reports by Ralph Parsons in Hudson's Bay Company Archives.
15. St. Matthew's Anglican Church Records, Bay Roberts.
16. Frank Ryan, "Forty Years on the Fur Trail," *The Beaver*, June 1940 (Outfit 271), p. 20.
17. "The Tale of a Lonesome House," in R.A. Parsons, *The Tale of a Lonesome House*, p. 14.
18. Information from Frank G. Mercer.
19. Jack Hambling, *Stage Heads and Warm Dandelions* (St. John's, Newfoundland: Harry Cuff Publications Ltd., 1985), pp. 19-32.
20. Information from Jack Hambling.
21. Information from David R. Parsons.
22. Henry Gordon, *The Labrador Parson*, ed., F. Burnham Gill (St. John's, Newfoundland: Provincial Archives of Newfoundland and Labrador, 1972), Chapter 10.
23. Jack Hambling, *The Second Time Around: Growing Up in Bay Roberts* (St. John's, Newfoundland: Harry Cuff Publications Ltd., 1992).
24. R.A. Parsons, *Reflections* (Toronto, Ontario: The Ryerson Press, 1954).

25 Harry A. Cuff and Daphne Benson, "From the Editors," R.A. Parsons, *Curtain Call*, eds., Harry A. Cuff and Daphne Benson (St. John's, Newfoundland: Harry A. Cuff, 1980), p. ix.

26 Linda A. Parsons, "Dr. Arthur Barnes," *Encyclopedia of Newfoundland and Labrador*, vol. I, eds., Joseph R. Smallwood and Robert D.W. Pitt (St. John's, Newfoundland: Newfoundland Book Publishers [1967] Ltd., 1981), p. 131.

27 "In Memoriam: Dr. Arthur Barnes 1865-1956—The Teacher," in R.A. Parsons, *Curtain Call*, p. 15.

28 Information from Jack Hambling, who heard it from his mother, Floss, Ralph Parsons' sister.

29 James Fraser, Certificate of Character, dated December 29, 1900.

30 Peter C. Newman, *Merchant Princes* (Toronto, Ontario: Viking, 1991), p. 185.

Chapter 2

First Years With the Company

"...[H]e had a way of making the men under him feel that he was not only one whose orders had to be obeyed but also a friend on whom they could rely. Thus he got the best out of them and became a fabulous image of power and fame."
—Archibald L. Fleming, *Archibald the Arctic*, 1956, p. 259

he Hudson's Bay Company had asserted its claim to territorial rights in Labrador in 1752, but it did not move into the region until 1834. At that time, it set up its first trading post at Rigolet, located at the bottom of Groswater Bay near the "Narrows" that led into the great saltwater inlet, Lake Melville. It was there that young Donald A. Smith had laboured as a clerk with the Company. He was later post manager at North West River. Moving to Montreal and later London, England, he became, in time, Governor of the Company and, as Lord Strathcona, a prime mover in the building of the Canadian Pacific Railway.

In 1836, the Company established a second post in Labrador. The site was North West River, located at the upper end of Lake Melville. The following year, a third site was acquired, this time at Cartwright, located on the eastern side of the entrance to Sandwich Bay, along the southern coast of Labrador.[1] A.P. Dyke wrote in 1969 that Cartwright's "existence today is a direct result of the Hudson's Bay Company's post which is still being maintained."[2]

Ralph Parsons' first job, after exchanging the rugged coasts of Newfoundland for the equally-rugged coast of Labrador, was to become tutor for two years to the two sons of the Hudson's Bay Company's agent at Cartwright, James Fraser. He was the individual who recommended

Parsons to join the Company. In his letter of reference for Parsons, written from Cartwright on December 29, 1900, Fraser declared: "I found him at all times upright, honest, and invariably most attentive to his duty, and it gives me pleasure to recommend him to any position he may find."[3] Young Ralph must have been delighted with such a positive appraisal of his efforts as a tutor.

Parsons began his professional career at nineteen at Cartwright by entering into the service of the Hudson's Bay Company as an apprentice clerk and for general service for the term of five years without leave, with the option of a sixth year. The relationship turned out to be a most congenial one, for he would remain with the Company until his retirement four decades later. His initial responsibilities were a mixture of office and store duties, including wood-chopping. His contract outlined the pay scale of twenty pounds sterling for his first year, twenty-five for his second, forty for his third, forty-five for his fourth, and fifty for his fifth.[4]

He spent six years commuting between Rigolet and North West River, the wilderness posts once managed by Donald A. Smith. Promotion came quickly for the Bay Roberts native. From 1900 to 1904 he apprenticed at Rigolet, where he sat at the very desk where Smith had worked in his day. "Truly the mantle of Strathcona fell upon his successor," The Right Rev. Archibald L. Fleming, the Anglican Bishop of the Arctic, wrote in 1939, "for step by step, through hard persistent work and sheer ability, Ralph Parsons rose until now he is the key man in the fur trade in Canada."[5] From 1905 to 1906 Parsons was in charge at the North West River post, and, from 1907 to 1909, the Cartwright post, where he had started his career. He received eighty pounds sterling annually for his sixth to eighth years with the Company.[6]

Parsons quickly earned respect from those with whom he associated. When he retired in 1940, a poem in his honour was inscribed on a sealskin and presented to him. The first stanza speaks of his popularity among his associates:

Nigh one and forty years ago,
'Way back in nineteen double O,
R.P. was sent to work in Labrador.
When they saw the new apprentice,
They cried, "Look what they have sent us!"
But soon they welcomed him at every door.[7]

In 1909 Parsons was transferred to Hudson Strait to open up a post at Wolstenholme, a momentous event which he related in rich detail years later.[8]

In 1908 information had been received at the Hudson's Bay Company's Montreal office that the master of its supply ship had called at Cape Wolstenholme, an austere, isolated, rocky, windswept cape where Northern Quebec swings down to Hudson Bay. (Henry Hudson, the English navigator associated with the search for the Northwest Passage, had christened the entire cape "Wolstenholme" after one of his backers, and named the sheltered cove where the Company's post stood in 1940 "Erik Cove." Hudson had put in there for fresh water. Hunting knives, produced in England and sporting the Wolstenholme trademark, were still being used by the Company in this area to trade with the Inuit as late as 1940.) The supply ship's master had found a single family of Inuit at Cape Wolstenholme.

Based on this information, the Company decided to establish a trading post there the following year, 1909. Parsons was given the responsibility to establish the first of the Arctic fur trade posts, a task which would firmly establish his own reputation as the builder of more posts in the North than any one man in the history of the Company. However, he almost lost his life in this hair-raising adventure. "These were the days of the chief factor regime," wrote Frank Ryan, "of arduous trips without communication, without sail or power boat or aeroplane."[9] These difficult conditions taxed Parsons' endurance, but he persevered, leaving an indelible mark upon the course of Arctic, not to mention Hudson's Bay Company, history.

In July 1909, at which time he was in charge of the Cartwright post, Parsons received from the Montreal office orders to travel to Wolstenholme and establish a post there. He was given only one week's notice to prepare for his journey. Added to this, he had no knowledge of conditions of trade in the Far North. Requisitions covering the supplies, which were thought necessary, were designed by the Montreal office and, as circumstances later showed, proved inadequate and unsuitable for the requirements of such an expedition, and could have resulted in dire consequences for the founding party.

Nothing was said to Parsons about a boat, but an "outfit" was sent. (The year of the Hudson's Bay Company's incorporation—1670—is referred to as "Outfit 1," and each year thereafter is numbered accordingly.) The Wolstenholme outfit was made up by a man who knew nothing of the North. There were no engine-driven boats in the fur trade in that part of the country, so Parsons supplemented the outfit by purchasing an old whaling boat. The expedition personnel consisted of Parsons; seventy-five-year-old John Ford, Sr., a retired pensioner of the Company, and his wife; William Dickers and Mark Mukke (both nineteen-year-old Inuit); and Amesso, a carpenter, who would rejoin the supply ship on her return from Hudson Bay ports and proceed to Montreal. Together they set out to find a site for a post on the comparatively unknown shore of Hudson Strait.

Parsons, knowing of Erik Cove, at the southwest outlet to the Strait and the source of fresh water for the Company's ships, headed there. On Friday, August 13, the party arrived at Wolstenholme aboard the Company's supply ship, the S.S. *Pelican*. After consideration, Parsons decided it was as suitable a spot as any on that barren coast. The expedition looked around for a day for Inuit, but located none. Nor did they know of other places where there was a harbour. The ship barely had time to supply the other posts in Hudson Bay, so a decision was made to erect the buildings at Wolstenholme, hoping to locate Inuit later.

Parsons instructed the carpenter, Amesso, assisted by the elderly Ford, to start erecting the post buildings. When the foundations were laid, Parsons, accompanied by Dickers and Mukke, took the sailboat and proceeded to the east along the Hudson Strait coast in search of Inuit. They knew that a post was of no commercial value without customers from whom to buy furs.

On their first day out, they encountered good weather, with a favourable northwest wind which enabled them to make about thirty-five miles. Calling at several coves along the coast, they found signs of Inuit, sites where they had camped four or five years before.

On their second day, the wind was still in their favour, and they sailed about thirty miles. But toward evening the wind veered to the southeast and was accompanied by a heavy swell. Parsons and the young men with him were prevented from making further progress. Beaching their boat at the nearest cove, they pitched camp for the night. They pulled up their boat as far as they could, with their meagre stock of supplies intact. Exhausted, they fell asleep in the tent, which had been placed about thirty yards from the boat.

About 2:00 A.M., they were awakened by a noise. The trio realized they were drenched and, a moment later, they knew the reason. A fierce storm had blown up, and the seas were breaking over them. The rain was

Ralph Parsons and Crew on the deck of the *Pelican*, 1911. Parsons is seated on the left.

coming down in torrents, and their tent was being swept away from them. They looked out to see how their boat was faring. To their surprise, it was completely filled with water and most of their provisions were being washed away. They tried to save the boat, but there was such a heavy sea running that the craft soon became broken up on the rough beach, the cause of the noise they had heard shortly before. Within moments, their flimsy boat was nothing more than driftwood being tossed about by the breakers. All they had were the remains of their supper of the previous evening.

There was nothing left for them to do but to wait until daylight, when they would return on foot to Wolstenholme. They were at least sixty miles from Erik Cove—i.e., sixty miles in a straight line—but it was virtually impossible for them to travel in a direct line. The land in the vicinity was about 1,000 to 1,500 feet high, rising perpendicularly from the sea-coast. Every mile or so along the coast there was a small cove, backed by gulches running inland for ten or more miles. Fifty miles under ordinary circumstances would have been nothing unusual, but there was no way to cross that rough, ripped-up northern coastline, with hundreds of inlets 2,000 feet deep that pierced the coast like jagged needles, some of them going inland twenty miles. The three intrepid explorers were faced with the discouraging task of threading their way inland around the tips of the inlets, time after time, before working their way back to the coast to determine their bearings. To compound the situation, with only enough provisions for a single day, they knew there was a tricky job ahead of them, but they did not think it would be nearly so tough as it turned out to be.

For the first day they followed the coastline, scaling the side of one mountain and down another, until they tired, realizing they were making little progress. They advanced no more than five miles as the crow flies. The only food they had was in their pockets. They continued walking all night, but quickly began to realize the impossibility of their mission, as the distance they would have to travel might be as much as 200 miles.

The next day they went inland for about twenty miles and then turned west, thinking the land would be easier for walking. But when they reached fairly level country, fog settled down and they could not even see the sun. As a result, they made little progress that day, as well. At sunset, confused about their location and wanting to ensure that they were not overshooting their mark, they went to the coast to get their bearings. They had no compass, and the only way for them to plot their course was by two islands off the coast, which they thought were Nottingham and Salisbury Islands.

It was the roughest country Parsons had ever crossed. In a short time the jagged edges of the rocks had completely cut away their sealskin boots. They tore off bits of their clothing and bound it around their feet, until they were reduced to bare feet on the flint-like stones.

On the third day the fog cleared somewhat, and they went inland again, expecting shortly to see the post. But there was to be no such luck for them. By this time they were completely exhausted, having had nothing to eat all day, except the legs of their sealskin boots, on which they chewed continually. Most of their clothing had been used to bind their feet from being cut by the rocks, and their sealskin boots had become completely worn out. At the end of the day, they were convinced they were lost beyond any hope of discovery. Apparently there was not an Inuit, much less a white man, in the country. But that bulldog determination which was to often characterize Ralph Parsons in later years, carrying him through in the face of almost insuperable obstacles, was to move him along now. Dickers and Mukke almost despaired of ever getting through. They had nothing on their feet, and practically no clothing, guns, or food, but Parsons encouraged them to keep moving.

On the fourth day Dickers could go no further. The last coverings on their feet were worn through, and all three were naked. Parsons himself was near exhaustion, but he realized that unless someone went on ahead and reached the post, and sent back food and clothing, none of them could survive. Parsons and Mukke slowly carried on, hoping to find the post shortly and return for Dickers. Telling the latter they would return with food, Parsons and Mukke continued their journey barefoot, scarcely conscious of what they were doing. At sunset many hours later—they lost track of time—after walking and crawling the entire day, they reached the summit of another of many mountains, but their bodies refused to go any farther. The end seemed close at hand. Suddenly, their semi-conscious brains aroused them, making them wonder whether what they saw at the foot of the mountain was the post or just a mirage brought on by delirium. They had reached Wolstenholme Gorge, from which vantage point they could see the post about two miles distant. They inched themselves along to the post, staggering into the quiet little cove about three hours later. They stumbled down the last few terrible rocks and collapsed on the sharp stones, their feet raw and bleeding. Parsons was surprised but happy when he saw the pile of lumber left there by the company ship for building the post. He was able to tell Amesso and Ford in terse language what had happened, to point, to say "food and clothes," and to instruct them to go after Dickers. The two set out in search of the second Inuit, returning to Wolstenholme with him the following day.

Parsons and his associates made no further exploration trips that fall because their feet were badly cut. In addition, the only boat they had was a fourteen footer salvaged from the *Paradox*, an abandoned whaler from Dundee, Scotland.

With the establishment in 1909 of the Wolstenholme post, twenty-eight-year-old Parsons had begun to leave his distinct imprint upon the Hudson's Bay Company. In 1985 A. Dudley Copland, Chief Trader with the Company from 1923 to 1939, referred to Ralph Parsons as "no ordinary man."[10] The Wolstenholme adventure served to create a portrait of an individual of great daring and perseverance. Frank Ryan, on the occasion of Parsons' retirement, spoke of the days

> ...when the young apprentice dreamed of fur trade regions beyond the known shores and gulfs, and of taking ships through the Northwest Passage. He refused to accept the Company's traditional custom of ignoring the Hudson Strait area. If there were rich furs in

adjacent regions there must be furs all along that southern shore of Hudson Strait and northeastern coast of Hudson Bay. Trappers hinted at great empires untouched by the Company's fur traders, and Ralph Parsons wanted to tap these resources—to gather wealth wherever it was, even in the shadow of the North Pole.[11]

Even in 1909 Parsons was setting his sight, not on narrow, provincial aspirations, but on expanding the influence of the Company he was beginning to love.

Parsons' determination is evident in that he waited at the Wolstenholme post two years before the first customers showed up. A lesser person would have succumbed to discouragement and moved on to another location and other pursuits; Parsons saw the broader picture and remained for the long haul. However, this is not to suggest that he walked about Wolstenholme with his head in the air. He was realistic enough to admit that he lived in an inhospitable environment that, at times, discouraged him, making him wish he lived and worked elsewhere. He noted in his journal on April 20, 1909, "Snowing fast, very rough, wind blowing a gale...This place should have been called 'Windholme' or something worse. Great place for a lunatic asylum, that sort of thing would *pay*."[12] On May 10 he wrote:

> This is a terrible life. Would that we could only see a strange face to break the monotony. Even now when we might reasonably expect a little warmer weather to get away from the place for a week or so, it's impossible unless we wished to stay for good and all.
> If the sun shines *it's foggy* on hills, and when the sun doesn't shine it's as cold and rough as almost midwinter on southern part of Labrador... .This is an admirable place to practice *patience*, another year would finish mine.[13]

He was determined to stay at least until he made contact with Inuit, his customers.

The only means of travelling with any degree of comfort in the North was according to the Inuit style, that was by living in snow-houses and travelling by dogs and komatiks. Parsons and his party had neither dogs nor komatiks. Not having yet located Inuit, they were unable to build snow-houses. Instead, they did the next best thing: they constructed small sleds on which to haul provisions, and made a thick canvas tent. They were then ready for the trip in search of Inuit in the winter.

It was bitterly cold camping in a tent at -40° F, especially considering that there was no firewood within 500 or so miles. Added to this, their outfit, supplied by the Montreal office, did not contain the usual kerosene oil stove. Prior to departing from the post, they had substituted a stove made from a biscuit tin, by soldering three lamp burners to it and using coffee tins for funnels, thereby managing to melt sufficient snow for drinking water. But there was no luxury such as tea or coffee.

On several occasions during their first winter, they travelled inland from Wolstenholme, probably fifty or sixty miles in all directions, but without catching a glimpse of Inuit. In the spring, when the snow became too soft to travel over, they were compelled to abandon this means of exploring because they had no snowshoes. Now they waited for open water and the arrival of the supply ship to bring them a new boat.

Ralph Parsons at Cape Wolstenholme, 1910.

All during the next summer, they travelled both east and west along the coast for a distance of 120 or 130 miles each way, but still found no recent signs of Inuit. In the second summer, the whaler *Active* called at Wolstenholme post and gave Parsons and his party four dogs, which proved to be of great assistance to them during the following winter. From the *Pelican* they obtained a secondhand coal/oil stove, with two good burners, which was a luxury.

During the second winter, when the snow was sufficiently hard, they started out with their usual tenting outfit and their dogs, as well as their much-prized kerosene oil stove. Travelling all day, they decided to pitch their tent on a sturdy snowbank, fastening the structure with blocks of ice and snow.

By the time the dogs were fed and the men had their lunch, they were beginning to feel comfortable. They climbed into their sleeping-bags, leaving one of the kerosene oil stoves burning. Exhausted, they quickly fell asleep, but were awakened about 2:00 or 3:00 A.M., only to find everything—including themselves—in blackness!

They looked at each other, but failed to immediately recognize themselves. A thick layer of lamp-black soot on their faces made them feel even more miserable. On the tent overhead and along its walls was a collection of frost—about one and one-half inches thick—through which was mixed a buildup of soot which had escaped from their lamp. Glancing around, they observed that their clothing and provisions too were covered with a dense layer of soot.

Wondering about the source of the trouble, they concluded it must have originated with their stove, which they were now unable to locate. They threw open the tent door for awhile and let the smoke clear away. Only then did they see that their stove had melted a three-foot hole in the snow. Down in the hole they spotted a faint glimmer.

It was bitterly cold as they tried to change their faces back to a recognizable condition. It was impossible for them to get more sleep, although they retrimmed their kerosene oil stove, getting it going at full blast, which scarcely made any impression on the temperature inside their tent.[14]

On one occasion during their second winter at Wolstenholme, some of the men were away, tending their traps, leaving at the post an Inuit boy, James Palliser, and Ralph Parsons, together with an Inuit dog and three pups. The guardians of the post decided to check their early traps, which were about one and one-half miles away. At the same time they planned, with the assistance of the dog, to attempt to break in the pups.

After considerable difficulty with the pups, the group reached the north shore of Wolstenholme Cove, following the dog's lead for a mile or so inland. Suddenly, Jimmy, the Inuit boy, stopped, shouted, then pointed to the hilltop. Looking up, Parsons saw a bear, about 1,000 yards away, that was acting strangely.

Nearing the animal, Parsons discovered she had two small cubs with her, and she was trying to get them up a 1,000-foot-high hill, the surface of which was frozen, slippery snow. The bear would take one cub in her mouth and go halfway up the mountain, drop it, then come back for the other. But she no sooner reached the one at the base of the mountain when the cub halfway up the mountain-side would slide back. The mother repeated this procedure two or three times, until the men arrived within 700 yards, at which point she forsook her offspring and galloped up the hill, disappearing over the crest.

Parsons, swinging into action, fired two shots at her, one of which struck her in her flank, but did not impede her progress. The men approached the cubs, both of which they dispatched, delighted to have them, as their supply of fresh bear meat was dwindling steadily.

Parsons realized that a young Inuit dog would usually chase and overtake a polar bear, and that the latter would turn and chase the dog—or its tracks—for awhile, eventually bringing the bear within easy shooting distance of 100 or so yards. Parsons thought they should take the dog with them and follow the tracks of the mother bear, hoping to get a shot at her. As they had only one gun with them, Parsons instructed Jimmy to take the dog.

At the crest of the mountain, they saw where the bear had disappeared into her cave, which consisted of a twelve-foot tunnel in the snow, at the apex of the mountain, the top of which was fairly level. Seeing the large amount of blood on the snow, the older man thought the bear might already be dead. Passing his rifle to Jimmy, Parsons told him to fire into the hole, while he leaned in as far as he could.

When Jimmy fired, the bear rushed out of the cave, mad with rage, its mouth open wide. The boy immediately slid down the mountain, taking the rifle with him. Parsons, not caring to take such a steep dive himself, ran as quickly as he could in the opposite direction. Glancing around once or twice, he saw the bear lumbering toward him. Then he thought he could hear her breathing.

Suddenly, he faced the bear, less than eight feet from him, expecting her full weight to be thrown directly at him. The animal stopped abruptly, standing on her hind legs, fore-paws shading her eyes, and looking, as Parsons thought, a short distance beyond him. He was both surprised and relieved!

Parsons did not linger to discover the object of the bear's attention, but retreated swiftly. Looking around a moment later, he spied the bear beating a hasty retreat to her cave. Then he realized the object of her staring; she had seen the dog, no more than fifty feet away, tethered to a rock.

Parsons saw that Jimmy was crippling a little, but he thought the young boy would still accompany him in trying to finish off the bear. At first Jimmy refused, but was finally persuaded to creep up to the cave and listen while Parsons shot the animal. Should the bear come out on the second occasion as she had done on the first, Parsons intended to stand his ground and meet her with another shot.

They gingerly crept up to the cave, but Jimmy did not do much listening; instead, he gave the entrance a wide berth. Parsons fired several shots into the hole, but the bear did not appear. They concluded that one of the shots must have killed her.

But they still did not know how to retrieve the animal. Parsons could think only of smoking her out of the cave, assuming she were still alive. He stood guard over the entrance, sending Jimmy back to the post for a shovel and some old linnet, the latter of which they saturated with oil. Setting fire to the linnet, they tossed it into the cave. They stepped back, waiting for the bear to emerge.

Ten to fifteen minutes later, they again concluded the bear was dead, but they preferred not to take any more chances. They shovelled snow into the cave, intending after filling it to cut a hole into one side of it to get the bear out. Half an hour later, the cave was nearly full. Suddenly, they heard the animal thrashing about, clawing her way out. A minute or two later, her head appeared, at which point Parsons' rifle did the rest. Parsons wrote later:

> This is the first and only instance that I have ever heard of a white bear attacking a white man, and, on this occasion, I am sure it would not have done so, had it not been wounded and its two cubs taken, and, afterwards had been greatly tormented.[15]

The following spring the men at Wolstenholme Post started out early in their boat, determined to find Inuit. They were forced to haul their boat two or three miles over the frozen harbour in order to reach open water. They could travel for only three or four hours each day because the tide would, at every chance, take the ice in on the land.

Three or four days later they had travelled a total of only fifty miles, arriving at a point of fairly clear water. However, the ice on their side of the point was coming in on the land very fast. Parsons called on the boys with him to pull their best in order to manoeuvre around the point before the ice got to them. As they were rounding the Cape, the sheet of ice, which had entered the tide, crowded in on their boat, crushing it badly. Water rushed into the craft. By this time, the ice jam had reached the land and had lifted their boat completely out of the water.

The land where the ice had caught them ran perpendicularly for a distance of nearly 2,000 feet. Consequently, they were unable to get around or up the base of the mountain. Every now and then the ice would move off a short distance and they would have to stand on the barricade of ice frozen on the shore. It was midday and the sun was high in the sky. Occasionally, a large stone would thaw from the mountain-side and tumble down, not more than a few feet from them. But they dared not move as there was barely sufficient standing room. They expected every moment for the next rock to hit them and knock them off the edge, which would signal their end. They stood still for over an hour, Parsons never fully understanding how they managed to do it. When the ice cleared, their boat lay on a sheet of ice grounded nearby.

Parsons decided that he and his party—two boys and another man—would repair their boat by wrapping a large tarpaulin around it, then proceed on their journey of exploration. However, the man refused to go on, insisting that he would not permit the boys to continue because they were frightened.

Parsons declared that he was going on, but that the others could remain where they were. He also made it clear that he was taking the boat, a decision that raised strenuous objections. Parsons wrote years later that "it was only by threatening to finally shoot the man that he consented to go on."[16] Would Parsons have shot him? We will never know, but if he had, the subsequent course of his life would have been altered substantially. They continued for two more days, during which time nothing was spoken between them. In the midst of such strained relations, Parsons got no sleep.

In the evening of the second day, they finally came upon a group of Inuit tents. The Inuit were as pleased to see them as they were to see the Inuit. The Inuit rushed down the side of the hill, their faces covered with blood and looking as if they had been fighting with each other. The man and the boys with Parsons, although ordered ashore, were fearful to do so, thinking the Inuit were intent on harming them. It was later learned that the Inuit had recently killed a seal and were enjoying a banquet of raw meat.

Parsons' party transported some of the Inuit back to the Wolstenholme post with them, and sent the others further along the coast to spread the news of the new post. The two-year waiting period at Wolstenholme and the frequent forays inland had paid off for Parsons. Once he found the Inuit, the trade grew briskly.[17]

Parsons exhibited certain personal qualities which in time would lead to his becoming in charge of the Hudson's Bay Company's entire transportation system. As well, his resourcefulness in assisting business in the fur trade was always evident. For example, in the Eastern Arctic District, he was not provided with Company trading tokens. As early as 1909,

Wolstenholm Post, 1934.

however, he made his own tokens from scrap copper traditionally used for strappings around casks, and later from lead commonly sold to the trappers for moulding into musket balls. To identify them, he stamped on each one his name, or a portion of it, with a die normally used to stamp his tools. These crude tokens were of various sizes and in the form of squares, triangles and rectangles. They were mainly used in the areas of Lake Harbour and Cape Dorset, Baffin Island. Today they are very rare. In recent years, a fortunate purchase of a few pieces has been made, preserved by chance on an old Indian coat, as medicine balls. Canadian coin catalogues list these tokens and show them to be of fair market value.[18]

Although Frank G. Mercer did not work for Ralph Parsons, the former, as a policeman in Northern Labrador for many years, knew the latter well. Mercer wrote recently, "That he possessed qualities of leadership was evident to all who knew him. His word was his bond."[19] Again, "Arctic travel held no terrors for him, for he went where few white people had ventured before his time."[20] By joining the Company as a nineteen-year-old apprentice at Cartwright, Labrador, Parsons had found a professional career to follow, a passion to develop and a cause to defend. From then on he lived for the Company. His natural ability and work ethic were twin assets which enabled him to endure in an often inhospitable environment. He never sought an easy life, a fact evident from as early as 1909 during the founding of the Wolstenholme post. If his many and varied adventures were too overwhelming and demanding for him, that would have been the ideal time for him to resign from the Company and seek a less strenuous vocation in life. Instead, his activities, beside adding to a wealth of invaluable experiences, whetted his appetite for adventure and drove him relentlessly to succeed and advance the cause of the Company.

Cape Wolstenholme   Sketch by John Parsons, 1964

NOTES TO CHAPTER 2: FIRST YEARS WITH THE COMPANY

1. Frederick W. Rowe, *A History of Newfoundland and Labrador* (Toronto, Ontario: McGraw-Hill Ryerson Ltd., 1980), p. 476.
2. A.P. Dyke (1969), cited in Dermod C. Madden, "Cartwright," *Encyclopedia of Newfoundland and Labrador*, vol. I, eds., Joseph R. Smallwood and Robert D.W. Pitt (St. John's, Newfoundland: Newfoundland Book Publishers [1967] Ltd., 1981), p. 377.
3. James Fraser, Certificate of Character, dated December 29, 1900.
4. Employment form for Ralph Parsons, dated at Cartwright, Labrador, July 31, 1900.
5. Archibald L. Fleming, "People I Meet in the Arctic," *The Evening News and Evening Mail* (London, England), April 14, 1939, p. 8.
6. "Memoranda for Sir William Schooling Record of Hudson Bay Service—Ralph Parsons."
7. First stanza of poem inscribed in India ink on skin side of sealskin, presented to Ralph Parsons on his retirement, 1940.
8. The story of the establishment by Ralph Parsons of the Wolstenholme post is drawn from Ralph Parsons, "Post Established in Hudson Strait and Instances in Connection With the Same," part of "Memoranda for Sir William Schooling Record of Hudson Bay Service—Ralph Parsons," pp. 1-11. See also Frank Ryan, "Forty Years on the Fur Trail," *The Beaver*, June 1940 (Outfit 271), pp.20-21; R.H.H. Macaulay, *Trading into Hudson's Bay: A narrative of the visit of Patrick Ashley Cooper, Thirtieth Governor of The Hudson's Bay Company, to Labrador, Hudson Strait and Hudson Bay in the Year 1934* (Winnipeg, Manitoba: The Hudson's Bay Company, 1934), pp. 45-46; and Ralph Parsons' Journal of Wolstenholme post.
9. Ryan, "Forty Years on the Fur Trail," p. 21.
10. A. Dudley Copland, *Coplalook* (Winnipeg, Manitoba: Watson and Dwyer Publishing Ltd., 1985), p. 83.
11. Ryan, "Fur Trail," p. 20.
12. Ralph Parsons' *Journal of Wolstenholme Post*, April 20, 1909 entry.
13. *Ibid.*, May 10, 1909 entry.
14. Ralph Parsons, "Looking for Eskimos in Winter," in "Post Established in Hudson Strait and Instances in Connection With the Same," pp. 4-5 in *Journal of Wolstenholme Post*.
15. *Idem*, "Polar Bear," in ibid., p. 9. The entire incident is found on pp. 6-9.
16. *Idem*, "The Finding of the Eskimos," in ibid., p. 10.
17. This entire incident is found in *ibid.*, pp. 9-11.
18. Canadian coin catalogues of modern vintage.
19. Frank G. Mercer, "W. Ralph Parsons (1881-1956): The Last Fur Trade Commissioner of the Hudson's Bay Company," unpublished article, p. 3. See also reference to Mercer's unpublished article in Heather May, "W. Ralph Parsons," *The Compass*, Carbonear, Newfoundland, Vol. 26, No. 45, Nov. 9, 1993 — Sec. B.
20. *Idem*, letter to the editor, *The Evening Telegram*, March 21, 1991, p. 10.

Chapter 3

Adventure in the North

"... [T]he qualities we value are not natural gifts but human achievements which must be preserved with effort and sacrifice."
—Evelyn Waugh, Commentary to T.A. McInerny,
The Private Man, 1962, p. viii.

n the fall of 1910, twenty-eight-year-old Ralph Parsons was stranded for the winter at Erik Cove, a sheltered spot at the southwest outlet to Hudson Strait and the source of fresh water for Hudson's Bay Company's ships. He was supposed to trade for furs and ivory during the winter; however, because the cove was so remote, the Inuit did not know he was there until the following spring. In the interim, he spent the entire winter alone, lacking even a dog team for companionship. "But intrepid young Newfoundlanders are not easily put off by such trifles," comments Richard Brown, author of *Voyage of the Iceberg*.[1] Rather than despair because of his predicament, Parsons patrolled his traplines on snowshoes, logging literally hundreds of miles before the arrival of spring. His hard work paid rich dividends; word spread through the surrounding settlements that he had amassed an excellent haul of furs in that virgin territory. Now he waited for the Company's supply ship, the *Pelican*, to call at Erik Cove for his precious cargo.

But there was someone else who had a marauding eye on the result of Parsons' labours. That individual was Osbert Clare Forsyth-Grant, who planned to engage Parsons in a short-lived conflict over the latter's furs,[2] a high-stakes gamble doomed to failure almost before it began, mainly because of mistakes caused by Forsyth-Grant's own arrogance. Even if he had succeeded in his planned act of piracy, he would have done so only at the expense of a titanic struggle with the Company's contact at Erik Cove,

Ralph Parsons, an individual of "iron-willed determination," according to Cyril Goodyear.[3]

The youngest son of a wealthy Scottish landowner, Forsyth-Grant had been educated at the famous English public school, Rugby.[4] He entered Sandhurst to prepare for a career as an officer in the British Army, but bought his way out of the army after a run-in with a superior officer. A visit to Canada and a voyage on a Scottish whaler to Greenland and Baffin Bay left him captivated by Arctic life. He bought the whaler, the *Snowdrop*, as well as the whaling station at Cape Haven, on the Davis Strait. He later replaced the *Snowdrop* with the *Seduisante*.

By 1911 he was extremely proud of his *Seduisante*. French-built, she was an elegant two-masted barquentine. In 1910, armed with a harpoon gun in the bow for bowheads and a smooth-bore swivel gun on both sides for seals and walrus, she had reaped a bumper load of walrus hides and tusks, whale oil and blubber, seals, white foxes, polar bear skins, narwhal horns, and eiderdown. Traditionally he sent his ship back to Scotland for the winter, preferring to enjoy the Arctic's free lifestyle year-round. Hoping to reap as rich a harvest in his second hunting season as he did in 1910, Forsyth-Grant instructed Captain Connon to take the *Seduisante* into Hudson Strait late in the year, much against the better judgment of her Dundee captain and crew. But Forsyth-Grant had an ulterior motive; Ralph Parsons' bounty of furs had not gone unnoticed by this buccaneering Scot, who was more than willing to take enormous risks with his ship and crew on the Arctic ice, especially if it meant a sizeable harvest of walrus at Nottingham Island, off the western end of the Strait. More to the point, he desperately wanted Parsons' exceptionally fine haul of furs.

Richard Brown describes Forsyth-Grant as "a tough, handsome young man with a sardonic sense of humour, an utter contempt for convention and a set of sceptical opinions which border on Godless anarchy."[5] This portrait is borne out by the Rev. Archibald L. Fleming, first Anglican Bishop of the Arctic, who recalled in 1957 that Forsyth-Grant "stood about six feet in height, had a clearly chiselled profile, searching eyes, slightly hollow cheeks, sensitive mouth expressive of both wit and sarcasm and a very determined chin."[6] A practical joker, on one occasion Forsyth-Grant induced the Bishop to eat brains that were oozing from a caribou head dropped onto his plate by the Scot's Eskimo concubine. Although a person of positive convictions, Forsyth-Grant held no belief in the Christian God, instead he recognized an impersonal mind behind the universe. Man's purpose, he felt, was to squeeze as much pleasure as possible out of life. "I was sure he would be dangerous if thwarted," Fleming observed ominously.[7] Whispers among the Inuit intimated that he had murdered another trader for his furs; while this was patently untrue, he *could have* committed such an act. This was the individual Ralph Parsons would encounter at Erik Cove.

A loner, Forsyth-Grant looked askance at what he perceived as competition from the Hudson's Bay Company. Irritated by Parsons forcing himself into *his* territory, he decided to sail to Erik Cove, make his move on a black night, and pick the site bare. "The next morning," he said to himself, "Parsons can whistle all he wants for his furs." Forsyth-Grant was fully aware that the closest Law—the Royal North-West Mounted Police—was 300 miles away at Cape Fullerton, on the far side of Hudson Bay. "By the time Parsons can get news of this across," he schemed, "his furs and ivory will be halfway to Scotland." The intruder realized he was the only white man aboard who might be recognized, but he reasoned that as long as he kept his head lowered, he could return to his idyllic life at his Cape Haven whaling station and nobody would know about his actions. Admittedly, he was not planning to hurt Parsons, as long as the Company man behaved reasonably. However, if Parsons responded with unreasonable behaviour, Forsyth-Grant thought that his crew would be capable of virtually anything.

Much to Forsyth-Grant's surprise, not all of his crew shared his freebooting policy. "The fact that we're living in a civilized world has to count for something," they figured, "and tactics that might've worked in the old days won't wear well now. We're in this for money and adventure—but not the way you're planning." Although his crew protested, Forsyth-Grant, a persuasive individual, forced his crew into submission.

On Saturday, September 9, 1911, the *Seduisante* furtively slipped into Erik Cove. Once the boats were lowered, the crew rowed ashore; however, because the place appeared to be deserted, Forsyth-Grant could see no reason why he and his men should not be safely on their way again by midnight, if not earlier.

But this is where Forsyth-Grant made a miscalculation. He was unaware that Parsons had reinforcements. The Company had bought him a thirty-foot motor launch, the *Daryl*. A couple of able American yachtsmen on holiday from Yale University—Bob English and Pete Rowland—had taken the *Daryl* from the Grenfell Mission at Mecatina,

Quebec, and with the help of a Labrador pilot, George Ford, brought her north, delivering her to a grateful Parsons. Until the *Pelican* arrived to return them home, they were lounging about Erik Cove for a day or two.

After sunset, English, Rowland, and Ford bid Parsons good-night and slowly picked their way down to the launch, where upon arrival they saw what appeared to be a small spurt of light out at sea. Then the first spurt was followed by another, and another, each one moving from east to west. English and Rowland were mystified. "Are they from a lost hunting party?" they asked each other. "No, they're moving too quickly for that." Ford, a livyere who had been born and raised in Labrador, and wise in the ways of life along the coast, suggested that someone was igniting matches and dropping them into the water from a moving ship, or "Maybe someone's lighting his pipe?" he suggested tentatively. "Or perhaps it's a signal to someone on shore." Ford's words were met with further questions from the university students, "But what ship can it be, and more importantly, what's she doing here?" Whatever was going on, it was obvious to all three that it was most unusual.

Ford and English dropped a dory into the water and rowed out to look around. Edging cautiously along the high, imposing cliffs, Ford spied the silhouette of a small sailing vessel. Then they heard the muffled squeak of paddles. Two boats, loaded with men packed like sardines in a can, passed them. It was light enough to observe that the occupants were carrying guns. "This is no longer odd," commented English. "This is downright dangerous!" He fired his rifle as a warning. Onboard the launch, Rowland, knowing nothing about what was happening directly ahead of him, on impulse started her up and headed toward them. He pushed every switch within sight; the *Daryl* lit up like a Christmas tree. Ford and English boarded the motor launch.

Forsyth-Grant and the men in the boats were astounded. The latter rested uneasily on their oars, with the *Daryl* between them and the *Seduisante*. The Scot's mind raced through a litany of possibilities. "Of all nights to choose for this," he muttered, "I had to settle on one when the Cape Fullerton Mounties are on the prowl! This throws my plans into confusion." The Mounties may—or may not—have been able to prove that he had designs on Parsons and his bountiful harvest, but there was no doubt in his mind that they could charge him with illegal hunting. Too late he realized he should have obtained a whaling permit. Then a sickening thought entered his mind: he was in danger of having his entire season's cargo, possibly including his trusty *Seduisante*, confiscated. That thought was more than he could bear. He knew he was unable to fight off "the Mounties"; even the hardiest members of his crew would disapprove of such action. Neither could he run away, what with most of his men still in the boats. Trapped, his nerve momentarily failed him.

As for English and Rowland on the *Daryl*, the thought that they were supposed to be the Mounties never entered their minds. The only thing they knew was that they were sandwiched between two groups of armed men in the middle of something strikingly similar to a pirate raid, and that they were both outnumbered and outgunned. They were unsure of their next move.

Out of desperation, Rowland attempted a bluff. Putting the *Daryl* into gear, he roared directly toward the strange ship, hailed her in his most authoritative voice, and demanded her name.

"The *Seddy-santy*," responded the lookout, seventeen-year-old Fred Livie, the secret match-lighter, before Forsyth-Grant could quell him.

"Why are you showing no lights?" Rowland asked indignantly.

Taken completely off-balance by the second question, Forsyth-Grant replied, "I see no need for them in such a deserted neck-of-the-woods." Concerned with the possibility that he was being chased by "the Mounties," the authoritative voice now had him on the run.

Rowland could think of nothing further to say, especially since the other side had all the weapons. After a long pause, he demanded to board the *Seduisante*, but by now his voice sounded less authoritative, even to himself.

Forsyth-Grant, who had regained his courage, absolutely refused to cooperate. To his surprise and relief, the launch turned away.

Their bluff having failed, English and Rowland felt ridiculous.

Forsyth-Grant was not overly pleased with himself, either. Because he had volunteered too much information, there was no prospect of pursuing his planned raid. "What's more," he thought to himself, "whoever these people were, they certainly weren't the Mounties." Once he saw the *Daryl* anchored inshore, he signalled his men to return to the *Seduisante*. It is no understatement to claim that everybody in Erik Cove—both afloat and ashore—spent a disturbing and sleepless night.

The following morning, much to everyone's surprise, the *Seduisante* was still anchored in Erik Cove, the reason being that during the night Forsyth-Grant had decided on an alternate course of action. "The best thing for me to do," he said to himself, "is to brazen the whole thing out and pay Parsons a social call." He and Captain Connon rowed ashore. An individual of great charisma, he switched it on as soon as he sat close to the stove, drinking his host's coffee and making small-talk. "I should point out," he said, "that we only put into Erik Cove to take on water." Then, as an afterthought, he inquired casually, "Isn't this where the Hudson's Bay Company's vessels take on water? Now that we're here, though, I'm wondering if there's any news of the walrus herds?"

Parsons, according to Bishop Fleming, had "a tremendous understanding of human nature," knowing "exactly how to deal with men."[8] Now he put his expertise into action. "I've heard nothing," he responded in an equally-mannerly voice. He was careful to say nothing about the unusual events of the previous evening, but made it clear that he was expecting the *Pelican* to arrive at Erik Cove any day. "Maybe she'll be here this afternoon," he said offhandedly.

Forsyth-Grant and Parsons shook hands, after which the Scot and Captain Connon returned to the *Seduisante*, but they spoiled the effect somewhat by neglecting to collect the water they allegedly had come for. Getting his ship underway, he took her out into the rising westerly gale. Undeterred by the fiasco at Erik Cove, Forsyth-Grant was still determined to send a bumper cargo to his homeland. He had failed in his attempt to wrest it by an act of piracy from Ralph Parsons, but he was prepared to hunt for it. Later that same year, however, he lost his life when the *Seduisante* was wrecked in a gale. The *Pelican* arrived at Erik Cove, where she collected Parsons' valuable cargo, and proceeded down Hudson Strait, taking Bob English and Pete Rowland with her. As for Parsons' own perception of the Erik Cove incident, Pete Rowland wrote, "The factor inclined to make light of the whole affair."[9]

Partly as a result of this incident, Parsons' own stature with the Company increased. In 1957 Bishop Fleming referred in glowing terms to his "amazing powers of detachment." He "never appeared to be surprised no matter how unexpected or absurd a report or incident might be."[10] The Erik Cove episode—unexpected and absurd in many respects—is a prime example of such studied reserve and discipline.

By the summer of 1911, Ralph Parsons was still dreaming — some people might have termed it *day*dreaming. Prior to 1909, when he had established the Company post at Wolstenholme, trading had been in the bottom of the bay, primarily up the Labrador coast, around Ungava, and

Hudson's Bay Company Post at Lake Harbour, Baffin Island, about 1939.

Hudson and James Bays—mainly below the tree line—across the Prairie provinces, and into what is presently British Columbia. There was limited trading — mainly in white foxes — with the Inuit on the outskirts of their territory.[11] But Parsons was dreaming of fur trade regions beyond the known shores and gulfs.

Parsons now felt confident enough to select Lake Harbour, on the opposite side of Hudson Strait, for another advance post of the Company, thereby installing its first Baffin Island post in 1911. Indeed, he would be honoured in 1934 as "the first man to realize the great possibilities of Baffin Land and of the country to the east of the Bay up to Hudson Strait."[12] He constructed the new post from supplies brought by the *Pelican*, the Company's supply ship, on which he had travelled in 1909 while establishing the post at Wolstenholme.

Lake Harbour, which takes its Inuit name, "Kingmeeghock," from a light-coloured, rounded headland, resembling the heel of a foot, is located at the head of a winding inlet, about twenty miles in length. The strong tidal action — rising and falling twenty-eight feet — creates problems for boats. During the winter, the tides cause the ice along the coast to heave up twice a day. Steaming up the inlet, one experiences an uncomfortable rise in temperature. In Hudson Strait, in the midst of the ice fields, the temperature can be in the forties, but while dropping anchor at Lake Harbour one can be sweltering in a temperature of 85°F. The channel leading into the anchorage is rather narrow.[13]

By 1929, Lake Harbour was the base for the Southern Baffin Island Section, which consisted of the posts at Lake Harbour itself, Amadjuak (established by Parsons in 1921), Cape Dorset (established by him in 1913), and Frobisher Bay (established in 1914 while he was in charge of the District). In the summer of 1928, Ernie Lyall, who spent sixty-five years in Canada's North, had left Cape Smith for Lake Harbour. He remembered it later as

> ...a really beautiful place. From the ship as you get near, you can see great big high land that looks like it's straight coast, but then you come into a long narrow harbour, and there is a sort of cliff edge around you.[14]

A year later, in 1929, A. Dudley Copland, the Company's Chief Trader from 1923 to 1939, was sent to Lake Harbour as manager of the Southern Baffin Island Section. He recalled in 1985 that the site

> ...had a tidy appearance. The few buildings sat snugly at the bottom of a gravel hill where every spring the staff worked hard to cover the entire post area with fresh sand. In this way the grounds were levelled up and were always in immaculate condition. All the walks between the buildings were lined with white-washed stones. The buildings themselves were fresh-painted in the standard colours: white with green trim, and a red roof.[15]

Parsons took a brief holiday in 1911-12, during which time he made a winter inspection trip along the North Shore of the Gulf of St. Lawrence, extending from Bersimis to St. Augustine. He then returned to Hudson Strait. From the nucleus of the two posts he had established—at Wolstenholme and Lake Harbour—the northern portion of the District was developed.

In 1913, by which time he was making 200 pounds sterling annually,[16] Parsons established a post at Cape Dorset. By 1930, A. Dudley Copland found this isolated post to be the most prosperous one in the Southern Baffin Island Section.[17] In 1914, another post was established under Parsons' personal supervision, this time at Stupart's Bay, a Northern Quebec post. In the same year, a post was also established at Frobisher Bay, while Parsons was in charge of the District. The posts at Stupart's and Frobisher Bays marked the northward march of the Company. Already Parsons was beginning to bear the appellation by the Inuit on Baffin Island as "the white man who does all the thinking."[18]

When Great Britain declared war on Germany in 1914, Canada took immediate steps to aid the British war effort. The first Canadian soldiers landed in France on February 11, 1915. When Parsons heard in 1915 that Canada was at war, his initial thought was that the Company's supply ship might be unable to get through to the posts which had been established. If this indeed were so, he realized, then someone would have to make an effort to get out.[19]

One of the Company's motor vessels and the one which had figured prominently in the Forsyth-Grant fiasco at Erik Cove in 1911, the *Daryl*, had been beached for the winter in its rough dry-dock. She would usually be slipped into the water around July and deputized for demanding inter-post work. Unfortunately, she was at that time far from open water. Parsons realized that if she were to get out and return with supplies, she would have to start her journey long before July. The ship, which had been beached high above the water level, was now thirty feet above the ice. But seemingly insurmountable difficulties had never deterred Parsons before, nor would they stop him in his most recent predicament.

A heavy sled was constructed on the ice surface. A series of cribs was built, Parsons' intention being that the *Daryl* might be eased down to the structure. The workers were greatly relieved when her bow finally rested on the sled, but their sigh of relief was short-lived. As her great weight pressed down on the weakening ice, it began to belly. Parsons quickly saw that if she sank where she was, she would be held up indefinitely. The ship would have to be moved by other means.

The only other alternative was to move the ship by humans and dogs, fifty of each were available. Assembling both, Parsons hitched the dogs in front, while he instructed the men and women to push from behind. Grudgingly, the *Daryl* moved and was gently eased onto firmer ice.

Then the tough trip — fifteen miles over ice to open water — began. Cheers from the men and women mingled with howls from the dogs as the *Daryl* eventually crashed through the ice near the water's edge and was safely launched.

The voyage from Lake Harbour to Cape Dorset began on Monday, May 24, 1915. The fourth day out, the *Daryl* encountered heavy running ice, which badly damaged her keel, rudder, propeller, and stern-post. The crew barely succeeded in keeping her afloat by using pumps and by bailing with pails until she was beached on the barricade ice. The pressure on the crew was intense, for everything would be lost if the *Daryl* sank and no supply ship came.

There were few tools available for a job of this magnitude, and few men capable of performing such repairs. But Parsons again displayed his keen leadership qualities, and sent one of his men to the post about five miles away, to obtain available tools.

When the tide went out, exposing the *Daryl*'s hull, it was discovered that her keel had been half ripped away. Parsons and the other men worked feverishly to repair the damage caused by the treacherous ice-shelf. Using wood handsaws, they managed to saw the iron keel from the ship. At low-tide, they worked constantly, sawing through the one-inch-thick bolts which fastened the keel to the keelson. The teeth were worn from all the saws, but eventually the *Daryl* was set free from the damaged keel and was ready for repair. Since there were no materials for a shipyard, odd parts were used. At last, the stout-hearted ship, in a patched-up fashion, slipped off to complete her entire Eastern Arctic trip and out to Port Burwell, a tiny settlement snuggled in a valley on a barren island near Cape Chidley.

After his adventurous 1915 voyage in the *Daryl*, Parsons was eventually picked up by a patrol from Newfoundland and brought to St. John's. In 1916 he visited the capital city again and was appointed inspector of the three eastern Districts—Labrador, Ungava, and Hudson Strait. In November 1916, while he was in St. John's, he tried to enlist in the Royal Newfoundland Regiment to serve in the war, but because of an accident suffered up North, he was rejected by the medical officer and found ineligible for war service.[20]

Parsons compensated for the rejection by returning to the North and carrying on in the fur trade empire. However, he personally supervised the establishment of no more posts until after the war. Some of the most famous and memorable stories related about him had their origin in those days when he was attempting almost the impossible. It is necessary to add that it was rare for anyone outside Parsons' close circle of friends to hear of his spine-tingling experiences, as his nephew, Jack Hambling, admits in *The Second Time Around: Growing Up in Bay Roberts*.[21] Bishop Fleming acknowledged in 1939, a year before Parsons' retirement, that the latter was "[a] man of few words, inclined to avoid the society of other men."[22] This observation is borne out by Henry Toke Munn who wrote, "He appeared to me to have no intimates."[23] One of those stories was the record-breaking trip for a man and dog team from Cape Dorset to Lake Harbour—a distance of 250 miles—which Parsons covered in two sleeps, a record unheard of before and unequalled since.

In 1917 Parsons was made inspector of the Labrador District, and shortly later, was appointed in charge of the combined District of Hudson Strait, Labrador, and St. Lawrence. It was in this year, 1917, that a post was established at Fort McKenzie, in the Ungava Bay Section, while Parsons was in charge of the St. Lawrence-Labrador District.

During the 1917 season, he took an inspection trip on the *Daryl* of the Hudson Strait posts. During the trip, which lasted from July 26 to October 6, he maintained a diary, which provides moment-by-moment coverage of his activities.[24] Leaving Montreal at 7:00 A.M. on Thursday, July 26, he stopped for various lengths of time at St. John's, Grady, Burwell, Wareham Bay, Lake Harbour, Wolstenholme, Charlton, Nelson, Churchill, Chesterfield, back to Wolstenholme, Dorset, back to Lake Harbour and Wareham Bay, concluding his inspection at Fort Chimo.

During the ten-week trip, he, among other activities, noted the progress of the posts; made suggestions on how they could be improved; dispatched cargo; noted the price of salt and salmon; suggested how best the codfishery could be developed; commented on firewood, vessels, and furs; surveyed harbours; delivered mail; and explored mineral deposits along the coast. On August 4, he was concerned that, in his opinion, some of the Labrador post managers knew

> ... practically nothing about grading and valuing furs; they know so little that we are compelled to work under the great disadvantage of not allowing them to purchase for cash, which to a great extent is reducing our trade and leaving an opening for opposition to get the better of us every time.

He was especially pleased with the Stupart's Bay post, which, he noted on August 10, had

> ... made a record hunt, not only in foxes, but in all other returns. In

white foxes alone, they have secured 450, as compared with 137 for last year. This has been a fairly good year for furs in this locality. . .

Nor were there any complaints about the Cape Dorset post, as he noted on August 23.

En route to Wolstenholme, the *Daryl* steamed through literally thousand of walrus. He noted in his diary on August 24: "Had to alter our course many times to keep clear of them." August 25: "Near the shore the water was in a continual foam made by the walrus, and appeared like a long string of breakers."

There were problems—some minor, others, major. One gentleman was being troubled greatly by a toothache. "After giving him a stiff glass of whisky," Parsons wrote on August 25, "he had courage enough to let me pull out three teeth for him . . . ." A more serious problem arose when Parsons tried to repair the *Daryl*'s engine. "The cylinder head had rusted so badly," he noted in his diary on August 14, "that there was a hole in it . . . ." He plugged it temporarily with red lead and cement to allow the vessel to continue her trip. Scraping the paint and rust from the outside of the cylinder, he discovered that the entire cylinder head had been eaten away by the saltwater and that only one-sixteenth of an inch of metal remained about halfway around the object. Even that fell away when it was scraped. Twenty-four hours later, he had to abandon any hope of placing a clamp over the head because there was insufficient metal to hold the screws. Another temporary solution was to fill the cavity with cement and attempt to get around to the Strait posts, but he was practical enough to realize they would be exceptionally fortunate to succeed.

From 1910 to 1918, Ralph Parsons continued the tradition he had begun much earlier by applying himself wholeheartedly to the work at hand. Being in the employ of the Hudson's Bay Company continued to provide him with an honour to defend, an occupation to enjoy, an adventure in which to be involved—in short, his *raison d'être*. His voracious appetite for hard work was the stuff of which legends are made. By 1918 Ralph Parsons was well on his way to becoming a legend in the North.

NOTES TO CHAPTER 3: ADVENTURE IN THE NORTH

1. Richard Brown, *Voyage of the Iceberg* (Toronto, Ontario: James Lorimer & Co., 1983), p. 78.
2. The story that follows is taken from *ibid.*, pp. 77-85. See also John T. Rowland, *North to Baffin Land* (New York: Seven Seas Press, 1973), Chapter 6.
3. Cyril Goodyear, "Nunatsuak: Arctic sovereignty," *The Evening Telegram*, October 3, 1987, p. 1A.
4. This portrait of Forsyth-Grant is drawn from Archibald Lang Fleming, *Archibald the Arctic* (Toronto, Ontario: Saunders of Toronto Ltd., 1957). p. 123.
5. Brown, *Voyage*, p. 77.
6. Fleming, *Archibald*, p. 123.
7. *Ibid.*
8. *Idem*, "People I Meet in the Arctic," *The Evening News and Evening Mail* (London, England), April 14, 1939, p. 8.
9. Rowland, *North to Baffin Land*, p. 66.
10. *Idem, Archibald*, p. 259.
11. Goodyear, "Nunatsuak," p. 1A.
12. The Governor's Speech at Farewell Dinner Given by the Fur Trade On R.M.S. Nascopi, August 11, 1934, in R.H.H. Macaulay, *Trading into Hudson's Bay: A narrative of the visit of Patrick Ashley Cooper, Thirtieth Governor of The Hudson's Bay Company, to Labrador, Hudson Strait and Hudson Bay in the Year 1934* (Winnipeg, Manitoba: The Hudson's Bay Company, 1934), p. 103.
13. Macaulay, *Trading into Hudson's Bay*, p. 44; and A. Dudley Copland, *Coplalook* (Winnipeg, Manitoba: Watson and Dwyer Publishing Ltd., 1985), pp. 114-115.
14. Ernie Lyall, *An Arctic Man* (Halifax, Nova Scotia: Formac Publishing Co. Ltd., 1983), p. 62.
15. Copland, *Coplalook*, pp. 114-115.
16. Record book of the Hudson's Bay Company, pp. 24-25.
17. Copland, *Coplalook*, p. 124.
18. Frank Ryan, "Forty Years on the Fur Trail," *The Beaver*, June 1940 (Outfit 271), p. 21.
19. This story is taken from *ibid.*, pp. 21-22.
20. Certificate of Rejection from the First Royal Newfoundland Regiment, November 16, 1916.
21. Jack Hambling, *The Second Time Around: Growing Up in Bay Roberts* (St. John's, Newfoundland: Harry Cuff Publications Ltd., 1992), p. 58.
22. Fleming, "People I Meet in the Arctic," p. 8.
23. Henry Toke Munn, *Prairie Trails and Arctic By-Ways* (London, England: Hurst and Blackett, Ltd., 1932), p. 270.
24. What follows is taken from "Journal. Ralph Parsons, 1917." Cf. "Extracts from Diary of Ralph Parsons on Inspection Trip of Hudson Strait Posts per Daryl—Season 1917," *passim*.

Fur Trade Conference, 1937. Ralph Parsons is in the centre of the first row. Hayward Parsons is on the far left of the first row. A. Dudley Copland and Robert H. Chesshire are second and third on the left in the third row and George Watson is second from the right in the first row...

Courtesy of Norma (Cave) Sparkes

Chapter 4

Years of Joy and Years of Sorrow

"To every thing there is a season, and a time to every purpose under the heaven: A time to be born, and a time to die...A time to weep, and a time to laugh; a time to mourn, and a time to dance...A time to get, and a time to lose..." (Ecclesiastes 3:1-6).

o Ralph Parsons, life *was* work, a self-imposed discipline, which left little time for socializing. His love of work left little time for anything else. Naturally reserved, he released his energy and strength in a hardy, outdoor lifestyle. But in 1918 his life would be permanently altered; he would enter into a loving relationship with the woman of his choice. However, death intervened and the joy he was to experience with his young bride was to be short-lived. Thereafter, he would devote his energy primarily to the Hudson's Bay Company and his surviving son, David.

Like all families, the Parsons family of Bay Roberts experienced years of both joy *and* sorrow. Marriages and births were associated with joy, and sickness and death, with sorrow. Between 1917 and 1924 there were far too few of the former, and far too many of the latter. Children were born to brothers Hayward and Gus and their spouses, and to sisters Etta, Florence, Winnifred, and Mildred and their spouses. Almost a year after Parsons' marriage, his wife gave birth to a healthy son. Their second child, also a son, died mere hours after his birth. This tragedy was followed closely by another traumatic event, the death of Parsons' beloved wife. Less than a year before, he had lost a sister who died in childbirth. In 1924 sorrow entered the Parsons family again when his ten-year-old nephew was killed in a tragic accident, an event which seemed only to highlight the fine line between joy and sorrow. Life was a mixture of both, with sorrow always seeming to override the brief interludes of joy. Parsons was made to realize the transitory nature of joy and the almost constant sorrow that accompanied his life and that of other members of his family.

In 1918 Parsons married Flora May House of Pool's Island, Badger's Quay, Newfoundland. The youngest of twelve children—five girls and seven boys—born to Peter (1840-1923) and Mary House, Flora was born on Tuesday, May 3, 1887. Her mother was a daughter of William Kean of Greenspond, one of the famous seafarers of his day. Several of Flora's brothers emigrated to the United States and Canada, where they eventually died after successful careers. Details of Flora's early life are scanty, but it is known that between 1906 and 1909 she travelled back and forth between her hometown and the United States, particularly New York. She later compiled a large scrapbook of post cards, now in the possession of her son, sent to her from relatives and friends while she was in the States.

Flora met Ralph Parsons through her older sister, Caroline ("Carrie"), who several years earlier had married the Rev. Evelyn Clench, an English cleric. The Anglican minister, who had served at Cartwright, had already met Parsons, probably while the latter was at his Hudson's Bay Company post in Labrador. Shortly before 1918 the Clenches moved to Spaniard's Bay.

The Rectory in Spaniard's Bay was situated in a picturesque setting with spacious grounds and a wooded area. As a small boy David Parsons often visited the Clenches at Spaniard's Bay, and remembers the spacious park-like rectory grounds, with its wooded paths, rustic benches alongside a clear-flowing little brook, an idyllic refuge for a few domesticated ducks and stocked trout. At those times, Carrie reminisced as she showed the young boy the spot where Flora and Ralph had sat when they were courting.

Ralph and Flora were married by the Rev. Clench at Holy Redeemer Anglican Church in Spaniard's Bay on Wednesday, October 30, 1918.[1] On the day of her marriage, Flora was presented with a certificate in commemoration of her six years as a member of the Girls Friendly Society, founded in 1875. The document, signed by Caroline W. Barnes, Associate Branch Secretary, and the Rev. Clench, Rector of the Spaniard's Bay parish, displayed the classic passage on women from the Book of Proverbs:

Ralph Parsons and his wife, Flora May House with infant son David, 1920.

A virtuous woman is a crown to her husband: her price is far above rubies. The heart of her husband doth safely trust in her. She will do him good and not evil all the days of her life. She worketh willingly with her hands. She stretcheth out her hand to the poor; yea she reacheth forth her hands to the needy. Strength and honour are her clothing and she shall rejoice in the time to come. She openeth her mouth with wisdom; and in her tongue is the law of kindness. She looketh well to her household and eateth not the bread of idleness. Favour is deceitful and beauty is vain but a woman that feareth the Lord she shall be praised.[2]

The happy couple may have spent their honeymoon in St. John's.

On Saturday, September 27, 1919 the Parsons household was blessed with the birth of a child, a moment of great joy. He was given the names of David Ralph. Flora so named him because, as she explained it to her sister-in-law, Datie, "David was a good man." She was referring to the David in the Bible.[3] The parents' delight in their offspring knew no bounds. From day one the proud father lavished love on his son. While Parsons was in Montreal on business in July 1920, Flora wrote him that his son was

> ...a good, sweet boy and do you believe it he missed you very much the first 3 or 4 nights. He used to cry and look all around and look at your empty pillow and cry & cry. And when I used to say "Poor Pa Pa gone" it seemed that he knew what I meant. He loves his dear pop alright.[4]

Some of Flora's feelings towards her husband are preserved in the tender and newsy letter she wrote to her "dear, dear Ralph" from St. John's while he was in Montreal. The letter, dated July 10, 1920, was written on the same day as she had received a message from him. "What a shame you did not stay on longer," she wrote. "To think I might have had my dear Ralph with me a week or so longer, instead of being parted this week...."

Although she was keeping busy, his absence, if only for a short time, had left a noticeable void in her heart. She expressed her thoughts this way:

> Well my dear how empty and lonesome it seems here without you. I've often thought since you've been gone but I know you can never realize what your love and companionship mean to me; for, like all good things in life, we (and I especially) are too apt to take them for granted, or more as a matter-of-fact. But you must know dear that you mean *everything* in life to me. I feel at times that I would give worlds to be able to kiss you and say again & again "Ralph I love you." But it will be a long time yet before I can kiss you and love you and feel your strong loving arms about me.

She reflected on the "sweet, comfortable home" her husband had provided her, thinking "of all the thought & work & worry" he had put into it. Their house, which was located on Leslie Street, was evidently within sight of the "poor house." David's Aunt Datie later recalled his mother jokingly saying, "David's going up the hill to the poor house when he grows up!"[5] Although Parsons' building project had been worthwhile, Flora regretted that she was "getting all the comforts" but that, as long as he was away, he would be unable to "enjoy it at all."[6] She assured him she would not be alone in the house, what with a steady stream of visitors, including Parsons' sister, Datie; her sisters, Jane and Carrie; and Parsons' mother. She stated that little had happened at home since her husband had left, but her letter indicates that her life kept a steady pace. Carrie had been doing her best to get Flora "to go gadding around town," but Flora, who was pregnant, resisted her sister's persuasions.

Parsons' mother, who was visiting from Bay Roberts, was "worn and tired." She wanted to return home within a week to put caplin as fertilizer on the ground and attend to things she had left undone. Flora informed Ralph that his mother "thanks God He gave her such a *son* (that's you)." She was also charmed by her "sweet and good" grandson, David.

A significant portion of her letter was reserved for chatting about their son who, Flora told her husband, was sleeping much better in his crib than in his basket. David "looks so sweet in his bed," she continued. "Oh! if his Pop could only see him. He is a dear, sweet boy. Your mother says he is *just* like you were." Flora then had David hold her pen and "write" his father "a little letter" before falling asleep. In the process of his scribbles, David received "a mustache & a black nosey" which caused his mother to laugh heartily. The infant, Winnie Butt, Parsons' niece, was staying there with Datie and her mother at the time. She was "a dear little girl," but Flora felt she was not "as quiet as our dear little boy." Flora was grateful that Parsons' mother, "a dear old soul," was visiting, too, for she was "trying to keep Winnie quiet."

Flora could hardly restrain her excitement at the prospect of being reunited with her husband. Her endearing remarks in her letter undoubtedly served to make him homesick for his wife and son. "It seems endless to look forward to the time when you will be home again...," she wrote almost despairingly. "You know my dear you are ever in my mind," she reminded him. She missed him cuddling up to her at night. "Do you miss me!" she asked rhetorically. Meanwhile, she hoped to hear from him by letter or telegram: "A word from you means everything to me." She and David prayed "every night for God to keep dear 'Ba-ba'! and bring him back safely to his dear little boy & me." She encouraged her husband to join her in praying for each other and for their son. She was confident "that God will spare us both... ."

Flora informed her husband: "The lawn seeds are coming up. I can see green in places. I sowed some flower seeds all along the walk. Hoping they will be in bloom to greet you when you come home to us." Ironically, when Parsons did return home, it was to witness, not the blooming of the flowers Flora had planted in their garden, but the wilting of his own special, delicate flower, Flora, who was near death.

On Tuesday, July 13, Flora dispatched a message to her husband who was staying at Queen's Hotel in Montreal. It stated: "Know you will be surprised to hear seven-month [premature] baby boy was born this morning." Undoubtedly Parsons' heart leapt with joy. Flora's second bundle of joy had made his entrance into the world at 11:45 A.M., attended by Dr. Will Roberts, then head doctor at the Grace General Hospital in St. John's. Parsons' mother, who had also been present for the momentous occasion, was a "great comfort" to the new mother. The latter had no doubt that Parsons' mother or sister, Datie, would stick by her and take care of any necessary matters. She encouraged him not to worry.[7] The child was named Robert. However, the unbounded joy accompanying the birth of the Parsons' second child was to be brief.

Later that day, Parsons' mother rushed a telegram to her son. It began with a resolute promise, "I can assure you, my boy, Flora will not be neglected." It had been difficult enough for him to be away from home during the latter stages of his wife's pregnancy, but to have been absent during the birth of their second son had been exceedingly difficult. However, the realization that Flora was being well cared for eased his troubled mind somewhat. But then the remainder of this second terse telegram intensified the pain he felt. It required five words for a barb to pierce his heart: "Baby boy lived four hours." *Dead?* It was impossible. Admittedly, he had been surprised earlier that day to receive the telegram announcing the premature birth of a second son. *But now dead?* Through his blinding tears he read on that his baby boy would be buried at 11:15 the following morning. His mother was quick to assure her heartbroken son that his wife was doing well, and she wished God's blessing on him.[8]

On Wednesday, the day the baby was buried, Dr. Roberts sent a telegram to Parsons, informing him that the cause of the baby's death was unknown. In the meantime, Parsons' wife was doing splendidly; the doctor was anticipating a speedy recovery and saw no cause for alarm.[9] A little more than three hours later, Flora sent her husband another telegram: "No danger whatsoever," she assured the distraught husband and father. "Getting stronger every minute. Having best possible attention. Mother says there is no need to worry. Cheer up, dear, for I am quite well."[10] Cheer up with his second son just having been buried? An admonition difficult for him to follow, so far away from his home and loving family.

On Thursday, Parsons still assumed his wife was progressing favourably, but later that evening he received from Dr. Roberts a foreboding telegram. "Your wife not doing so well today," the doctor declared in his professional manner. "Complications but not dangerous. Advise you come if convenient."[11] Parsons was understandably nervous, but in all likelihood the thought that his darling wife's complications could be life-threatening never entered his mind. The doctor had put him at ease a little.

On Friday, Flora was still unwell and, on Saturday, was very low. However, by Sunday she was slightly better, a brief interlude of hope. On Monday, when he arrived in St. John's from Montreal, she was better than she had been the day before.

But at 3:30 A.M. on Tuesday, July 20, Flora May Parsons died, seven days after giving birth to her second son, Robert, who had lived only four hours.[12] She was thirty-three, and had been married to Parsons for less than two years. Their first son, David, was ten months old when his mother died.

The best source of information on Flora's last hours and her subsequent death is a letter written in 1926 by her brother, Arthur House, who had been at her bedside when she died.[13] He had gone to St. John's on business, not knowing that his sister was seriously ill. He arrived at Flora's house just in time to take charge of the final two hours she lived. The others present—Jane, Carrie, Parsons, and his mother—had gathered around Flora's bed, stricken with grief. "That was a hard sad scene that I shall never forget," Arthur recalled six years later. "A young strong woman just in the prime of life dying before us and we were helpless."

Not more than five minutes before she died, Flora's eyes followed every move her brother made. "It was so sudden that nobody could realize she was dying," Arthur remembered with obvious pain. Indeed, nobody had known she was seriously ill. The doctor and nurse watched Flora closely, but made it clear to Arthur that nothing could be done for her.

"You don't mean to tell me that she has to die like that," Arthur said to the doctor.

"There's no aid that can save her," he responded.

Arthur walked over to Flora's bedside. "Flo," he said gently, "do you know you're dying?"

"Don't let me die!" she called desperately. Then she asked weakly to be moved. Although she was strong enough to help Arthur turn her, she died within a few minutes.

The reality of the situation was almost impossible to fathom. "We were all like fools," Arthur wrote. "Poor Flo, she had so much to live for, just married, a splendid home, with all the comforts that could be desired and a splendid husband."

The effect of Flora's death—both immediate and long-term—on Parsons was traumatic. "Imagine what I was up against for 3 or 4 days," Arthur commented. The funeral service for her was conducted on Wednesday, July 21. Parsons spent Thursday caring for various matters related to her death and the funeral. On Friday he left for Spaniard's Bay, arriving there late in the day.

Flora's death was most certainly the darkest day of Parsons' life. Even though his mother was with him at that nadir in his life, Flora's death was a crushing, almost devastating, event. And it will not be considered strange that a number of years were required for the recovery of a semblance of the stability he had had before. He was probably *too* dependent on his wife—more dependent than she would have wanted him to be. Her death forced on him a "release" which he did not want, for which he was unprepared, and which he would not be able fully to accept for the rest of his life. There is no doubt that he was grief-stricken. Six years later his brother-in-law, Arthur, wrote, "Poor Ralph has hardly smiled since. I pity him." In short, the shock of his wife's death was great indeed, and the adjustment to the fact of it was difficult. Some of what he had thought were the secure foundations of his life were severely shaken. *He* was the bereaved person; death had taken from sight one with whose life his own had been so closely intertwined for almost two wonderfully fulfilling years.

Some family members maintain that Flora died of pneumonia, but according to the best modern medical authorities, she had likely died of an embolism, a blood clot, a diagnosis which is consistent with the series of extant telegrams.[14] While an embolism is uncommon, some women do develop it after giving birth. In 1920 such a condition would have been much more difficult to deal with than in 1995. As the years wore on, Parsons' grief may have been exacerbated by the realization that a condition which had been life-threatening in 1920 could now be treated by medicine.

One of Parsons' immediate and chief concerns was how to provide care for his surviving son, David. It would have been rather difficult for a single father, so heavily involved in his multifaceted work with the Hudson's Bay Company, to care adequately for his young son. Parsons arranged for Flora's older sister, Carrie, to assume responsibility for his son. But this relationship was unable to continue because Carrie had three children of her own, the youngest being only a few months older than David.[15]

Parsons then wrote a letter to his sister, spinster Datie, who was a schoolteacher, asking her to leave her profession and take care of David. The letter, dated November 16, 1920 and written from St. John's, reads:

> Dear Datie:
> Better make definite arrangements to camp out next & send in your resignation.
> You & I will camp it out together for the rest of our lives and I will always look after you and make provision for you—no matter what happens. The little boy is well provided for and you will share alike with him.
> You and mother go and talk the matter over with Mrs. Clench, and make the best arrangements possible. I will telegraph you from Montreal as to when I expect to be home. In any case if you sent in your resignation now you would be free by Christmas.
> I know you are making a sacrifice for me and I appreciate it very much, but we will try & make the best of things & let's trust that we will make a "go" of it.
> Good bye for now. See my little boy as often as you can and remember *this* that you are the one who will have to act as his mother and bring him up as you consider his dear natural mother would like. It's a great responsibility and I know you realize that. It's a life's work and one that will I hope yield good results by seeing my little boy grow up to be a good man, worthy of his mother.
> Love & kisses to dear old mother & tell her she is the only one left to love now.
>
>   Your brother
>   Ralph[16]

Datie accepted the responsibility, and David was taken to the home of his grandparents, Dorcas and William Parsons, in Bay Roberts, where he was raised with his cousin, Winnifred ("Winnie"), whose mother had died in childbirth just over a year earlier. By 1926, David was, according to Arthur House, "growing 'a fine boy'."[17]

After death usually comes recovery and renewal and going on with life. However, Parsons found it very difficult to overcome the grief he felt. In addition to being devastated by the death of his second child and then his wife, he was probably still reeling from the death in childbirth of his sister, Winnifred Butt, only ten months earlier on September 7, 1919. Two young women, who held a special place in his heart, had died in childbirth, a little more than a year apart. In 1923 Parsons' father-in-law, Peter House, died. He was buried beside his beloved daughter, Flora, another reminder to Parsons of his own loss.

Just as the Parsons family was nearing the end of what might be termed a period of mourning, tragedy struck again. On March 29, 1924 George Butt, the nine-year-old son of Charles and the late Winnifred Butt, fell over the 200-foot cliff at Jones' Head in Bay Roberts East and was killed. He was buried next to his mother in the old Anglican Cemetery.

There is no doubt that Flora greatly influenced her husband's life, even in death. Only on very rare occasions when he and his son were alone did Parsons mention Flora's name. "David," he would say heavily, "your mother was a wonderful woman." He would try to say more, but would be too emotional to continue.[18] Had Flora and their second son lived, Parsons would have had a wife and children to dedicate his life to. After his wife's death, he showered his affection on his surviving son and compensated for his loss by immersing himself in his work with the Hudson's Bay Company. Indeed, according to Henry Toke Munn, "the great Company is Parsons' god. He thinks of it, and works tirelessly day and night for it."[19] His subsequent "marriage" to the Company was in all likelihood a coping mechanism to enable him to deal with the anguish of the tremendous pain he had lived through.

The sad passing of his wife left Parsons so grieved, he could not think of another marital affair. He never remarried. David never saw his father dressed without a white shirt with detachable starched collar and black tie, regardless of his activity, including hunting, fishing, etc.[20] In 1926 Parsons' brother-in-law, Arthur House, wrote, "It seems that he intends to live it alone now."[21] Admittedly, other women were thought by some to be interested in him. There were, for example, Harriett Crossman of St. John's; Annie French, formerly of Bay Roberts but a nurse in the New England States; and Kate M. Keddie.[22]

Kate M. ("Kitty") Keddie (1887-1966), daughter of James A. Wilson and secretary to Donald A. Smith, was born at Seven Islands, Quebec.[23] Wilson later joined the Hudson's Bay Company Fur Trade Division as Chief Factor, and Kitty lived most of her early life in Northern Quebec and Labrador. As a teenager she moved to Montreal, where she worked as a stenographer. In 1916 she relocated to Cumberland House, Saskatchewan, where she met and married Philip Keddie. An influenza epidemic broke out in the community, and only three individuals—including Kitty—escaped. Her husband of only six months was one of the many who died. Kitty then moved to The Pas, Manitoba, where she held a number of positions, including Court Reporter, Public Stenographer, and Commissioner of Oaths. In 1930 she joined the staff of the International Grenfell Association, later becoming its Industrial Director.

> Mrs. Keddie's devotion to excellence in craft work created many highly skilled craftspeople in her jurisdiction. To this day people can be identified as "Mrs. Keddie's workers" or descendants of them by the quality of their products.[24]

Kitty visited the Parsons family in Bay Roberts when David was a boy, but *not* necessarily when his father was present. She may have had strong feelings towards Parsons, but the family witnessed no outward demonstrations of them in their presence. Actually, those three—Harriet Crossman, Annie French, and Kitty Keddie—and others were family friends, and it was not always readily clear whether or not they had ulterior motives.[25]

Following his father's death in 1956, David found in his safety deposit box at the Bank of Nova Scotia in Bay Roberts, a number of priceless mementos of his late mother. In a leather case there was a series of notes and telegrams. Also in the package was a ladies' small leather purse which held some coins from that period; a ladies' lace-trimmed handkerchief; a couple of invoices showing small purchases, one of them a purse; and the above-mentioned letter from Flora to her husband.[26]

In the leather case which Parsons carried with him at all times, David found a white envelope containing a single light-grey kid glove. The year 1994 was the first time David looked inside the glove, which contained a lock of dark-brown hair with a reddish sheen, and an old-fashioned wire hairpin. In relating this to the authors, David wrote,

While gazing upon this lock of beautiful hair, I held it in my hands and was strongly compelled to kiss it; and at the moment of doing so I had an overpowering sense of her presence in the room with me, and I felt closer to my dear mother than I ever had before.[27]

NOTES TO CHAPTER 4:
YEARS OF JOY AND YEARS OF SORROW

1. David R. Parsons to John Parsons and Burton K. Janes, April 20, 1994.
2. See Proverbs 31:10-30. Certificate presented to Flora M. House by the Girls Friendly Society, October 30, 1918.
3. Information from David R. Parsons.
4. Flora M. Parsons to Ralph Parsons, July 10, 1920. What follows is taken from this letter. Emphasis in original.
5. David R. Parsons to John Parsons and Burton K. Janes, April 20, 1994.
6. Flora May Parsons to Ralph Parsons, July 10, 1920. What follows is taken from this letter. Emphasis in original. "Poor House" refers to an institution for the destitute.
7. Telegram from Flora M. Parsons to Ralph Parsons, July 13, 1920.
8. Telegram from Dorcas Parsons to Ralph Parsons, July 13, 1920.
9. Telegram from Dr. Will Roberts to Ralph Parsons, July 14, 1920.
10. Telegram from Flora M. Parsons to Ralph Parsons, July 14, 1920.
11. Telegram from Dr. Will Roberts to Ralph Parsons, July 15, 1920.
12. The chronology of these events is taken from an undated note in Ralph Parsons' handwriting.
13. Arthur House to Nathan House, October 21, 1926. What follows is taken from this letter. Emphasis in original.
14. Interview with Dr. Nigel Rusted by John Parsons, June 20, 1994.
15. David R. Parsons to John Parsons and Burton K. Janes, April 20, 1994.
16. Ralph Parsons to Datie Parsons, November 16, 1920.
17. Arthur House to Nathan House, October 21, 1926.
18. David R. Parsons to John Parsons and Burton K. Janes, April 20, 1994.
19. Henry Toke Munn, *Prairie Trails and Arctic By-Ways* (London, England: Hurst and Blackett, Ltd., 1932), p. 271.
20. Information from David R. Parsons.
21. Arthur House to Nathan House, October 21, 1926.
22. David R. Parsons to John Parsons and Burton K. Janes, April 20, 1994.
23. On Kate M. ("Kitty") Keddie, see the special issue of *Them Days* devoted to her (XIX:3, April 1994).
24. "These Days at *Them Days*," ibid., p. 2.
25. David R. Parsons to John Parsons and Burton K. Janes, April 20, 1994.
26. *Ibid.*
27. David R. Parsons to John Parsons and Burton K. Janes, September 26, 1994.

Chapter 5

Expanding the Fur Trade in the North

> *"Most people who have lived and travelled in the North learn to accept risks as part of living there, and just carry on. An old-timer once described the country as: 'A land of death, desolation and disaster.' Certainly, at times, there were elements of each, but no one dwelt on them for any length of time."*
> —Archie Hunter, *Northern Traders: Caribou Hair in the Stew*, 1983, p. 135

ollowing the death of his wife, Ralph Parsons transferred his energy primarily to the Hudson's Bay Company and his surviving son, David. From 1918 to 1929, a number of new posts were established, some under the supervision of Parsons, and others while he was in charge of the St. Lawrence-Labrador District (see Figures 1 and 2 below).[1] Each site was chosen after careful thought and with keen precision. A. Dudley Copland wrote:

> Each of the tiny arctic settlements was a memorial to Parsons' vision, for each area had been carefully studied and the location of the post decided upon, so that the maximum amount of produce might be obtained from the hunters.[2]

FIGURE 1: List of Posts Established in the St. Lawrence-Labrador District (1920-29) Under Management of W. Ralph Parsons

Northern Quebec
Port Harrison   1920
Cape Smith   1925
Sugluk West   1925
Sugluk East   1929

Baffin Land
Amadjuak	1921
Blacklead Island	1921
Pangnirtung	1921
Pond Inlet	1921
Clyde	1923

Chesterfield Section
Southampton Island	1924

Labrador Section
Frenchman's Island	1928

FIGURE 2: List of Posts Established in the St. Lawrence-Labrador District (1918-29) While W. Ralph Parsons was in Charge of District

Northern Quebec
Coat's Island	1918
Povungnetuk	1921
Mansel Island	1928

Ungava Bay Section
Payne Bay	1921

Baffin Land
Tukik	1926

North Somerset Island
Sikinik	1926

Chesterfield Section
Padley	1926

St. Lawrence Section
Natashquan	1926
Oskelaneo	1926
Chibougamau	1928
Havre St. Pierre	1929
Mutton Bay	1929

Port Harrison, located on the east coast of Hudson Bay, had a particularly good harbour that was sheltered by several islands. Cape Smith was mostly south and a little west of Wolstenholme. The Cape Smith post itself was actually situated on an island of low, rolling, rocky hills. Unfortunately, it had the worst anchorage of any of the Hudson's Bay Company posts. Because there was no harbour, ships had to lie in open sea about a mile offshore and two miles from the post, ready at a moment's notice to weigh anchor. Sudden storms were frequent. The post was built on a stretch of very rough shingle about 200 yards long and 100 yards deep.

A post was established at Amadjuak when the Company, not unlike what Wilfred T. Grenfell had done at St. Anthony in 1906, began an experiment with reindeer brought from Lapland. The herd, numbering around 600, was transported across the Atlantic on the Company's vessel, the *Nascopie*, along with a supervisor for the project and four reindeer herders with their families and dogs. When the herd gradually diminished for a variety of reasons, not the least of which was a lack of nourishment in the local moss, Parsons in 1924 decided to terminate the project.

In January 1930, when A. Dudley Copland inspected the Amadjuak post, six years had failed to erase all evidence of the reindeer experiment. He found some leather driving harnesses, reindeer bells sporting a Scandinavian Royal Coat of Arms, bunches of ear-tags, and a number of quaint coal-oil-burning lanterns. Two years later, he passed the time at Amadjuak by looking at the relics of the ill-fated experiment: the tags, equipment, and registration books.[3]

"Pangnirtung, to people who know the north," wrote Ernie Lyall, "is one of the prettiest places of all because of the fjord there." A ten-bed hospital was built there in 1928. "I don't know why Pangnirtung had a doctor and hospital when practically nowhere else I've been had one," Lyall complained in his autobiography, *An Arctic Man*.[4]

Pond Inlet, located on the north coast of Baffin Island, well over 1,000 miles from Port Burwell, was, according to Archibald L. Fleming, "so far north that for all but a few brief weeks each 'summer' the cold is so intense and the snow and ice so abundant that it is impossible to differentiate between the land and sea."[5] Nevertheless, A. Dudley Copland thought that the spectacular scenery in such a high latitude would capture the interest of tourists. The trim Clyde River post was, Copland claimed, "the loneliest on Baffin Island."[6]

In the spring of 1924, a group of Inuit discussed with the Hudson's

Bay Company the possibility of establishing a trading post on Southampton Island. Their proposal was accepted, and a site was selected in the general area of Coral Harbour, which was most central to all the winter camps. Unexpectedly, the S.S. *Bayeskimo*, one of the Company's main supply ships, was anchored in the bay. Surprised by her appearance, the builders in Coral Harbour rowed out to her in a whaleboat. District Manager Ralph Parsons was aboard and, not having heard of the decision to establish a post on Southampton Island, was equally surprised. Ironically, he had closed the small Northern Quebec post on Coat's Island and had on board the twenty to twenty-five families from that area for relocation to Southampton Island. He also had on board a prefabricated building and Sam Ford, who was to be the new post manager. Parsons gave A. Dudley Copland the option of returning to Chesterfield Inlet or remaining at Coral Harbour as clerk. Copland chose the latter.[7]

The poem, written in Parsons' honour when he retired in 1940 and inscribed on a sealskin, tells of his activities through the years:

He dreamed of fur trade empire flung
From Arctic Bay to Pangnirtung.
He said, "I'll hang my washing on the pole.
The Canadian Committee
Can sit around the city,
But I'm going up to Baffin Land to stroll."

Tough Eskimos stood all agape
When once he strolled to Dorset Cape
Three hundred miles in three days and two nights.
He could have done it in a day
But as it was, he lost his way,
And sometimes stopped en route to see the sights.

White foxes, seals and polar bears
Were traded in for H.B. wares.
A "skin game"—and a credit to the bay.
And up and down the Arctic coasts,
The sight of shiny, new-built posts
So pleased the dogs, they fought to pull his sleigh.[8]

In 1922 Parsons gained greater public visibility by receiving appointment as a Justice of the Peace in Quebec. On October 31 of that year, he had written the Department of Justice in Ottawa, seeking to secure a commission as a Justice of the Peace to take affidavits in the Province of

Quebec.[9] His rationale was simple enough. Occasionally while making his annual visits to the Company's most northerly trading posts in Quebec—Stupart's Bay, Fort Chimo, Wolstenholme, Port Harrison—where there were no Government representatives, he was considerably inconvenienced when sworn statements were required in connection with personal investments of employees, and various other matters, such as Income Tax forms, collection of royalties, and sundry other matters.[10] He was assured that the Company itself had no objection to the appointment.[11] The Department of Justice, grateful for the valuable service which both Parsons and the Company had rendered in connection with the Labrador Boundary Dispute, recommended his appointment.[12] On November 28, 1922, Parsons was officially informed that he had been appointed a Justice of the Peace with jurisdiction over the Province of Quebec.[13]

Parsons' generosity with those individuals who expressed a desire to work with the Hudson's Bay Company is legend. Cecil E. Bradbury (1901-1996), a young Newfoundlander, applied for employment with the Company, but in 1917 joined the Royal Newfoundland Regiment and left the island to serve in the First World War. Parsons, undoubtedly thinking back to his own unsuccessful attempt in 1916 to enlist in the Royal Newfoundland Regiment to serve in the war, wrote to Bradbury, congratulating him on his decision to go overseas:

> ... I much regret in the Company's interests to hear that you have enlisted. It has, however, proved that you are a man of mettle, which is the type of man that this Company demands. Were it possible, we would like very much to offer you employment now, but as this is out of the question, we hereby request you that when you have left the army, will you please call at this Office where I feel sure you will hear of employment which will be to your advantage.[14]

The year 1919 found the eighteen-year-old Bradbury back home in St. John's, looking for work. One day Parsons approached him, inquiring if he wanted to go north. He did, and appeared at Parsons' office for an interview. "It was not easy to find work in St. John's at that time," Bradbury admitted in 1994, "and Parsons' invitation stirred exciting memories that caused me to say 'Yes.'"[15] He subsequently served with the Company from 1920 to 1930 under the leadership of Parsons, whom William Rompkey in 1994 referred to as "that eminent son of the Island and outstanding builder of the [Hudson] Bay's Arctic empire."[16]

Starting at age eighteen in 1930, Hugh Mackay Ross worked with the Hudson's Bay Company for forty-one years. In his 1989 autobiography, *The Manager's Tale*, he spoke of the privilege of having worked "under three great men who were keen businessmen. They had to be to occupy their high positions. But to me, they all had one common bond. They were humanitarians." One of them was the legendary Ralph Parsons, who in Ross' words,

> ... was reputed to be a stern man and a strict disciplinarian, qualities he required to pull the fur trade out of the lethargy into which it had fallen and to make it a viable business. To me, he showed another side with his complete understanding of the cares and worries of a young post manager taking his city bride to a rundown bush post.[17]

A. Dudley Copland, whose hero seems to have been District Manager Parsons, spoke endearingly of his former boss in an emotion-laden passage in his 1985 autobiography, *Coplalook*:

> ... Parsons ... was a natural leader, a man of vast arctic experience. .... When he had at length convinced the London [England] office that the arctic trade was worth developing, he rapidly organized and expanded his 'kingdom' until the Company was trading with every group of Inuit throughout the Eastern Arctic.[18]

The Company bought furs, walrus hides and ivory, sealskins, whale and seal oil, salmon and trout, and even mica and garnet crystals.

Early in August 1926, Parsons met with his staff at Chesterfield Inlet and was presented with the most thorough briefing that anyone had ever been given on the Arctic from Eskimo Point inland to Baker Lake and up to the Arctic Circle and beyond.

That summer, Parsons had arrived aboard the newly-constructed vessel, the S.S. *Bayrupert*. His inspection boat, the *Fort Amadjuak*, was carried on the foredeck. A. Dudley Copland later recalled how the party of eight—Parsons, Copland, Lorenzo Learmonth, Sandy Macpherson, Harry Ford, Stephen Bradbury (engineer), and Oblate Fathers Thibert and Pigeon—reached Eskimo Point, a feat requiring great stamina:

> When the *Bayrupert* was hove to in order to lower the *Amadjuak* into the water, we could see that the waves were much higher than we had thought them to be. The crew got the launch over the side where she bobbed around in an alarming way, rising as high as the deck level,

Ralph Parsons on the deck of the *Fort Amadjuak* somewhere in Hudson Strait. About 1930.

then plunging down into an abyss—or so it seemed to those of us who were going to have to jump aboard. We got the whaleboat over the side, had her tied to the launch and then each of us, one after the other, jumped onto the *Amadjuak*'s small stern platform. We huddled aft in the little cockpit, while the waves broke over the bow and cascaded along a canvas canopy which protected the crew and the engine from the weather. We shivered on the receiving end of a lot of water.[19]

Moving away from the *Bayrupert*'s side, the *Fort Amadjuak* slammed into the full ferocity of the storm. The whaleboat began to ship water and, losing control, veered off to one side. Pupik, who had volunteered to steer the whaleboat, shouted to be lifted off. The engineer on the launch pulled the clutch, which allowed the *Fort Amadjuak* to drop back to the whaleboat. Once Pupik was aboard the *Fort Amadjuak*, Copland cut the whaleboat free. All in a day's work for Parsons and his associates in the North.

On occasion, ominous clouds arose. One such incident occurred late in 1926. An investigation was initiated in Ottawa concerning a tragic incident that had transpired in 1920 at Lake Harbour. The significance of this matter to this biography is that until it was satisfactorily resolved, a cloud of suspicion hung precariously over Ralph Parsons' head. The question revolved around whether or not he had participated in a coverup of the murder of an Inuit.

On October 9, 1926, W. Stuart Edwards, the Deputy Minister of Justice in Ottawa, drafted a solemn letter to Charles V. Sale, Governor of the Hudson's Bay Company, who happened to be in Ottawa at the time. Reports received by the Minister of Justice intimated that some Company officials on southern Baffin Island had assumed sole responsibility for the administration of criminal justice. More specifically, those individuals had evidently conspired with the Inuit to prevent reports of the murder from reaching the Royal Canadian Mounted Police and obstructed them in their inquiries once the matter was uncovered.[20] A Company official, later identified as David Wark,[21] had evidently informed a police officer that the Company was absolute ruler of the Inuit in their districts. W. Stuart Edwards hoped that Company officials would be instructed to cooperate wholeheartedly with duly-constituted authorities.[22]

Charles V. Sale, responding two days later, expressed sincere regret at the reported incident — "one demanding very serious discipline" — about which he was hearing for the first time, and promised to immediately investigate it fully. As for the Company officials' remarks, they were, Sale assured Edwards, "entirely contrary to the views and to the policy of the Company."[23]

The Governor of the Company then called District Manager Parsons, requesting a statement about the incident. Parsons based his recollection upon a verbal report made to him several years earlier by S.J. Stewart and Lorenzo A. Learmonth, respectively the officer in charge and the clerk at the Lake Harbour post in 1920. Arriving at Lake Harbour in August 1920, Parsons was told by Learmonth that during the year an Inuit man—named "Davey"—had become insane, shooting and killing an entire party of Inuit, with the exception of a catechist. The armed man then positioned himself at the rear of the post. As a result, the Inuit in outlying districts were unable to obtain their supplies at the post. Both they and the people at the post, fearful of their lives, took steps to protect themselves from the violent man. Eventually, the Inuit at the post requested protection. The men at the post, including at least one of the Company's staff, surrounded Davey's snow-house and killed him.

There was no police base close to Baffin Island. Parsons reprimanded S.J. Stewart for participating in what he perceived as essentially an Inuit matter. Consulting the day after with his confidant, the Rev. Archibald L. Fleming, Parsons decided that nothing further remained to be done. He assured Governor Sale that he had always recognized police functions. He had never tried to suppress the facts; indeed, he had conscientiously reported similar incidents. However, Sale noted at the close of his letter to the Deputy Minister of Justice that neither Parsons nor Stewart had filed a report of the Lake Harbour incident with the Company.[24]

On October 12, 1926, Parsons dispatched an urgent message to James Cantley, his assistant, inquiring into the month and year in which Davey was killed. He also wondered if an entry of the circumstances was made in the post journal. More to the point, he wanted to know if the journal was retained at Lake Harbour, because it was unavailable to him in Montreal.

Cantley, responding a day later, thought that the book itself was at Lake Harbour, as there were no duplicates. To his recollection, there was no entry on the incident, although he was of the impression that one was made, stating only that a search for the victim had been conducted and Davey had been found. However, the cause or particulars would not likely have been given.[25]

On October 19, Parsons wrote S.J. Stewart and Lorenzo A. Learmonth, reminding them of the seriousness of the action that had been taken against Davey. With the circumstances of the case now revealed, he stressed the importance of their providing a statement "absolutely without bias or reserve." His memo continued:

> It should be clearly understood that all incidents of an untoward character, in connection with either the direct actions of the natives with whom you trade, or come in contact, or their indirect relationship with the Company, which may in any way adversely affect the good feeling it is our object to maintain with the Government, must, without fail, be reported to me at the first convenient opportunity.[26]

On the same day, Charles V. Sale requested Stewart and Learmonth to afford the Royal Canadian Mounted Police "*every possible assistance*," especially in light of the fact that the Company's rule in Canada had terminated with the Deed of Surrender in 1870.[27]

S.J. Stewart's 2,000-word statement, sworn before Ralph Parsons, now Justice of the Peace for the Province of Quebec, verified Parsons' earlier statement, but provided a more detailed reconstruction of the events surrounding Davey's murder. The portrait of the Inuit, Davey, that emerges from Stewart's description is that of a person who, usually industrious, well-liked and of good character, had changed to become a brooding, impulsive, temperamental loner, a paranoid religious fanatic. Stewart's defense was categorical:

> The peculiar circumstances of the case .... demanded, in my opinion, that immediate steps be taken to protect ourselves. The natives would have taken action had I not done so and to prevent this I took the responsibility of leading the party. Davie [sic] was a desperate character and I am convinced that he would have again made a raid on some of the camps as soon as his ammunition was exhausted, with probably disastrous results.[28]

As for the statement by the Deputy Minister of Justice that Company officials at Lake Harbour had conspired with the Inuit to prevent reports of the crime from reaching the Royal Canadian Mounted Police and to obstruct the police once the matter came to their knowledge, Stewart was appalled, but nevertheless promised to cooperate fully with justice.[29]

On May 16, 1927 Parsons wrote a stern rebuke to David Wark, an official at the Amadjuak post, who had evidently refused to cooperate with the police in investigating the murder:

> You should remember that whatever your personal feelings may be, you are an official of the Company and, as such, your actions will reflect upon it and be taken as an official expression of the Company's attitude.[30]

This statement is an important key to understanding Ralph Parsons. The Company of Adventurers was his life and, as long as he was associated with it, he would fight with great resiliency to defend it from opportunists and its detractors. Not without reason did Henry Toke Munn write in 1932, "His interest is submerged in his service to his Company."[31]

In his autobiography, *Archibald the Arctic*, Archibald L. Fleming, the first Anglican Bishop of the Arctic, recalled Davey's murder. However, he failed to acknowledge the account as originating with Parsons, but gave the credit to Joseph Pudlo, the Bishop's Inuit assistant. Fleming had listened "with a sad and almost unbelieving heart" to the tale of the ill man whose "mind unhinged so that he developed into a homicidal maniac." As for who shot Davey, nobody knew, because in each man's rifle there was one empty cartridge. "For days after hearing this story," Fleming wrote, "I felt as if something cruel had been at work among these people whom I loved. I understood the belief in evil spirits."[32]

The Davey incident at Lake Harbour was strangely reminiscent of another one that had occurred on the Belcher Islands in Hudson Bay in 1919. On September 30 of that year, Inspector Philips and Sergeant A.H. Joy went there to investigate rumours of the murder of two Inuit, Ko-Okyauk and Ketaushuk, who had been killed there under circumstances almost identical to the murder of Davey in Lake Harbour — "deviant behaviour that marked them out as a threat to their society." The investigation lasted twelve days and, when the Royal Canadian Mounted Police left Belcher Islands, no charges had been pressed against the guilty individuals.[33]

If wrongdoing, in the form of an obstruction of justice in the North, was shown to have taken place in Davey's murder, the embarrassment to the Hudson's Bay Company, following the chain of command to the top, would be significant. As it turned out, it is highly unlikely that any action was taken against either the perpetrators of the deed, or Ralph Parsons, who had effectively defended his actions, but it made him realize, undoubtedly as never before, the importance of analysing events fully before acting, cooperating with the Government, keeping accurate records, demanding the undivided loyalty of those who worked under him, and at all times acting in a forthright, if cautious, manner. And this, not only to protect himself, but to retain the good reputation of the honourable Company of which he was a part.

Meanwhile, Parsons was increasing in stature with others because of his strong leadership abilities. Wilfred T. Grenfell spoke in glowing terms about both the Hudson's Bay Company and Parsons. In July 1927 Grenfell expressed pleasure about what he perceived as "the new notes of hope that have come to Labrador." One such note was "the new way of sending salmon home frozen," thereby saving the fishermen expense, increasing their earning capacity, and greatly improving salmon for consumption. "It is really excellent," he noted, "and the Hudson['s] Bay Company certainly [does] deserve our gratitude and support for their plucky persistence in making it a success." He was also delighted that the Company had taken up the line of new industries, including mat-making, weaving, knitting, ivory-carving, skin-embroidery, basket-making like the Innu, model-building, and toy-making. His praise for Ralph Parsons and his brother, Hayward, was boundless: "we are proud of the Newfoundland boy who directs it in our country and who sits in power in Montreal, while his brother at Cartwright embodies his fine attitude to the workers of the country."[34] A year later, Grenfell made reference to Ralph Parsons' appointment as one of the Hudson's Bay Company's Commissioners:

> This is a signal honour, but a very well-deserved one. We have known Mr. Parsons for many years and he has been, as has his brother Hayward, most helpful in every good work to advance the best interests of the people of Labrador.[35]

We have arbitrarily selected Parsons' annual report of Outfit 258—1928—to provide a glimpse of his keen eye for detail in recalling the activities of the District—St. Lawrence-Labrador—over which he held responsibility. In this forty-four-page report, he was intent on covering every possible angle which had any bearing on his District. The report is instructive as an indication of the obvious pride he took in his duties and the care which he exercised in carrying out his functions.

While the buildings at the majority of the posts in his District were in good condition, Parsons offered a number of suggested improvements to existing buildings which, if carried out, would result in practically all of the territory within his District being covered with posts well-equipped to handle the trade requirements. He was particularly concerned about the Newfoundland-Labrador Section, where the condition of the buildings leased from the Moravian Mission was most unsatisfactory.[36]

An unusually poor fur hunt in Outfit 257—1927—was, he suggested, almost entirely responsible for a significant decrease in total sales (from $852,085. to $685,732.), although merchandise inventory had increased by $69,402. Nevertheless, he thought the overall merchandise situation to be satisfactory.[37] He acknowledged the scarcity of practically all classes of furs. There had been an increase in the furs of black and white bear, ermine, silver fox, mink, raccoon, skunk and wolf, but a decrease in the furs of beaver, fisher, cross, red, blue and white fox, lynx, marten, musquash and otter.[38]

He felt that the fisheries—salmon and dried salt cod—in Newfoundland-Labrador and on the North Shore of the Gulf of St. Lawrence were primarily the sole industry which offered possibilities of extensive development, although he realized that the profit margin on the fisheries would always remain narrow.[39] The comparatively poor fur hunt was blamed for the fluctuation in the Innu and White debts at year-end.[40]

With regard to competition, Parsons had little to add to what he had written in earlier reports—no material change had taken place. There were, he maintained, two main sources of competition: the activities of the Clarke companies, that practically controlled the transportation facilities on the North Shore of the Gulf of St. Lawrence; and the facilities that would be offered by the Hudson Bay Railway in 1930 to outside traders to enter the North country. He reiterated the need to meet competition on an equal footing in order to strengthen the Hudson's Bay Company's position in the Gulf and prevent the Clarke companies from extending to new territories. An agreement for a cooperative trade, acceptable to the Hudson's Bay Company and Clarke's, might benefit both. If such an agreement failed to materialize, Parsons suggested that the Hudson's Bay Company would have to put its business in an equal, if not a superior, position to Clarke's. However, Parsons, with an obsession about competitors, was still eager to block new ones, regardless of size, from entering the Bay.[41] He wrote:

> We should be prepared, therefore, to throw every obstacle in their way at the outset and to leave no stone unturned to prevent any competitor [from] obtaining a foothold in the country. The returns to be obtained in the Bay have been greatly exaggerated to the general public but it will only take a few years, provided the proper tactics are used, to convince these traders that Hudson Bay is not the El Dorado which they at present imagine it to be.[42]

Parsons' preoccupation with competition also comes through in the final stanzas of the poem, written in his honour when he retired in 1940:

When competitors appeared,
Their foul tactics were not feared
He'd hoist the flag and shout, "Pro pelle cutem!"
If we can't undersell them
We'll then be forced to tell them
They'll have to pack their bags or else we'll shoot 'em.

Since then the trade has made great gains
Through radios and aeroplanes—
All tributes to your thought and guiding hand.
And so, each loyal Eskimo
And all who your achievements know
Proclaim you rightful King of Baffin Land.[43]

He was pleased with the individual post accounts.[44] The steamer, the *Nascopie*, had surpassed the *Ungava* in delivering supplies to the northern posts and depots. He proposed that the *Baynain* be stationed at Churchill, Manitoba, to supply Eskimo Point, the M.S. *Fort Garry* supply the three posts in Davis Strait, and the *Nascopie* supply the remainder of the northern posts. The Newfoundland-Labrador posts were being adequately serviced by the Government mailboats and chartered schooners. Transport facilities to the Gulf posts would be improved if and when the Hudson's Bay Company decided to operate its own transportation there. The coming of the Hudson Bay Railway to Churchill in 1930 would, he admitted, require minor rearranging. Local distributing vessels—the *Fort Rigolet*, *Fort Chesterfield* and *Nannuk*—completed their respective itineraries, but regretfully one of the coastal boats and its cargo had been lost the previous autumn in Wager Inlet. Authorization had been granted to increase by fifty percent the purchase price of white foxes in the Chesterfield territory, in anticipation of competition resulting from the completion of the railway into Churchill.[45]

For some time, according to A. Dudley Copland, there had been a decided change in the outlook in the fur trade. In 1925 Charles Townsend, the new chief of the Company's development department in London, England, was engaged to bring his expertise to the marketing of country produce. Copland was not long with Townsend before realizing that he intended to adapt his expertise to the fur trade. "The old traders were to be jostled by the engineers of change," Copland wrote in his autobiography, "and Mr. Townsend was the most vocal of them." According to Copland, Townsend had intoned,

"Markets can and will be found for the by-products of the hunt. Of course we must not forget that as far as our arctic posts are concerned, the white fox is still of paramount importance. In fact we are giving some thought to a campaign to publicize the white fox. We might have a tennis star, perhaps Madame [Suzanne] Lenglen herself, wear one as she comes to the courts. We will associate the white fox with some article of her attire—possibly with the brilliant in her famous headband...."[46]

Although a new era was dawning, Copland, for one, was unprepared for it. District Manager Ralph Parsons accepted Company policy, but he continued to maintain that white foxes must remain the mainstay of the Arctic trade.[47] In his 1928 report, Parsons reiterated that conviction.[48]

District expenses amounted to $406,470. for 1928, an average of $7,500. for each unit operated, a decided increase over 1927 expenses, attributable to increased staff. However, Parsons promised that expenses would decrease as District business became more settled.[49] He admitted that staffing continued to be a difficult problem. All too often, he claimed, experienced businessmen were unobtainable, and young men, after a few years with the Company in the North, could see no future in their positions and either deteriorated or retired, leaving behind those with less ambition and possibly weaker natures. He felt that the terms of the apprentices' contract in effect were unsatisfactory, the wages being too low and the term of five years too long.[50]

Experimental fox farming was too young to analyze, but he hoped it would eventually prove to be a great success.[51] He wrote:

> In fact, I think that fox farming of this nature will eventually prove to be the salvation of many of our Posts which are at present non-producing fur units and are playing a losing game.[52]

The accounts of the Newfoundland sealfishery were being handled by Job Brothers and Co. Ltd. in St. John's, and Parsons anticipated a sizeable profit margin.[53] During the previous ten to fifteen years, the Hudson's Bay Company had attempted to discover minerals in the District. Parsons felt it was to the Company's advantage to investigate the possibilities further.[54] Another consideration was the importance of Labrador as a potential timber-producing country.[55] Almost in the same breath, he suggested that shell deposits in Labrador were negligible.[56]

The general health of the Inuit had been maintained, but the epidemic of influenza and the presence of a sickness resembling chicken pox was disquieting and took a severe toll at some of the posts. He recognized the need for a small hospital at a central point in the northern part of his District. He warned against unnecessary intermingling between the

Whites and Inuit, the latter being "our principal asset in the North country." The Inuit had

> .... no immunity from even the simplest diseases of civilization, the danger of their being allowed to freely intermix with any visitors to the territories, particularly vessels' crews [being] at once apparent....[57]

He reported on the work being done by the *Fort James* expedition[58] which, according to Cecil E. Bradbury, had a fourfold mandate: to investigate the commercial possibilities of a water route between the eastern and western Arctic, to survey a route to supply the Company's western Arctic posts from the east, to study the hunting and trading potential in the vicinity of Cockburn Bay, and to connect with the M.V. *McPherson*, the Company's western-based supply ship that was sailing to find the Northwest Passage—taking the western route—and to follow plans to meet the *Fort James*, the Company's schooner.[59] The potential for east-west trade across the top of North America would be first demonstrated in 1930. The *Fort James* had left St. John's, only to spend two winters frozen in at Gjoa Haven on King William Island. When the *Fort McPherson* pulled in and anchored near her, it was the first time since the Northwest Passage had been bridged since Roald Amundsen's history-making crossing of 1903-06.[60]

Parsons was fearful that the establishment of the Royal Canadian Mounted Police throughout the North had not, despite the Davey murder investigation two years earlier, generally reacted favourably on Company business. He attributed the problem to the unfortunate selection of the police personnel sent north, many of whom abused their authority. "As far as we are concerned," he wrote, "we realize that the situation is a delicate one and we will continue to deal with it locally as diplomatically as possible."[61]

Mansel Island had a rather lucrative trade, and the fox cycle on Coat's Island was rising, but he recommended that the Blacklead Island post be relocated.[62] The Labrador Section office, too, should be moved from Cartwright to the capital city of Newfoundland, St. John's.[63] Of all the District posts, the five Moravian ones in Labrador were the most unsatisfactory. The Moravian Church had created, in his opinion, not a self-reliant group of Inuit, but "a lazy, degenerate race, spoiled by a hundred years of pampering, who think that the Mission or the Company owed them a living without their being called upon to make any effort," thereby "utterly ruining them."[64] The only method of dealing with them, he contended, was by a process of education designed to encourage them to become self-supporting, rather than summarily cut off all supplies to them until they had earned them.[65]

He was pleased to report that relations between the Hudson's Bay Company and Revillon Frères of Paris, France, the only serious longterm rival faced by the Company in the North, "continue to be harmonious, and cooperation has been found to be more fruitful of practical results than the competitive spirit of the past."[66] No longer were post managers being subject to misgivings about their competitors' movements, but were devoting their entire energies to the welfare of their hunters.[67] Likewise, relations between the Missions in the area—Anglican and Roman Catholic—and the Company were amiable. Both Missions appeared alert to the dangers posed to the Inuit of large influxes of traders or prospectors and seemed to be assisting in protecting them from such derogatory influences.[68] However, he took issue with the suggestion that the incorporation of the Chesterfield Section of his District with the Nelson River District would strengthen the Company's position.[69]

Parsons recognized that Outfit 258 would probably show little more than a nominal profit gain and about break even as opposed to a net profit of a million dollars the year before. But he reminded the head office that the results of a District's operation can be judged only over a period of the cycle. The success of Outfit 259 depended upon the fur hunt; barring any unexpected contingency, the prospects looked bright.[70] "The territory is now well-covered," he noted, "and is capable of considerable development yet of a more intensive character than we have been able to attend to during the years of pioneer work."[71] As well, Parsons was concerned with other products and markets:

> Besides our furs, we are in a position in this District to obtain many other products, provided that markets can be obtained to absorb them, and it would be in disposing of such products and in suggesting new products that this Department can be of real service. If markets can be found and if we are kept fully informed of such markets we will obtain the requirements, if they *are* obtainable.[72]

Although he was personally devoted to the Company, Parsons never forgot his son, David. When he was ten, the boy suffered an attack of acute appendicitis, which eventually burst, causing peritonitis to set in which nearly killed him. His father, hearing of his only son's illness, must have remembered the sorrow he had experienced only a few years before with the unexpected death of his wife and second son. Parsons immediately rushed to David's bedside at the old General Hospital in St. John's. When David recovered nine weeks later, his father gave him a get-well present—a Majestic combined radio and record player. In 1945, when David returned from serving overseas with the Royal Canadian Air Force, he saw his radio again, but his father had removed the inner mechanisms and converted the instrument into a cupboard![73]

Sometime prior to April 2, 1929, Parsons wrote his sister, Datie, in Bay Roberts, suggesting that his ten-year-old son, David, go North with him that summer on his annual trip. This was a demanding request, because the boy's aunt was so protective of him that she could not bear the thought of his leaving home. Parsons declared that his son needed to have the "rough edges" rubbed off him. On April 2 Parsons expressed the hope to Datie that she would still favourably consider his earlier suggestion, as he believed that such a trip would do his son much good. Parsons promised Datie that David would be back in Bay Roberts in the fall early enough for school. Predominant in his mind, however, was the pain he knew she would experience in parting with David, even for a short time. Parsons pledged to "try to take good care of him and hand him back to you."[74] From June to August 1930 David accompanied his father on a memorable journey to the northern posts.

Datie, David, and Winnie, his cousin, left St. John's in late June in the Company supply ship, the S.S. *Nascopie*, under the command of the trusted Captain Thomas Farrar Smellie, and sailed to Montreal. Datie, who could stand no type of travel motion, became deathly sick as soon as the ship left port and continued so until it arrived in Montreal. Datie and Winnie returned home several days later.

David and his father had a stateroom on the upper deck of the S.S. *Nascopie*, by the landing of the stairs to the ship's bridge. Father and son were welcome and frequent visitors, with Captain Smellie's approval, on the bridge where David was impressed by what he saw.

Another passenger was Archdeacon Archibald L. Fleming, Ralph Parsons' friend, whom David found to be a delightful and friendly individual. He took a photo of David and his airedale dog, Nibs, which his father had given him at the beginning of the trip. Fleming later published the photograph, along with an article about David on the trip, in an Anglican Sunday school paper.

During sailing they observed a regular routine. Out of bed for breakfast at 7:00 or 7:30 A.M., they enjoyed the ship's regimen throughout the day. Their nightly ritual was to retire to their cabins, dress for bed at 10:00 P.M., then eat a piece of Aunt Carrie Clench's fruit cake (which she had baked especially for the journey), washed down with a glass of Canada Dry ginger ale, David's favourite beverage. A temperate drinker, Parsons, or Pop as his son referred to him, usually had a drink of Hudson's Bay dark rum. After saying their prayers, Parsons would turn out the lights. "Good night, Pop," David would say, and his father would respond lovingly, "Good night, my son."

David Parsons with his dog, Nibs, on the *Nascopie* at Port Burwell, 1930.

Courtesy of David R. Parsons

Eventually they arrived at their first post in Labrador, where Parsons assumed his responsibility of inspecting the stores—examining furs and commenting on the previous year's accomplishments. Sometimes, to David's embarrassment, his father found it necessary to openly chastise the entire staff on their performances. At some of these posts, David was told that he was the youngest white boy that some of the "Esquimaux"—a non-derogatory term for the Inuit in those days—had ever seen.[75]

At one of the northern posts, a corpse, probably that of Chesley Ford, was taken aboard. The body was placed in a casket in one of the staterooms below deck. David recalls sneaking into the room and fearfully stealing a glance at the corpse. On board the ship there was also a phonograph with a large selection of records. Most popular among them was Sir Harry Lauder singing "Keep Right On to the End of the Road," "Six Feet of Earth" and "I Belong to Glasgow."

At his father's suggestion, ten-year-old David kept a diary of his trip, a portion of which is extant.[76] The sensitive boy was devoted to his dog,

Nibs, but he was nevertheless ready to assist in odd jobs when needed. On Tuesday, July 29 he wrote:

> Then I got Nibs' breakfast, which was biscuits, milk and porridge. He liked that very well. After breakfast I unchained Nibs and brought him about the deck. After that I chained him up, and then I went ashore in an H.B.C. boat.
>
> As soon as I got ashore I went up in the place where the people keep all their goods, and the people were taking some of the boxes down to the shore, and I brought one small box down and rolled two barrels down which had nothing in them.
>
> After that Mr. Richie told all the boys that belonged to the *Nascopie* to get on the boat that was going out to the ship, for this was the last boat going for the boys.
>
> When we got on the steamer it was dinner-time, so I got a wash and went to dinner. Pop was coming out on a different boat, so I had my dinner the first before Pop. We stayed on the boat for the rest of the evening.
>
> After dinner I got Nibs' [dinner] which he liked very well. After Nibs had his dinner, I unchained him and let him run about the deck. Then I called him and he wouldn't come. So I put the leather leash on him and then he obeyed me. There was a little boy who is taking the trip with us who cried when he left the Eskimos. That little boy must have liked them.[77]

The Great Depression of the 1930s wrought havoc in the Fur Trade, not unlike the reality in numerous other fields of commerce. Markets were demoralized and values dropped to a fraction of their former strength. As a result, the purchasing power of the Company's customers throughout the Fur Trade was drastically reduced. "Nothing but stern measures of retrenchment and comprehensive overhaul of the entire Fur Trade Department would suffice to restore its fortunes," Frank Ryan wrote in retrospect.[78]

In 1930, after successfully extending the Company's fur trade to the remotest north, after being initially a post manager in the field, then a manager of the original Straits District with headquarters at Lake Harbour and, later, district manager for all the Eastern and Eastern Arctic districts of the Company, Parsons was asked to assume the duties of the Fur Trade Commissioner's office. At that time, he was given a clear explanation and understanding of his responsibilities, the Company fully realizing it was a fateful hour. "We knew the Fur Trade Department was badly disorganized and extravagantly operated," the Company's Canadian Committee wrote in 1937.[79] On January 1, 1931, Ralph Parsons officially became the Fur Trade Commissioner of the Hudson's Bay Company, a post he held until his retirement on May 31, 1940.

Parsons, putting his typical tireless energy to work, sent a terse message—a call to action and for restoration—to the remotest post. He began his numerous shuttle trips into the north, east and west throughout the Company's fur trade domain, in addition to several trips to Beaver House, the Hudson's Bay Company building in London, England. An all-out attempt was made to restructure the Fur Trade Department and thus to make it more profitable. In Frank Ryan's words:

> Thus were the fortunes of the Fur Trade restored, and in so doing, Ralph Parsons accomplished a very fitting climax to an outstanding career of achievement; a record which will earn him a place with the historic figures of the Fur Trade.[80]

No doubt Parsons' tenure as Fur Trade Commissioner was the climax of an outstanding career in the Hudson's Bay Company, but to say, with Ryan, that Parsons restored the fortunes of the Fur Trade Department in the 1930s is an oversimplification. It is true that he worked hard as Fur Trade Commissioner and accomplished much, but the economic downturn in the world economy in the 1930s caused him considerable difficulties as he tried to reorganize the fur trade and make the total operation more economically efficient. By the time the Fur Trade Department was reorganized and once again on a firm economic footing, Ralph Parsons was long since gone and others were in control.

NOTES TO CHAPTER 5:
EXPANDING THE FUR TRADE IN THE NORTH

1. Drawn from Appendix to R.H.H. Macaulay, *Trading into Hudson's Bay: A narrative of the visit of Patrick Ashley Cooper, Thirtieth Governor of The Hudson's Bay Company, to Labrador, Hudson Strait and Hudson Bay in the Year 1934* (Winnipeg, Manitoba: The Hudson's Bay Company, 1934), p. 106.
2. A. Dudley Copland, *Coplalook* (Winnipeg, Manitoba: Watson and Dwyer Publishing Ltd., 1985), p. 83.
3. *Ibid.*, pp. 123-124, 142-143.
4. Ernie Lyall, *An Arctic Man* (Halifax, Nova Scotia: Formac Publishing Co. Ltd., 1983), pp. 88-89.
5. Archibald L. Fleming, *Archibald the Arctic* (Toronto, Ontario: Saunders of Toronto Ltd., 1957), p. 276.
6. Copland, *Coplalook*, pp. 180, 179.
7. *Ibid.*, pp. 34-35.
8. Stanzas 2-4 of poem inscribed in India ink on skin side of sealskin, presented to Ralph Parsons on his retirement, 1940.
9. C.P. Plaxton to Ralph Parsons, November 2, 1922.
10. Ralph Parsons to Charles Lanctot, November 7, 1922, and Ralph Parsons to the Hudson's Bay Company, November 7, 1922.
11. A. Brabant to Ralph Parsons, November 11, 1922.
12. C.P. Plaxton to Ralph Parsons, November 21, 1922.
13. C.P. Plaxton to Ralph Parsons, November 28, 1922.
14 Ralph Parsons to Cecil Bradbury, April 17, 1917, in Cecil E. Bradbury, *Ten Years in the High Canadian Arctic* (St. John's, Newfoundland: RB Books, 1994), pp. 3-4.
15. Bradbury, *Ten Years*, p. 5.
16. William Rompkey, introduction to *ibid.*, p. ix.
17. Hugh Mackay Ross, *The Manager's Tale* (Winnipeg, Manitoba: Watson & Dwyer Publishing Ltd., 1989), p. 236.
18. Copland, *Coplalook*, p. 83.
19. *Ibid.*, p. 84.
20. W. Stuart Edwards to Charles V. Sale, October 9, 1926.
21. See Charles V. Sale to S.J. Stewart and L.A. Learmonth, October 19, 1926; and Ralph Parsons to David Wark, May 16, 1927.
22. W. Stuart Edwards to Charles V. Sale, October 9, 1926.
23. Charles V. Sale to W. Stuart Edwards, October 11, 1926.
24. Charles V. Sale to W. Stuart Edwards, October 12, 1926.
25. James Cantley to Ralph Parsons, October 13, 1926.
26. Ralph Parsons to S.J. Stewart and Lorenzo A. Learmonth, October 19, 1926.
27. Charles V. Sale to S.J. Stewart and Lorenzo A. Learmonth, October 19, 1926. Emphasis in original.
28. S.J. Stewart to Ralph Parsons, May 13, 1927.
29. *Ibid.*
30. Ralph Parsons to David Wark, May 16, 1927.

31. Henry Toke Munn, *Prairie Trails and Arctic By-Ways* (London, England: Hurst and Blackett, Ltd., 1932), p. 271.
32. Fleming, *Archibald*, pp. 201-202, 281.
33. Ray Price, *The Howling Arctic* (Toronto, Ontario: Peter Martin Associates Ltd., 1970), p. 51.
34. Wilfred T. Grenfell, "New Developments in Labrador," *Among the Deep-Sea Fishers* (XXV:2), July 1927, p. 67.
35. Idem, *Among the Deep-Sea Fishers* (XXVI:2), July 1928, p. 75.
36. "Buildings," in Ralph Parsons, "Annual Report—St. Lawrence-Labrador District—Outfit 258," pp. 1-4.
37. "Stocks," in *ibid.*, pp. 4-5.
38. "Furs," in *ibid.*, pp. 5-8.
39. "Fisheries," in *ibid.*, pp. 8-9.
40. "Debts," in *ibid.*, pp. 10-11.
41. "Competition," in *ibid.*, pp. 11-15.
42. *Ibid.*, p. 14.
43. Stanzas 5-6 of poem inscribed in India ink on skin side of sealskin, presented to Ralph Parsons on his retirement, 1940.
44. "Accounts," in *ibid.*, pp. 15-16.
45. "Transport," in *ibid.*, pp. 16-19.
46. Charles Townsend, cited in Copland, *Coplalook*, pp. 48-49.
47. Copland, *Coplalook*, p. 49.
48. "Transport," in Parsons, "Annual Report . . . . Outfit 258," p. 19.
49. "Expenses," in *ibid.*, pp. 19-20.
50. "Staff," in *ibid.*, pp. 20-23.
51. "General: Fur Farming, McLure and Mackinnon Silver Fox Farms Limited, Fur Purchasing Agencies," in *ibid.*, pp. 23-27.
52. "General: Fur Farming," in *ibid.*, p. 24.
53. "General: Newfoundland Sealfishery," in *ibid.*, pp. 27-28.
54. "General: Minerals, Coal Mining at Pond's Inlet," in *ibid.*, pp. 28-29.
55. "General: Timber on the Labrador," in *ibid.*, pp. 29-30.
56. "General: Shell Deposits on Labrador," in *ibid.*, pp. 30-31.
57. "General: Native Welfare," in *ibid.*, pp. 31-32.
58. "General: M.S. *Fort James* Expedition and the Wager-Cockburn Transport," in *ibid.*, p. 33.
59. Bradbury, *Ten Years*, p. 41.
60. See Peter C. Newman, *Merchant Princes* (Toronto, Ontario: Viking, 1991), p. 222.
61. "General: Royal Canadian Mounted Police and Other Government Activities," in Parsons, "Annual Report . . . . Outfit 258," pp. 33-34.
62. "General: Mansel, Coat's and Blacklead Islands," in *ibid.*, pp. 35-36.
63. "General: Labrador Section Office," in *ibid.*, p. 36.
64. "General: General Trade Conditions at Moravian Posts," in *ibid.*, p. 37.
65. *Ibid.*, pp. 36-38.

66. "General: Agreement With Revillon Freres Trading Company Limited," in *ibid.*, p. 38.
67. *Ibid.*, pp. 38-39.
68. "General: Missions," in *ibid.*, p. 39.
69. "General: Proposed Transfer of Chesterfield Section from the St. Lawrence-Labrador District to the Nelson River District," in *ibid.*, pp. 39-42.
70. "General: Review," in *ibid.*, pp. 42-44.
71. *Ibid.*, p. 43.
72. *Ibid.*, p. 44. Emphasis in original.
73. Information from David R. Parsons.
74. Ralph Parsons to Datie Parsons, April 2, 1929.
75. David R. Parsons recalls that in those days there were Esquimaux (Eskimos) and Indians, and there was never any mistaking the two.
76. July 29 to August 19, 1930.
77. Extracts from David R. Parsons' diary, July 29, 1930 entry.
78. Frank Ryan, "Forty Years on the Fur Trail," *The Beaver*, June 1940 (Outfit 271), p. 22.
79. Memorandum from Canadian Committee to Ralph Parsons, December 16, 1937.
80. Ryan, "Forty Years," p. 22.

Chapter 6

North to Adventure—
The Odyssey of 1934

"There is a local atmosphere to a place which must be felt at first-hand before you can fairly weigh up a situation or the men on the job; for, in order to form a right judgment of a man, you should always meet him on his own ground."
—From Governor P. Ashley Cooper's speech at a farewell dinner given by the Fur Trade Department on the R.M.S. *Nascopie*, August 11, 1934. An Appendix to R.H.H. Macaulay, *Trading into Hudson's Bay: A narrative of the visit of Patrick Ashley Cooper, Thirtieth Governor of The Hudson's Bay Company, to Labrador, Hudson Strait and Hudson Bay in the Year 1934* (Winnipeg, Manitoba: The Hudson's Bay Company, 1934), p. 103.

ne of the highlights of Ralph Parsons' career occurred in the summer of 1934 when the Fur Trade Commissioner accompanied the Governor of the Hudson's Bay Company on a trip to the northern posts and into Hudson Bay as far as Churchill, Manitoba.

The Company ship, the *Nascopie*, carrying the Governor and Mrs. Patrick Ashley Cooper, Ralph Parsons, Major D.L. McKeand, and others, left Montreal on Saturday, July 7, 1934 and headed down the St. Lawrence River, across the Gulf of St. Lawrence, and up towards the Strait of Belle Isle. So began the first day of a journey which was to last forty-three days and cover 4,000 miles in the North.

R.H.H. Macaulay was the official reporter onboard the *Nascopie* for this trip. The Hudson's Bay Company in Winnipeg published a selection from Macaulay's journal late in 1934 under the title, *Trading into Hudson's Bay*, the subtitle being long and cumbersome, *A narrative of the visit* of *Patrick Ashley Cooper, Thirtieth Governor of The Hudson's Bay Company, to Labrador, Hudson Strait and Hudson Bay in the Year 1934.*[1]

Early in his journal Macaulay makes special reference to the *Nascopie*'s commander, Captain Thomas Farrar Smellie, and Parsons, the latter of whom "opened up the fur trade on top of the world."[2] Later Macaulay provides greater detail about the accomplishments of the illustrious Fur Trade Commissioner. Particular reference is made to the founding of the Lake Harbour post in 1911, the initial establishment of the Company on Baffin Island. During the dozen years following the opening of that post, Parsons personally established six more posts on Baffin Island, thereby earning for himself, by his popularity with the Inuit and his zeal, the unofficial title of "King of Baffin Land."[3] Parsons was, in Macaulay's words, the "builder of more posts in the north than any one man in the history of the Hudson's Bay Company."[4] Macaulay praises Parsons for his herculean efforts on behalf of the Company, and effectively tries to outline the importance of Parsons to the Company, so important, in fact, that Parsons was the individual who in 1934 was given the task of escorting the first Governor in the history of the Company into the northern territory and Hudson Bay, where the trade in furs had been carried on for 264 years.

Ralph Parsons on the *Nascopie* voyage, 1934.

Courtesy of David R. Parsons

Macaulay may be considered a prophet when in 1934 he wrote,

> The history of the establishment of these posts has yet to be written, but when it is, among other stories it will tell how to Ralph Parsons, at Cartwright, came orders to establish a post in Hudson Strait; nothing was said about a boat, but an "outfit" was sent.[5]

Mike Lubbock with Archbishop Fleming and Ralph Parsons at Churchill, Manitoba, during the *Nascopie* trip, 1934.

Macaulay then tells in some detail the establishment of the Wolstenholme post in 1909, and how Parsons, in the process, almost lost his life. It was hearing the dramatic story of the establishing of this post and the appellation, "King of Baffin Land," being conferred upon Parsons, which inspired another Company man, Michael R. Lubbock, to write the following tribute:

> *Never yet has history shown*
> *A cleric on a royal throne,*
> *But here we see before us stand*
> *A Parson, King of Baffin Land.*[6]

Parsons had come a long way from his time at Wolstenholme in 1909 to official escort of the highest official in the Company in 1934. If ever a man could feel proud of his achievements over a twenty-five-year period, then Parsons surely must have felt personally overwhelmed by his position during that memorable trip north on the *Nascopie* with Governor and Mrs. Cooper.

Some of Macaulay's descriptions of Labrador and the Arctic are among the best to be found anywhere. The following is a typical example describing the coast of Labrador:

> Wednesday, 11th July, and we were steaming north by west up the Labrador coast which, due to a mirage, seemed to have enormous cliffs falling sheer to the water's edge. Every few miles we met icebergs, the colours of which were beautiful — pure sparkling whites, light blues, and dark blue caverns cut out by the waves. Grotesque and awe-inspiring shapes; a castle of the Rhine, which, as it came closer and our view changed, became an old-fashioned cruet, even to the handle in the centre. Then on the horizon appeared a large shoe brush with a handle; gradually it changed into a worn old boot, then an armchair, and on the arms sat hundreds of sea birds which rose screaming at our approach. An old man's face cut in ice—ice which strangely carried with it the scent of spruce and a pocket of warm air — an old man's face with the nose and chin becoming more pointed every moment, until it turned into an eight-pointed crown, and, finally, as we drew level, was a little hump-backed canal bridge with the wind rippling the water through the arch.[7]

Official photo of those on the *Nascopie* voyage, 1934. Governor and Mrs. Cooper are seated between Ralph Parsons and Captain Smellie.

Soon the settlement of Cartwright came into view and, for many on this voyage, this was their first sight of that well-known Labrador landfall founded by George Cartwright over 150 years earlier. In 1786 Cartwright had transferred his interests in that settlement to a partner, Collingham. Twenty-seven years later, a report indicated that there were "eight or nine families of British settlers at Sandwich Bay."[8] By 1837 the settlement was owned by A.B. Hunt, the Company that sold it to the Hudson's Bay Company, along with the dependent posts of Round Island, Gready Harbour, and Sandhill. Cartwright subsequently became one of the Company's principal posts on the coast of Labrador.

At Cartwright, Governor and Mrs. Cooper and Fur Trade Commissioner Parsons were met by the officials from the settlement. The chief official was Stephen Hayward Parsons, manager of the Labrador District and brother to Ralph Parsons; John S. Blackhall, post manager; and Michael Murphy, Justice of the Peace for Labrador. A crowd had gathered onshore and, in Macaulay's words, "eager hands held the Governor's boat while he stepped ashore to be welcomed to Cartwright by the Justice of the Peace."[9] Later the official party paid a visit to the Anglican Mission to meet the Rev. Elijah Parsons, another Bay Roberts man and a second cousin to Hayward and Ralph Parsons.

On Thursday night, July 12, an official reception was held at the local Community Hall. Speeches were made by Hayward Parsons, Rev. Parsons, Dr. Harry Paddon and, of course, Governor Cooper. Hayward spoke of the debt they all owed the Governor for his exemplary guidance in Company matters. Cooper told his audience that although the world was in the throes of a great economic depression, he was convinced that the worst had passed, prosperity was returning, and only by hard work could everyone share in that prosperity. His words were an encouragement to those involved in the ceremonies at Cartwright that night, especially so coming from a man so prominent in, and abreast of, world affairs.

The reception was followed by the usual old-time dance, complete with an accordionist who pulled out tunes that were probably played by his great-grandfather in some English village a century before. The names of the people listed by Macaulay are the same ones found around Cartwright and Sandwich Bay today. But there was one other Newfoundlander there that night. Tom Dawson, a Bay Roberts man, was game warden for that area of Labrador at the time. A survivor of the Newfoundland sealing

disaster of March 1914, he had lost part of both feet, but learned to walk again and even was an accomplished dancer despite his disability.

The dance was not the end of the evening's activities. The crowd then gathered outside to witness a fireworks display by the ship's officers. "The accordion started again," Macaulay notes, "and passengers from the ship were persuaded to join in, but they could not keep the pace of those

Labrador people and the next morning several of them complained of stiff legs and backs."[10]

The next port of call was Port Burwell, on Killinek Island in Ungava Bay and within the boundaries of the Province of Quebec but in the general area of Cape Chidley and the Button Islands.

On Tuesday, July 17, word was received aboard the *Nascopie* that the Company's motor schooner, the *Fort Garry*, commanded by Captain James Dawe and his Bay Roberts crew, would meet the *Nascopie* at Port Burwell and take the freight destined for the Ungava Bay posts.

On Saturday night, while waiting for the ice to clear in order to pass the dangerous Button Islands, the Governor broadcast a message to the Company's posts in the District. Fur Trade Commissioner Parsons opened the programme by introducing the distinguished visitor. Those broadcasts became a regular feature of the trip and took place in all the districts visited by the *Nascopie*. Macaulay is at his journalistic best in describing those broadcasts:

> Sometimes the skirl of the pipes went out over the ether, while at other times the ship's gramophone was carried up to the wireless room, and the music of Leoncavello, Sullivan and Tin-Pan Alley was sent out over ice and fog.[11]

The following day the *Nascopie* reached Port Burwell and, as at Cartwright a week before, there were the official introductions, done by Parsons who was pleased to renew his friendship with A. Dudley Copland, section manager of the District, and the Rev. F. Nicholson who had travelled from Fort Chimo to meet the Company Governor.

At Port Burwell, the Governor and Fur Trade Commissioner met the employees of the post and inspected the Company's store. Both were pleased with what they saw, particularly certain items for sale, such as the sealskin boots for which the Inuit of Port Burwell were well-known. The Governor was told that the sealskin boots made in Port Burwell were shipped to places like St. John's and Halifax for use in the seal fisheries.

Parsons took an active part at all official ceremonies in Port Burwell that day and the next. It was he who coached, then invited, Harry Ford, a native of the area, to read the official message from the King of England which the Governor had brought with him. Parsons was also the one who arranged for Charlie, the head Inuit in the Killinek Island region, to give the official statement of thanks for the King's message. Macaulay writes:

> ...Charlie...—grey hair, whispy beard, glasses, grey flannel shirt,

dark trousers and seal-skin boots—stepped forward, hesitated, coughed, spat politely, and in Eskimo read the following reply to the King's message:—

"We, the Innuit of Killinek, our thanks give to you, our Great Ruler across the sea, whom we love greatly.

"From our King we have heard through the Company's Governor and we are happy.

"God be thy helper for a long time.

"Port Burwell, Quebec, Canada.

"23rd July, 1934."

Then with a shy smile he handed the message to the Governor.[12]

The Governor then delivered his own message to the Inuit of Port Burwell and the Killinek Island-Ungava area:

> Our men who live with you the year round and trade with you have often told me what good hunters you are and how you try your best to do their bidding, and I wish you to believe that we have your welfare at heart. If times are good with us, they are also good with you. If you make good hunts you benefit by them and are happy, but if your hunts are poor, we both suffer and are sorry.[13]

The remainder of his speech was appreciative and simplistic but well-suited to his audience. The Governor concluded by stressing the importance of working with the post manager:

> ...now that we have seen you we are happy and will leave you with confidence that you will work with our Post Manager as one large happy family, you following his advice as if he were your father, for he does the things which I tell him and I want you to do the things which he tells you.[14]

Macaulay must have been moved at the Governor and Parsons' simplistic approach in dealing with the Inuit of Port Burwell, a small segment of the northern hunting population whose way of life was from the beginning the reason for the existence of the Company. In Macaulay's words:

> There, at a sub-Arctic trading post, stood a man delivering a speech to an aboriginal audience, an audience which listened with mouths slightly open, an "Ah" every now and then as the interpretation of the speech sank in, and all the time brushing away mosquitoes. The speaker was a man who had put his signature to a report which saved England from financial crisis in 1931 — the report of the National Economy Committee. And now here he was giving fundamentally the same advice which, as a member of that Economy Committee, he

had given His Majesty's Government, but it was expressed in terms of foxes, seal hunts and the long cold winter moons.[15]

On Tuesday, July 24, the *Fort Garry* drew alongside the *Nascopie* and transferred the freight for the Ungava Bay posts. Late that afternoon and four days behind schedule, the *Nascopie* weighed anchor, three blasts on the siren echoed back from the granite, unclad mountains around Port Burwell as the Governor and his entourage headed towards Lake Harbour, on the southern coast of Baffin Island.

Upon arrival at Lake Harbour, there were the usual ceremonial introductions. People from this important Company post were anxious for mail from the outside world, and those on the *Nascopie*, especially Parsons, were eager to know the state of things in Lake Harbour. The two main items of news were, first, that had the *Nascopie* arrived on schedule she would not have gotten into the post, as the passage was blocked with ice, and, secondly, that the fur hunt in the Lake Harbour area for 1933-34 was quite satisfactory, which must have been welcome news to Parsons' ears.

The freight for Lake Harbour was unloaded. Macaulay comments on the surprisingly warm temperatures around Lake Harbour: " 'Sunny' Baffin Land lived up to its reputation, and Lake Harbour, 'the capital,' pleased us all very much."[16] He tells how Lake Harbour, the first post on Baffin Island, was established by Parsons in 1911 from the old S.S. *Pelican*. During the decade following its opening, he had established six more posts on Baffin Island and, in the process, earned that noble but unofficial title of "King of Baffin Land." Macaulay explains why the Fur Trade Commissioner was so well-liked by the northern hunters:

> At Lake Harbour we were to see the first example of just why the Commissioner is so popular with the natives. He radiated energy and enthusiasm, chaffed the Eskimos, and, even after an absence of so many years, seemed to know them all by name. He was essentially a jovial king, throwing himself wholeheartedly into the holiday amusements of his subjects. He acted as starter for all the races, personally demonstrated the "wheelbarrow" race, acted as coach and judge in the tugs-of-war, and, when in the women's tug-of-war one side was getting badly beaten, he threw in his weight and won the battle for that team.[17]

The usual scene of ceremonial welcoming and freight unloading was repeated a couple of days later at the Stupart's Bay post which Parsons had established in 1914. There again Parsons and the Governor gave their typical paternalistic speeches to those simple hunters of the North and those Company men who worked with them. The officials were well aware that the Inuit were the foundation of the Company, and the local hunters, in turn, fully realized that they needed the Company for their very existence as much as the Company needed them for their economic existence.

At Stupart's Bay a demonstration of harpooning was given for the Governor. The next day, when an Inuit came alongside the *Nascopie* in his kayak, the Governor called for the interpreter to ask the Inuit to lend his kayak and harpoon so that he might try his hand at harpooning and handling the double blade paddle. The Governor's handling of the kayak was a success, but the people on the *Nascopie* were a trifle nervous for his safety.

The next port of call was Wolstenholme, where no welcoming party came out to meet the *Nascopie* because the men at the post had no gasoline left. There the ceremonies were cut short out of necessity, but there was the usual inspection of accounts and buildings, while the Inuit were unloading and storing the supplies.

Parsons was at home in Wolstenholme, for this was the first post in Hudson Strait that he had established in 1909. The post held special memories for him because as a young man he had almost lost his life there in the performance of his duty.

The *Nascopie* in Hudson Strait, 1934.

On August 1, the *Nascopie* was anchored off Port Harrison on the east side of Hudson Bay and another post established years earlier by Parsons. Port Harrison was, according to Macaulay, a pleasant change from the Hudson Strait posts:

> Instead of the barren mountains, there were grass-covered hills; wild flowers grew everywhere in the grass, and here and there was a low bush—promise of trees not so far away. The harbour is good, being sheltered by several islands. The post buildings are on the bank of a river which empties into the harbour; Revillon Frères' buildings at the mouth, next the Anglican Mission, and then the Company building.[18]

At Port Harrison, the Governor, Parsons and other officials, along with the post personnel, took time out to go on a trouting expedition. It was later reported that the Governor showed real ability with the rod and reel and presumably caught more trout than anyone else.

In time, the *Nascopie* anchored near Charlton Island in James Bay. The Governor and his party, including Parsons, were carried by seaplane to Moose Factory and Rupert's House. On Charlton Island the Governor was greatly impressed by the Inuit-made furniture he saw during a visit to Tom Taylor's house. In addition to being sturdily built, the chairs and settees were extremely comfortable with their eiderdown cushions. The Governor was so impressed that he issued instructions that a few pieces be sent for preservation to the Company's historical museum in Winnipeg. Moose Factory was the second oldest Company post. It was at Rupert's House that the Company got its start in 1668. Two years later the Company was incorporated, receiving its seal and charter from King Charles II of England.

En route to Churchill (prior to 1934 known as Fort Churchill), Manitoba, a farewell dinner was held onboard the *Nascopie* in which the Fur Trade Commissioner toasted the Governor and Mrs. Cooper. Parsons congratulated the Governor on his extraordinary understanding of northern life. In a short time, Parsons said, the Governor had gained much first-hand knowledge of the fur trade and the people who carried on that trade. With tongue-in-cheek, Parsons suggested that the Governor had served his apprenticeship, and was now a full-fledged fur trader. Finally, Parsons expressed the conviction that the Governor's 1934 journey to the northern posts and Hudson Bay would be of inestimable value to the fur trade, for it had given everyone a measure of encouragement and an added incentive to succeed.

The Governor responded by thanking the captain and crew of the *Nascopie*. He also expressed his appreciation to Parsons for his help in planning and executing the trip north which, in the Governor's opinion, was a tremendous success. Summarizing Parsons' accomplishments to 1934, the Governor said the Fur Trade Commissioner had proved that "the road to fresh conquests is still wide open."[19] As a memento of the voyage and a token of his and Mrs. Cooper's affection and appreciation, the Governor presented Parsons with a gold cigarette case.

When the *Nascopie* dropped anchor outside Churchill harbour on Sunday, August 19, after a journey of six weeks and one day since leaving Montreal, the sea voyage for the Governor and Mrs. Cooper and his party, including Fur Trade Commissioner Parsons, had come to an end. During the official ceremonies at Churchill, Parsons presented the Governor with a desk set from his Department in commemoration of the historic voyage which saw the only Governor of the Company of Adventurers of England trading into Hudson Bay. History books would in time record the voyage of Patrick Ashley Cooper, the first Governor to visit the Company's posts in the barren land of the North. Ironically, in 1991, Peter C. Newman would refer to it as "Cooper's most notable — and most bizarre — adventure...."[20]

If a movie were to be made of the Governor's voyage to the northern posts and Hudson Bay in 1934 and the participants on that journey were asked to play their own parts, there is no doubt that Cooper would be playing the leading role, and Parsons, the best supporting actor. As well, Parsons would probably receive an award for the praises heaped upon him that summer by the Company Governor. The latter seized every opportunity to applaud Parsons for his dedication to and great work on behalf of the Company. And the Governor went even further by singling out Parsons as a unique type of individual who gave his best to every task to which he put his hand; in fact, there were times when the Governor seemed to over-praise the Fur Trade Commissioner.

The summer of 1934 must surely have been the climax of Parsons' career with the Company. The Fur Trade Commissioner was on more than one occasion singled out — and justifiably so — by the Governor to officials and Inuit alike as the ideal Hudson's Bay Company man, one who had gone from a junior apprentice at Cartwright in 1900 to occupying the top office in the Fur Trade Department three decades later. Two years before the Odyssey of 1934, Henry Toke Munn wrote that "the [Hudson's Bay] Company is a hard taskmaster, and Parsons serves it with cold-blooded efficiency."[21]

Macaulay ends his journal of the Governor's voyage on the *Nascopie* in 1934 by referring to the venture as another important chapter in the history of the Company:

> So another chapter has been added to the story of the Hudson's Bay Company; a story which began when Samuel Pepys was writing his diary and when a new London was rising from the ashes of the Great Fire; a story of loyal men and great leadership; pages which ring with names of men who guided the Great Company in other days—Prince Rupert; John Churchill, Duke of Marlborough; Sir George Simpson; Lord Strathcona and Mount Royal; and which now must tell of Patrick Ashley Cooper, the first Governor to visit the Company in the barren Northland.[22]

Here Macaulay could have made reference to the Fur Trade Commissioner and all he had accomplished for the Company during his thirty-four years of exceptional service, but if the journalist was remiss in paying tribute to Parsons in the last paragraph of his account, the Governor more than made up for it in earlier speeches at the various ports and onboard the *Nascopie*. The Governor devoted almost half of his speech at the farewell dinner on the vessel on August 11, 1934 to praising Parsons:

> And now, Gentlemen, I come to the central figure of the whole act, its originator, designer and executant, Chief Factor Ralph Parsons. I have travelled far with him, but this is the first occasion on which I have had the privilege of travelling with him through the North which he has made his own and which he knows so intimately. As we progressed from post to post, I gradually drew from him tales and reminiscences which together build up one of the most exciting and romantic chapters of our Company's history. Mr. Parsons was the first man to realize the great possibilities of Baffin Land and of the country to the east of the Bay up to Hudson Strait. Altogether he has been responsible for the establishment of no less than 35 posts. This is an achievement unparalleled in the Company's history and one of which most people know very little. In the course of this great work Mr. Parsons made many journeys by boat and sledge which for daring and endurance are equal to any accomplished in the old days. It is sometimes said that, under modern conditions, there is no longer scope for great deeds; but surely these exploits of Mr. Parsons must

prove that, given the necessary courage and imagination, the road to fresh conquests is still wide open.[23]

Hearing the Governor's reference to Parsons' numerous journeys by boat and sledge, the latter must have regarded it as confirmation from no less than the Governor himself that he was numbered with the greatest in the history of the Company's fur trade in Canada. The next day, when the Governor gave his final broadcast from the *Nascopie*, he continued to praise Parsons for his sizeable contribution to the Company and for his guidance and initiative.

> Last night you listened to the Commissioner, Chief Factor Ralph Parsons. He showed you what was needed. He explained in clear language the steps which you must take. When the Commissioner tells you how to go about your job, you know that you are listening to a man who has successfully put into practice the steps which he is telling you to take.
> He has explained to you the necessity of helping the natives to make themselves self-supporting. The help and guidance of the native is both your duty and your interest, and it is in the best tradition of the Company's service.
> Mr. Parsons has stressed the importance of learning the native languages. Only if you speak the language well can you hope to understand your natives; and it is only the man in close touch with the native mind who can hope to be a really successful trader. . . .
> Chief Factor Ralph Parsons is a great example to you — a man of initiative, imagination and endurance. He has risen from apprentice to Fur Trade Commissioner. He has established more posts than any other officer in the history of the Company. He has made astonishing journeys by land and sea. But remember, that at the back of these spectacular achievements, lies the greatest quality of all — industry, and Mr. Parsons' industry is proverbial.[24]

No doubt 1934 was the apex of Parsons' career. Anything of any significance that happened after this journey with the top Company official in the British Empire would surely be anti-climatic. The voyage north on the *Nascopie* that summer gave Parsons a chance to visit some posts that he had established and which must have brought back many memories for him. As well it gave him the opportunity to renew acquaintances and foster goodwill and fellowship with the men at the posts, some of whom did their apprenticeship under him when he was Post Manager or District Manager. Probably most importantly, it afforded him the opportunity — which he undoubtedly relished — to serve as guide and thereby demonstrate his expertise of the North to the first and last Governor of the Company to visit the very people—trader and Inuit alike — who were the backbone of one of the greatest trading companies in the history of the world. The governor concluded his final broadcast from the *Nascopie* this way:

> Now my last word to you is this. I am gratified with what has been accomplished. I know well the efforts and sacrifices which have been necessary. The Fur Trade has definitely turned the corner, but we must all recognize that there is still much to be done. You know that there is no Royal Road back to prosperity. You are succeeding, and your success comes from that which must always produce success—hard sacrifices, hard thinking, hard work. In your work of the last three years you have shown that you possess these qualities. It is for this reason that I leave you in Outfit 265 with complete confidence, for, having those qualities, there is nothing that can hold you back.[25]

And so the memorable visit of the Hudson's Bay Company Governor, Patrick Ashley Cooper, to the Arctic posts and Hudson Bay had come to an end, and from all accounts in 1934, and particularly from Macaulay's official journal, the voyage had been a success and everybody — those who were on the *Nascopie* and directly associated with the trip north — was well-pleased with what had transpired. Cooper, Parsons, and Smellie felt that much had been accomplished, and the traders and Inuit at the northern posts considered the year 1934 to be a very significant one in their history.[26]

On the other hand, the Canadian Committee in Winnipeg, headed by George W. Allen and the General Manager, Philip A. Chester, were not sure that much, if anything, had been accomplished. In fact, as far as Allan and Chester were concerned, the whole affair was somewhat ludicrous.[27] In their view, given the economic context of the times, the trip north made very little sense.

When he arrived in Winnipeg in late August 1934, Cooper gave a dinner for the Canadian Committee and employees of the Company, and just as he had presented engraved knives to the Inuit of the North a short while before, he now pinned special Hudson's Bay Company medals on more than a dozen employees and each member of the Canadian Committee.[28] But in Philip Chester's opinion, the most important happening in 1934 was the acceleration of a major reorganization of the Company, which was badly needed, among other things, to counter the economic realities of the Great Depression. He saw no benefit in the fanfare of a trip to the northern posts by Cooper, Parsons, and the others involved. Many years after the voyage, Chester wrote: "Within the Company the prospect of an Arctic pageant was received with misgivings and hopes that nothing would come of it."[29]

There is documentation that in the months and years after the summer of 1934, Cooper was somewhat condescending towards Ralph Parsons, but, unlike George W. Allan and Philip A. Chester, there is no evidence that Parsons held any negative feelings towards Cooper.[30] In fact, long after the summer of 1934 Parsons was writing to Cooper and commenting on the success of the venture; indeed, for Christmas 1934 the Fur Trade Commissioner sent Mrs. Cooper a pair of sealskin gloves, thereby fulfilling a promise he had made to her during the voyage.[31]

Finally, there is a puzzling aspect to the voyage of 1934 — the matter of the Governor's radio broadcasts. Apparently, the broadcasts did not go beyond the makeshift studio on the *Nascopie*. Certainly, Patrick Ashley Cooper was not aware of this, and likely neither was Ralph Parsons who, for his part, always rehearsed his dignified introduction of the distinguished visitor. Captain Smellie's biographer, Roland Wild, says that the *Nascopie* had been fitted with an expensive and somewhat sophisticated broadcasting unit,

> ...the idea being that the Governor would address each H.B.C. Post the night before his arrival, as a curtain-raiser to the ceremony to take place the following day... It was all very impressive, and there were great expectations of the enjoyment that must have been obtained by the personnel of the Posts on shore.[32]

Still, the next day when the ship reached the post and Cooper on occasion asked the post manager what he thought of the broadcast the night before, the latter appeared to be momentarily dazed, for he had heard no broadcast; the carefully rehearsed speeches by Parsons and Cooper were never heard outside the small studio that was formerly the Captain's dayroom. Some years later, Captain Smellie dismissed the broadcasts with this puzzling and ridiculous statement: "They kind of went up in the air and never came down."[33]

Peter C. Newman outlines three problems with the Governor's broadcasts: (1) because each post had only one radio receiver, which was usually located in the manager's staff house, the chance of an Inuit's actually hearing Cooper's voice was remote; (2) he spoke in English, so the Inuit

Captain Smellie of the S.S. *Nascopie*, with Fur Trade Commissioner, Ralph Parsons, c. 1934.

could not understand what he said anyway; and (3) officially Ottawa objected to a Hudson's Bay Company official speaking to Canadians on behalf of the King.[34] Neither Cooper nor Parsons seemed to be aware of any of this, for each "earnestly continued to perform his daily stint." Indeed, the post managers had been briefed to praise the top Hudson's Bay Company official for his non-existent broadcasts.[35] If this were indeed the case, then the question remains as to who briefed the post managers.

At the same time, all the nice things about Ralph Parsons that Patrick Ashley Cooper said in his non-existent radio broadcasts and various speeches on the *Nascopie* that summer did not go entirely to waste, for copies of Macaulay's official journal, *Trading into Hudson's Bay*, which included all the speeches and broadcasts, were widely distributed among Hudson's Bay Company personnel and given to some provincial archives and university libraries, while other copies found their way into the hands of the general public. Hence, the word had gone forth as to the kind of Hudson's Bay Company man Ralph Parsons really was. His accomplishments had been duly noted and recorded. Furthermore, his strong support for the Governor's voyage to the northern posts and Hudson Bay that summer ultimately did not go either unnoticed or unrewarded.

NOTES TO CHAPTER 6:
NORTH TO ADVENTURE — THE ODYSSEY OF 1934

1. R.H.H. Macaulay, *Trading into Hudson's Bay: A narrative of the visit of Patrick Ashley Cooper, Thirtieth Governor of The Hudson's Bay Company, to Labrador, Hudson Strait and Hudson Bay in the Year 1934* (Winnipeg, Manitoba: The Hudson's Bay Company, 1934).
2. *Ibid.*, p. 10.
3. *Ibid.*, p. 44.
4. *Ibid.*, p. 45.
5. *Loc. cit.*
6. *Ibid.*, p. 46.
7. *Ibid.*, p. 15.
8. *Ibid.*, p. 18.
9. *Ibid.*, p. 19.
10. *Ibid.*, p. 25.
11. *Ibid.*, p. 29.
12. *Ibid.*, p. 98.
14. *Loc. cit.*
15. *Ibid.*, pp. 37-38.
16. *Ibid.*, p. 44.
17. *Ibid.*, pp. 44-45.
18. *Ibid.*, p. 54.
19. *Ibid.*, p. 103.
20. Peter C. Newman, *Merchant Princes* (Toronto, Ontario: Viking, 1991), p. 295.
21. Henry Toke Munn, *Prairie Trails and Arctic By-Ways* (London, England: Hurst and Blackett, Ltd., 1932), p. 271.
22. Macaulay, *Trading into Hudson's Bay*, p. 89.
23. *Ibid.*, p. 103.
24. *Ibid.*, pp. 104-105.
25. *Ibid.*, p. 105.
26. *Ibid.*, p. 89.
27. Newman, *Merchant Princes*, pp. 295, 299.
28. *Ibid.*, p. 299.
29. Philip A. Chester, quoted in *ibid.*, p. 295. Quotation taken from Philip A Chester "The First 250 Years," an unpublished history of the Hudson's Bay Company, Chester Family Archives.
30. File RG2/37/161, Hudson's Bay Company Archives.
31. *Ibid.*
32. Roland Wild, *Arctic Command: The Story of Smellie of the Nascopie* (Toronto, Ontario: The Ryerson Press, 1955), p. 145.
33. *Ibid.*, p. 146.
34. Newman, *Merchant Princes*, p. 298.
35. *Ibid.*

Chapter 7

Conflict and Resignation

"At times the internal struggle was more important to these memo-warriors than trying to modernize the Company...."
—Peter C. Newman, *Merchant Princes*, 1991, p. xv

y the beginning of the 1930s, several individuals on both sides of the Atlantic appeared in important administrative positions in the Hudson's Bay Company. Patrick Ashley Cooper succeeded Charles Vincent Sale as Governor in London, while in Canada George W. Allan headed up the Canadian Committee, Philip Alfred Chester was General Manager, Ralph Parsons was Fur Trade Commissioner, and Francis F. Martin was Manager for retail sales.

Cooper, a member of the British political and economic elite, was adamant that the great Company was to be run from London, while Chester, an English accountant of lowly birth, thought otherwise. Chester, who had the support of Allan and the Canadian Committee, considered himself to be the key man in the overall administrative structure of the Hudson's Bay Company. He ran the Company from Winnipeg, in his opinion the site of the real action.

Initially, the Canadian Advisory Committee, set up in 1912, had no real authority, other than acting as a liaison between Winnipeg and London. By 1930 the name was changed to the Canadian Committee, and this group of Canadian businessmen, chaired by a lawyer, was given additional powers, including the naming of some senior officials to the Company. It was this committee that appointed Philip A. Chester as General Manager in 1930. Chester, a relatively unknown Englishman, would in time "exercise almost as significant an impact on the Hudson's Bay Company as had Sir George Simpson a century earlier."[1]

111

Robert H. Chesshire, 1960. Philip A. Chester, c. 1950.

Almost from the beginning, Chester became obsessed with making the Hudson's Bay Company economically efficient, which to him meant a total reorganization of the Company as it existed in Canada in the 1930s. In the transforming of the Company, Chester at times felt he was answerable to nobody, not even the aristocratic Patrick Ashley Cooper in London. And so began a type of struggle between Winnipeg and London that Peter C. Newman refers to as the "Trans-Atlantic Blood Feud."[2] In Canada, Chester had the full support of the Canadian Committee and its chairman, lawyer and former Member of Parliament, George W. Allan, who had been involved with the Hudson's Bay Company since 1914.

In September 1931, Cooper visited Canada in an attempt to familiarize himself with the reorganization that Chester was initiating to counter the economic realities of the Great Depression and to make up for what Chester considered the bad fiscal management of the previous decade. Arriving in Winnipeg, Cooper reported in his journal that he was amazed by what he found. He wrote, "the state of misunderstanding and tension between London and Winnipeg had almost reached an open breach... ."[3] Despite the "great and thoughtless extravagance" he encountered, the Governor was of the opinion that, if London and Winnipeg cooperated, Chester would be able to turn things around.[4]

Chester set out to impose economic "discipline on an organization that had spun out of control."[5] Retail operations were to be reorganized by an American merchandising expert, Francis F. Martin. Advertising was increased and a course in merchandising was instituted; unprofitable stores were sold, and each retail outlet was given a thorough going-over. By the end of 1936, the turn around in this division had taken place.[6]

In the Fur Trade Department, Ralph Parsons, the Fur Trade Commissioner who had succeeded Charles H. French on January 1, 1931, indicated that he was prepared to cooperate with Chester's attempt towards reorganization, although it was clear from the start that Parsons saw no need for the drastic changes in his department that Chester wanted to bring about. Parsons saw no reason for the large reduction in the number of trading posts in the Arctic. This was his territory, and he was reluctant to see posts closed down and people relocated or retired. A field man who had advanced through the ranks as Post Manager and District Manager, Parsons knew hundreds of people in the Arctic and had a personal loyalty to them, of which Chester and the Canadian Committee were not even remotely aware. Hence, wholesale reorganization within Parsons' department created tension between Parsons and Chester; by 1937 a conflict between the two men had developed, which only came to an end with Parsons' resignation three years later.

There was no blood feud between them and only a couple of serious confrontations, when Parsons was summoned to Chester's office, known among the staff as "the holy of holies."[7] Robert H. Chesshire, Assistant to the Fur Trade Commissioner, another Englishman not easily intimidated by Chester, often acted as a mediator in difficult situations. Still, Parsons, being the gentleman that he was, was unprepared to fight anyone to head off the changes which he must have realized were inevitable. By 1937, at the age of fifty-six, he knew the writing was on the wall and he often reported to his son, David, "Things aren't like they used to be."[8] Parsons was the oldest man in the organization and the only senior official who had come up through the ranks. He was unable to stop Chester's attempts to reorganize the Fur Trade Department, and he eventually reached the point where he had no desire to continue trying. He found himself working with much younger men than himself and, with a few exceptions, he found himself in a position where no senior officials could support him, not because they did not want to, but because their jobs were on the line. His staff was always supportive and remained so until the end, later transferring that support to Robert H. Chesshire, who proved to be one of the best-liked men in the Hudson's Bay Company in Canada.

George W. Allan and his Canadian Committee were on Chester's side. Ironically and despite the transatlantic blood feud, by 1937 Patrick Ashley Cooper, the Governor, sympathized with Chester and the difficulties he was having with Ralph Parsons.

Parsons was a field man and not a great administrative executive. His loyalty was to his staff and those within his jurisdiction, which included the personnel at the scores of posts from Labrador to the Mackenzie Delta and beyond. To Parsons' way of thinking, Chester and Allan and their economic reorganization of the Hudson's Bay Company, particularly the Fur Trade Department, disrupted the lives of many people. To Parsons, it was a simple matter of turning a profit versus the welfare of people.

Peter C. Newman writes, "Even if his methods were crude, Chester shook up the stores' bureaucratic lethargy and moved them into the twentieth century."[9] Chester was prepared to do the same for the Fur Trade Department, but in so doing he was invading Ralph Parsons' territory, thereby causing Parsons considerable anxiety which he was unprepared to take. He decided to resign, which he did in the spring of 1940. Parsons had had enough and in June 1940 he left Winnipeg, on friendly terms with everybody, including Philip A. Chester.[10]

On the evening of May 28, 1940, a retirement dinner was held in Winnipeg to honour Ralph Parsons and another Hudson's Bay Company man, Charles W. Veysey. At the time, Chester was in London, England, but he sent a message which was read by George W. Allan at the dinner: "Very disappointed cannot join you this evening to do honour to my old friends Parsons and Veysey to whom I send every good wish."[11] On May 2, 1940, Chester had sent a memo to the General Manager of the Retail Stores Department; the Manager of the Land Department; the Manager of the Wholesale Department; and the Fur Trade Commissioner, and a carbon copy to the Canadian Committee: "With deep regret the Canadian Committee has assented to the request of Chief Factor Ralph Parsons, Fur Trade Commissioner, that he be allowed to retire on pension on 31st May, 1940."[12]

Almost two and one half months earlier, Governor Patrick Ashley Cooper, not wanting to be excluded from the events leading up to Parsons' resignation and impending retirement, and echoing sentiments similar to those contained in his radio broadcasts and speeches aboard the *Nascopie* almost six years earlier, sent Parsons a well-worded letter:

> In view of your approaching retirement in May next, I am glad to take the opportunity of expressing, on behalf of my colleagues on the Board, as well as for myself, our appreciation and warmest thanks for the loyal, conscientious and valued services you have rendered to the Company over the long period of forty years.
>
> We recall with satisfaction that you joined our Fur Trade Staff, in the Labrador District, in 1900, as an apprentice, and by your tenacity of purpose and unstinted efforts earned promotion through successive stages to the post of Fur Trade Commissioner, the highest responsibility in our Fur Trade Department. This is an achievement which will serve as a example and an inspiration to all members of our staff, whose esteem and respect you have so well merited.
>
> We send you our best wishes for the future and hope that you may enjoy a full measure of good health and happiness during the leisure you have so well earned.[13]

Neither Chester nor Allan and the other members of the Canadian Committee had been in agreement with Cooper's voyage into the Arctic and Hudson Bay in the summer of 1934, when the Company's fiscal affairs were at an all-time low.[14] Neither were they in agreement with their Fur Trade Commissioner being involved in this "Arctic pageant," as Chester called it.[15] Naturally, the Governor reigned supreme and the voyage went ahead, and Ralph Parsons, with his expertise of the fur trade and intimate relationship with the Arctic, was the natural member of the senior personnel in Winnipeg to accompany the Governor.

Undoubtedly, Chester felt that Parsons' proper place was in Winnipeg, assisting with the reorganization of the Fur Trade Department which, in the opinion of most senior officials in Winnipeg, badly needed reorganizing. Parsons, for his part, saw no urgency for Chester's reorganizational plans and, in the couple of years following the Arctic voyage, half-heartedly cooperated and fully resisted at the same time. At various meetings with Chester and the others, Parsons would promise his full cooperation but then revert to his own way of operating, all the time resisting change as much as possible.

Eventually, this situation became intolerable, and official documents show that by the fall of 1937 Chester and Allan were pressuring Parsons and reporting to London every detail and action taken regarding Parsons, to the point where the Governor in London concluded that Parsons, who had been one of his strongest supporters during the 1934 odyssey and after, had now become "a difficult man" who was a thorn in the side of Chester and the Canadian Committee in Winnipeg.[16] On November 24, 1938, in a dispatch entitled "Notes on Senior Personnel," a terse note was sent to the Governor in London: "Ralph Parsons is not a good administrator or executive, and will have to be retired sooner or later."[17]

Between December 16, 1937 and the time of Parsons' resignation on May 31, 1940, many meetings and discussions were held between Parsons and Chester. Confidential memorandums began circulating, and Chester and Allan became experts at producing them. Undoubtedly, this professional wrangling caused all three men considerable anxiety and must have detracted from their responsibilities to the Hudson's Bay Company.

On the above-mentioned date and apparently with no consideration for timing—December 16, 1937, a few days before the season of goodwill—the Canadian Committee presented a confidential memorandum to Parsons, effectively laying down the law and informing him in no uncertain terms what was expected of him if he were to retain his job as Fur Trade Commissioner. This first tough, hard-hitting document was initialled by George W. Allan, R.J. Gourley. C.S. Riley, H.B. Lyall and J.A. Richardson, all members of the Canadian Committee.[18]

George William Allan, K.C., c. 1940.

Courtesy Hudson's Bay Company Archives

In the first few paragraphs of this document, Parsons was praised for his early attempts in bringing about improvements in the Fur Trade Department, but then he was informed bluntly that in recent times he had simply not been cooperating. The accusation was made that, instead of confronting problems head-on and turning to the Committee for assistance when things became difficult, he had kept his problems to himself and handled them his own way by "drawing farther and farther away from us."[19]

The Committee claimed to have been very patient with Parsons from 1934 to 1937 and tried to assist by giving him "a better understanding of our and your responsibilities, and ... assist[ing] you with those problems and weaknesses which were obvious to us, but with which little progress was being made."[20] It was clear that Parsons tended to keep to himself and handle the affairs of the Fur Trade Department without any reference to the Canadian Committee or the General Manager, Philip A. Chester.

The Canadian Committee referred to their responsibilities to the Board in London. Now, as a result of the difficulties in the proper procedure regarding the reorganization of the Fur Trade Department, the Board in London had asked the Canadian Committee

> ...to undertake, without delay, what they believe to be the necessary reorganization of the Fur Trade Department in Canada....You will understand that the Board and this Committee are unanimous in their view that your Department requires reorganizing if it is to survive and become vigorous and efficient.[21]

The message was clear. If Parsons was not prepared to do what Chester and the Committee wanted, then Chester, with the full support of the Committee, would do it himself—with or without Parsons' involvement:

> This means you will have to accept many things with which you have not been in agreement in the past year or two, and that you must change your attitude of mind towards this Committee and towards our General Manager....The changes to be made will have to be directed by us, but we wish to do this through you, and not only maintain the prestige of your position and of yourself, but give you all the credit for all that is done.[22]

In the last few paragraphs, Allan, who presumably wrote the memorandum, became very personal—"And if I may counsel you as a friend"—and reminded Parsons that his position as Fur Trade Commissioner was not the same as being a District Manager:

> As a District Manager the course you set yourself may have worked, but with the infinitely larger responsibilities of being Fur Trade Commissioner, it cannot work, and we hope you will see has not worked.[23]

This important memorandum to Ralph Parsons could be interpreted as a clear warning to him to cooperate with the plans for the reorganization of the Fur Trade Department or face the possible consequences. The message was clear, but did Parsons grasp the import of this memorandum, and if so, was he prepared to do what was required of him? Subsequent events over the next year and a half would answer that question.

In the minutes of a meeting of the Canadian Committee held on Thursday, December 23, 1937, Allan reported that he had interviewed Parsons, read the memorandum of December 16 to him, and discussed with him the necessity of reorganizing the Fur Trade Department. Chester had taken the matter up with Parsons, as well, and later reported back to the Chairman who in turn reported to the Committee.

> The General Manager reported that Parsons had stated he could not accept the view that there was any need for reorganization of the Department but he had intimated his willingness to cooperate with the Committee and the General Manager.[24]

On December 30, the Canadian Committee considered and then approved the report to be sent to the Board in London on the action taken to date with regard to the Fur Trade Department and its senior officer. The confidential report in question outlined in detail the situation involving the Fur Trade Commissioner. In the second paragraph, reference was made to the memorandum of December 16, "so that there could be no possible misunderstanding in the future."[25] The Chairman reminded Parsons of a private talk they had had about two years earlier, at which time Parsons had stated his opinion that "his Department was well organized and that if he were transferred tomorrow the staff he then had were thoroughly capable of carrying on."[26] Parsons acknowledged making the statement, and reiterated that he was still of the same opinion. It was his view "that he had tried to cooperate with the Committee and the General Manager but apparently had failed."[27] Reference was then made in the report to a meeting of December 20, 1937 between Parsons and Chester. Chester claimed that, at the end of the meeting, Parsons had promised "to cooperate loyally and thoroughly with the Canadian Committee and the General Manager, and do whatever he could to assist them with the changes they had in mind."[28] As a first step in this process, the Committee approved the appointment of David Robertson, Controller of the Winnipeg store, as Controller of the Fur Trade Department.

Robertson took up his duties on January 20, 1938 and, for most of that year, the organizational process within the Company appeared to go well. But all was not well, especially in the Fur Trade Department. On November 24, 1938 it was reported to London that the Fur Trade Commissioner "will have to be retired sooner or later."[29] Apparently, the dedicated Company man of long standing who had opened up the northernmost parts of Canada for the Hudson's Bay Company trade was having problems working with other senior personnel in Winnipeg, particularly Philip A. Chester, the one-time obscure English accountant with the "smooth and uncommunicative" facial features, "like those of the masked man in *The Phantom of the Opera*—not ugly, but expressionless...."[30] Peter C. Newman reports that, according to one Bay employee, "Even his handshake was bereft of feeling."[31]

No doubt Chester was a stubborn and uncompromising person, one who ultimately triumphed in the transatlantic feud with the Governor in London. Chester would also win his battle with the famed Hudson's Bay Company Arctic man and senior executive in the Fur Trade Department, but before the end came there would be more battles fought, for the most part in a gentlemanly and professional manner, for that was Ralph Parsons' nature. But if Chester believed he could talk Parsons into mute submission that would bring a complete turn around on the part of the Fur Trade Commissioner, he was in for a surprise. Yet it was an unfair struggle, for Parsons was on his own. Even Robert H.Chesshire, who had no fear of Chester, could do or say very little, even intimating at one point that at the time he and the others were holding on to their jobs by their eyebrows.[32]

Besides his staff, most of Parsons' other supporters were Hudson's Bay Company field men, particularly A. Dudley Copland, whose job it was to reduce the number of posts in the Western Arctic. Chester, on the other hand, had the support of Allan and the Canadian Committee, all of whom were prominent businessmen from the Winnipeg area. Even Patrick Ashley Cooper in London, Chester's other foe across the Atlantic, lined up on the side of the General Manager in Winnipeg. Still, although the mini-professional war raged in Hudson's Bay House on Main Street in Winnipeg for most of 1939, it was not destined to last for very long beyond that year. By the end of 1938 Parsons, fully realizing that he was fighting a losing battle, decided to retreat, which he did gracefully, setting his retirement date for May 31, 1940, and conducting himself in such a way that when he did retire, the Hudson's Bay Company gave him a pension of $6,000.00 per annum for life, a very generous pension at the time. Even then, the Company was unprepared to let Parsons go entirely and, in subsequent years, he continued to work part-time in a consulting role in the St. John's office and as an inspector of the posts on the Labrador Coast, for which he was paid a stipend and his expenses were covered. Thus in the end, Chester was successful in getting Parsons out of Winnipeg and, as if to wipe the slate clean, he even eliminated the position of Fur Trade Commissioner.[33]

During the winter and spring of 1939, the conflict and the struggle between Ralph Parsons and Philip A. Chester intensified. If Parsons were cooperating, then he surely was not doing so to the extent that Chester and Allan and the Committee expected. On March 1, 1939, fifteen months after Parsons had received the confidential memorandum from George W. Allan outlining what was expected of him as Fur Trade Commissioner, Chester drafted another private memorandum for the Canadian Committee. In this document, the General Manager referred to Parsons' "inability to reconcile himself to what I call, for want of a better term, the new ways of doing things."[34] Other significant parts of Chester's memorandum read as follows:

> I stated that it had been the wish of all of us to try to make the process of the reorganisation of his Department as easy for him as we could, and that there was no desire to force him out of the service. We knew that he had a great store of experience and knowledge about the Fur Trade which would be valuable for the new officers who had been introduced into the Department, and who still had much to learn about their work.
>
> From his own point of view, I suggested that, quite apart from any reorganisation of his Department, he was drawing near the end of a long and distinguished career in the service, which alone made it desirable for him now to be handing over duties and responsibilities to younger officers, and to take things more easily than had been possible in the past.
>
> In addition to this, he could give us valuable assistance with some of our problems, and that if he could reconcile himself to the new ways of doing some things, which really need not affect his position or the help he could give us, I saw no necessity for him to hurry his retirement.[35]

As a result of the discussion leading up to the memorandum, Chester continued, Parsons suggested that he should retire from the service on May 31, 1940. There is no diplomatic way to say it, but Chester's memorandum clearly indicated that he was rather anxious to have Ralph Parsons removed from his position as Fur Trade Commissioner. The last paragraph in the General Manager's memorandum reads:

> The trend of affairs in the Fur Trade Department was bound to result sooner or later, in Mr. Parsons wishing to retire, or perhaps our requesting him to do so, and consequently I find it difficult to express

adequately my sense of obligation to him for his attitude to his Department, and to me personally. As you will see, he places ungrudgingly at our disposal the remarkable and detailed knowledge he possesses of our Fur Trade, and is prepared cheerfully to render us assistance of great value in the next fifteen months.[36]

Was Parsons turning the other cheek, or was he treating Philip Chester with contempt? Undoubtedly, this paragraph expresses adequately the generous and gentlemanly person that Ralph Parsons really was. At this point in the struggle, there is no evidence of animosity on Parsons' part towards anybody. Still, what was in Parsons' mind during the discussions leading up to Chester's memorandum and after having read the document is open to speculation, but two things are clear. First, Chester expected more from Parsons than he could—or wanted to—give, and secondly, the Fur Trade Commissioner could not reconcile himself to the changes that were being made or were destined to be made in the Fur Trade Department.

Both prior to and after drafting this memorandum for the Canadian Committee on Tuesday, March 1, 1939, Chester had invited Parsons to his office for a man-to-man talk. Things did not go well and there is no record of what was really said, but the entire affair deeply affected Chester, and two days later he sent a letter to George W. Allan who was in Victoria, British Columbia at the time. The letter reads in part:

> This week brought a showdown from Parsons, and in a talk on Tuesday morning he allowed his feeling of irritation and annoyance to overcome his discretion, and poured out the works about getting out, as the present position was impossible for him.
>
> A two hour talk ensued, because I took him up, by saying that if that was the way he felt, then he had better plan to retire and so settle the matter, as there could be no question of our changing our plans with the reorganisation of the Department.
>
> I have the feeling that he was still clinging to the hope that we would let up and allow him to reign as "King" once more, and that he was a little taken aback by my acceptance of his wish that he should retire.
>
> I followed this up with counsel for himself, about what he was going to do, not to be in a hurry to get out, that he should undertake the Yukon development if we decide to go ahead with it, and that he still had a lot of valuable knowledge and experience to pass on to the younger officers if he could avoid being irritated by the new ways they were adopting, etc., etc.
>
> I then sent him off to sleep on it.
>
> The next day we had another long talk, and fixed the date of his

retirement for the 31st of May, 1940. In the afternoon I drafted a memorandum summarising, as well as I could, the results of our talks, and with the idea of showing it to Parsons before giving it to the Committee, so that there could be no possible misunderstanding between us.

We went over this memorandum yesterday morning; he took it away with him and brought it back to me this morning, stating that he thought it was an extremely kind and generous memorandum to him, and thanked me profusely for it. A copy is enclosed, which I should very much like you to read and let me have your views and comments thereon, before I consider having it brought up at a meeting of the Committee.[37]

The statement in the last paragraph above—"he thought it was an extremely kind and generous memorandum to him, and thanked me profusely for it"—is somewhat puzzling. Did this really happen as Chester maintained? If so, it appears that Parsons was treating Chester with utter contempt, whether or not the General Manager was aware of it. Maybe Parsons regarded the whole matter as nonsensical, and his relationship with Chester and Allan and the Canadian Committee as nothing more than a joke. One thing is certain: Ralph Parsons was no fool. The fight was heating up, and by now it was quite obvious that Hudson's Bay Company House in Winnipeg, big though it was, was not big enough for Chester and Parsons at the same time.

The mail moved swiftly in Western Canada in 1939, because two days later—March 5, 1939—Allan drafted his letter of reply to Chester. It reads in part:

I have read what you say about the inevitable show-down with Parsons and the memorandum. The show-down was due and is timely, and I feel that you have managed this difficult and delicate matter with great consideration for Parsons, and on really kind and generous lines, and I am glad that you were able to do this.

The memorandum is kind, generous and very fair to Parsons, and I am glad he appreciated it and thanked you for it.

The matter has been brought to that stage and it can now go before the Committee, and will I feel sure meet with their approval, as it does mine.

The matter will then be in shape to discuss with the Governor when he is in Winnipeg, and I trust will then take the form of a definite arrangement on lines wholly satisfactory to you, and which will enable you to proceed with your work of reorganisation of the Fur Trade Department, relieved of the continual difficulties with

Parsons with which you heretofore have had to contend... and which you have continuously met with great patience and forbearance, and always with the desire that he should make it possible to retire him on generous and fair lines and that he should be able to retire in a manner in every way befitting a long service accompanied for a long period with valuable performance, to enjoy a full pension.[38]

Although the Canadian Committee (made up of Chairman George W. Allan, a lawyer, and six prominent Winnipeg businessmen) was not directly involved in the day-to-day operations of the Hudson's Bay Company as was the General Manager, it is readily evident from the above statements that George Allan had completely lost patience with Ralph Parsons and was anxious to see him go. Chester, for his part, appeared to be preoccupied with the problem of Parsons; however, he now slept on it for almost two weeks. Then, being the tattletale that he was, he dispatched a letter to Patrick Ashley Cooper in London, informing the Governor of his problems with Parsons who by now had become the bane of his existence:

> I should mention that Parsons brought to a head his own position a couple of weeks ago, by losing his temper with me and saying that he might just as well get out and retire. I think he had faint hope that we might permit him to revert back to his autocratic rule and leave him alone, but I took him up by saying that we had better clear the atmosphere, allowed him a few hours to cool off, and then settled down for man to man talks.
>
> At the end of these I drew up a memorandum summarising them, which I asked him to read, so that there could be no misunderstanding between us upon the amicable conclusions we had reached. I enclose a copy of this memorandum for your information. Apart from sending a copy to Mr. Allan for his consideration, it has not yet come before the Canadian Committee, nor has it been seen by any other member of the Committee.
>
> When the members of the Committee return, it will be placed before them, and we shall then be in a position to discuss the question of Parsons with you during your visit.[39]

Cooper's pen was not as hot as Chester's, for it took him until March 31 before he replied to Chester's letter regarding "the question of Parsons." Cooper, who had come to know Parsons well on the *Nascopie* trip north in 1934 and who respected the Fur Trade Commissioner for his dedication to the Hudson's Bay Company, was more conciliatory in his attitude towards Parsons than Chester and Allan. Indeed, his letter of reply to Chester indicates a degree of sympathy for Parsons and the predicament

George W. Allan and Patrick Ashley Cooper, Governor of the Hudson's Bay Company, 1939.

in which the latter found himself. The main paragraph of Cooper's letter applicable to Parsons reads:

> I wish we could think of some way of keeping Parsons occupied when the time comes for him to lay down the Commissionership. He is so lonely a man and none too happy, and the Fur Trade is so completely the whole of his life that one feels there is grave risk of his breaking down when he finds himself with nothing to do. The Service must come first all the time, but we might be able to occupy him usefully. Money should not enter into the situation, for his pension I have no doubt will be ample for his apparently modest needs.[40]

In mid-April 1939, Chester wrote Cooper again. The Governor was planning a trip to Winnipeg, and the General Manager appeared anxious to discuss with him the matter of Parsons and the reorganization of the Fur Trade Department: "I think you will have a good picture of the Department after spending a week with it, and that the problem of Parsons will then be quickly settled."[41]

On April 13, the Canadian Committee met and discussed briefly Chester's memorandum of March 1 regarding Parsons. It was noted that the Chairman considered the proposals recommended by the General Manager in the memorandum to be "extremely considerate and generous" towards Parsons.[42] A decision was made to hold the matter over for discussion with the Governor during his forthcoming visit. A copy of the memorandum was to be sent to the Board in London, so the Governor could familiarize himself with it before his arrival in Winnipeg. Each member was given a carbon copy, but it is interesting to note that Hugh B. Lyall, not wanting the memo to become part of his official papers, subsequently returned his copy, which George W. Allan destroyed. There is a brief handwritten note to this effect, initialled by George W. Allan, at the bottom of an extant carbon copy of the memo in the Hudson's Bay Company Archives.[43]

In mid-May 1939, Chester received another letter from the Governor in London. Cooper's conciliatory attitude towards Parsons had now dissipated, and two members of the London Board, Sir Alexander Murray and Sir Edward Peacock, had come to the conclusion that the matter of Parsons "must come to a head."[44] On May 4, Cooper had also written a letter to George W. Allan:

> The memorandum regarding Parsons and his future has come in. At the same time that Chester sent his memorandum to you, he also sent me a copy. As you had not had the opportunity of considering it, I kept it private, but showed it to Murray and Peacock.
>
> I think you will be interested to know that the reaction that all three of us have in this connection is —first, that for a long time Chester has handled a difficult situation and a difficult man with a very great degree of patience and skill and—second, we feel gratified that Chester should send us unofficially and at so early a date his thoughts as expressed in the memorandum. It gives us the feeling that we are taken into your full confidence in a way which is helpful to our understanding of your problems, and makes it all the more easy for us to consider such matters when they come along officially.[45]

Apparently, for whatever reason, Cooper had developed a case of amnesia. All the highly complimentary things he had said about Ralph Parsons in his radio broadcasts and speeches on the *Nascopie* trip less than five years before were now forgotten. Parsons had clearly become the biggest villain in the Hudson's Bay Company in Canada.

On May 25, 1939, a meeting of the Canadian Committee convened, attended by the Hudson's Bay Company Governor who was visiting

Winnipeg. The matter of Parsons was discussed, and a decision was made that the Fur Trade Commissioner should be permitted to retire on a pension of $6,000.00 annually for life on May 31, 1940:

> In this connection the Committee were [sic] also unanimously in agreement with the Governor that every consideration should be extended to Mr. Parsons, so that his severance from the service was made as happy as possible.[46]

This was officially confirmed by the Governor and Board in London on June 13, and a communication dated June 23, 1939 was sent to the Canadian Committee to that effect.[47]

In the Annual Report of the Canadian Committee for the year ending January 31, 1940, the following reference was made to Parsons and the pitiful situation in which he found himself at the time:

> The present position of Mr. Parsons is a very uncomfortable one and he has all our sympathy. Officially he is still our Fur Trade Commissioner, but in some divisions of his Department changes and movements are taking place which he does not control, and with which he sometimes openly expresses his disapproval, and this cannot be a happy situation for anyone in the Fur Trade.[48]

Parsons knew that his days in Winnipeg were numbered, but his dedication to the great Company and all it embodied had not changed. In early December 1939, he had asked George W. Allan if it would be possible for him to purchase the *Fort Amadjuak*, the motor inspection boat which was no longer required in the Fur Trade Department. The Canadian Committee considered the matter and decided to present the boat to him as a retirement gift, and Allan wrote the Governor in London for official approval.[49] Cooper and the Board in London gave their decision, agreeing that the *Fort Amadjuak* would be "a very appropriate presentation."[50]

The battle was over, and Chester and Allan, with Cooper's blessing, had won. Parsons had lost, but he was not defeated. At the age of fifty-eight he was retired; given a good pension, the *Fort Amadjuak* as a retirement gift, and many gifts and mementos from his staff and others; and possibly more importantly, he left the Hudson's Bay Company after forty years of service with the respect and admiration of hundreds of Company personnel and thousands of Innu and Inuit from Labrador to British Columbia and from Winnipeg to Lancaster Sound.

Ironically, but true to Parsons' gentlemanly style, his final letter from the Fur Trade Commissioner's office was written on June 4, 1940 and addressed to Philip A. Chester, Hudson's Bay House, Winnipeg; but Chester was not at home at the time. When Parsons learned this, he rewrote his letter and had his secretary re-address it to the Ritz Carlton Hotel in Montreal. The letter, written on Hudson's Bay Company stationery with the words "Fur Trade Commissioner's Office" emblazoned across the top, read in part:

> I understand you are to arrive in Montreal on the 5th instant, but where you will be after that date nobody here knows, so that it seems somewhat uncertain where, and if, I shall meet you. However, should we miss meeting in the East this time for a final good-bye, I want to thank you sincerely for the many kindnesses you have shown me during the many years we have worked together.
>
> True, we have not always seen eye to eye, but that makes our relationship the more interesting.
>
> I would like to keep in touch with you and will write you when I have made my plans for the future.[51]

On Saturday, June 8, 1940, Ralph Parsons left Winnipeg and headed east. He did not connect with Philip Chester in Montreal. Maybe fate had deemed it so.

NOTES TO CHAPTER 7: CONFLICT AND RESIGNATION

1. Peter C. Newman, *Merchant Princes* (Toronto, Ontario: Viking, 1991), p. 277.
2. *Ibid.*, Chapter 14.
3. *Ibid.*, p. 285.
4. *Loc. cit.*
5. *Ibid.*, p. 287.
6. *Ibid.*, p. 288.
7. *Ibid.*, p. 289.
8. David R. Parsons to John Parsons, November 19, 1994.
9. Newman, *Merchant Princes*, p. 288.
10. Ralph Parsons to Philip A. Chester, June 4, 1940.
11. Philip A. Chester to George W. Allan, May 28, 1940.
12. Philip A. Chester to Senior Personnel, Winnipeg, May 2, 1940.
13. Patrick Ashley Cooper to Ralph Parsons, February 19, 1940.
14. Newman, *Merchant Princes*, p. 295.
15. *Ibid.*
16. Patrick Ashley Cooper to George W. Allan, May 4, 1939.
17. The Canadian Committee to Hudson's Bay Board in London ("Notes on Senior Personnel"), November 24, 1938. See also Arthur J. Ray, *The Canadian Fur Trade in the Industrial Age* (Toronto, Ontario: University of Toronto Press, 1990), p. 180.

18. Canadian Committee, "Private and Confidential Memorandum," Winnipeg, Manitoba, December 16, 1937.
19. *Ibid.*
20. *Ibid.*
21. *Ibid.*
22. *Ibid.*
23. *Ibid.*
24. Minutes of Meeting, Canadian Committee, Winnipeg, Manitoba, December 23, 1937.
25. Canadian Committee, "Private and Confidential Report," December 30, 1937.
26. *Ibid.*
27. *Ibid.*
28. *Ibid.*
29. Canadian Committee to Hudson's Bay Company Board in London, November 24, 1938.
30. Newman, *Merchant Princes*, pp. 285-286.
31. *Ibid.*, p. 286.
32. *Ibid.*, p. 289.
33. Philip A. Chester to George W. Allan, March 3, 1939.
34. Philip A. Chester, "Private and Confidential Memorandum to The Canadian Committee," March 1, 1939.
35. *Ibid.*
36. *Ibid.*
37. Philip A. Chester to George W. Allan, March 3, 1939.
38. George W. Allan to Philip A. Chester, March 5, 1939.
39. Philip A. Chester to Patrick Ashley Cooper, March 14, 1939.
40. Patrick Ashley Cooper to Philip A. Chester, March 31, 1939.
41. Philip A. Chester to Patrick Ashley Cooper, April 15, 1939.
42. Minutes of the Meeting of Canadian Committee, April 13, 1939.
43. See carbon copy of Philip A. Chester's memorandum, in Ralph Parsons' Personnel File RG2/37/161, Hudson's Bay Company Archives, Winnipeg, Manitoba.
44. Patrick Ashley Cooper to Philip A. Chester, May 4, 1939.
45. Patrick Ashley Cooper to George W. Allan, May 4, 1939.
46. Minutes of the Meeting of Canadian Committee, May 25, 1939.
47. Hudson's Bay Company Board (London), "Private and Confidential" (L.C.P. No. 5440) to Canadian Committee.
48. The Canadian Committee Annual Report for year ending January 31, 1940, dated February 23, 1940.
49. Canadian Committee to Governor and Committee (Board), London, January 5, 1940.
50. J. Chadwick Brooks, Secretary on behalf of the Governor and Committee (Board), London, to Canadian Committee, February 20, 1940.
51. Ralph Parsons to Philip A. Chester, Fur Trade Commissioner's Office, Winnipeg, Manitoba, June 4, 1940.

Chapter 8

Retirement Years

> "Retirement can be a very happy sequel to working years if it has been planned for. The busy worker who leaves his occupation and suddenly faces a life of aimless idleness may find that the sudden change proves a shock that impairs the health."
> —"The Business of Retirement," undated newspaper clipping in Ralph Parsons' "Pensions 1930-1940" file.

n May 31, 1940, in the wake of ongoing tension between Philip A. Chester and Ralph Parsons, the latter tendered his resignation with the Hudson's Bay Company. His decision must have been an agonizing one for him, despite the realization that it had been inevitable for some time. The Company was, after all, his life.

The editor of *The House Detective*, a monthly publication of the Company's employees' club, Beaver House, paid tribute in the June 1940 issue to a trio of retiring Company men, Alfred H. Doe, Charles W. Veysey, and Ralph Parsons: "The three are highly regarded men, almost institutions, and they are now retiring, each a loss to us all."[1] The record of Parsons' accomplishments alone was impressive:

> Forty years of Arctic experience when the Company realized more and more the possibilities of the vast trading empire within the Arctic regions; years of increasing responsibility and with it the opportunity to make trading north of Hudson Bay become a profitable reality....[2]

The writer of the tribute to Parsons characterized him as a courageous and sincere individual who had left his mark on the North: "A rigid disciplinarian, he demanded that all Company employees in the North maintain the high standard of the Company's tradition. His adventures and generosity are legend."³ Because of the way in which Parsons' life was tied so intricately to the Hudson's Bay Company, it was almost inconceivable that ties could be completely severed after his resignation. To its credit, the Company permitted him in subsequent years to work part-time in a consulting role in its St. John's office and as an inspector of its posts on the Labrador Coast.

As early as November 23, 1939, Parsons had been hoping to meet with Elwyn Ingrams, Manager of the Company's Fur Department in London, England, to "exchange news which one does not usually commit to paper."⁴ The exact nature of the anticipated conversation is unknown, but in all likelihood it revolved around Parsons' impending retirement and his feeling that he was being squeezed out of the Company. He expressed a similar thought in a letter to P.E.H. Sewell, also in London, on February 7, 1940:

> Things have changed tremendously in the old Company on this side, as well as in London, since first we met, and as one grows older I suppose it is only natural that they should think that the changes have not been for the better.⁵

He doubted that his friend, Michael R. Lubbock, would even "recognize the present setup," although most of Lubbock's old friends were "trying to be as happy as possible under the circumstances."⁶ Parsons admitted in a passing comment to J.S.C. Watt in Montreal that "none of us are getting any younger and I think that we require a holiday or rest more often than we did. . . ."⁷ To his Bishop-friend, Archibald L. Fleming, Parsons wrote: "I feel that a younger man should take hold of the 'reins' and I should try to live a little more leisurely." He added that he had been feeling unwell for the previous few months. "Nevertheless," he was quick to add, "there is quite a kick in the old horse yet and you may hear of me bobbing up at some unexpected place."⁸ Two days before his retirement, Parsons wrote to George Watson, "It is only natural I suppose on the eve of one's retirement to feel just a little blue. . . ."⁹ On the same day, Parsons informed Elwyn Ingrams that he thought his retirement from active service would be short lived, for following a month or so of holidays, he expected to assume more Government work in Ottawa.¹⁰ F.A. Hoyles in London, England, had heard and was somewhat grieved about Parsons' unhappy experience in the Winnipeg office during the previous few years.¹¹

Once news of Parsons' impending retirement filtered out, an innumerable assortment of tributes began pouring in. All of them were posi-

Archibald Lang Fleming, first Anglican Bishop of the Arctic, 1934.

tive, highlighting his many and varied adventures and accomplishments, but only a few were regarded by Parsons as sincere and worthy of personal response.

Patrick Ashley Cooper spoke of the "loyal, conscientious and valued services" rendered by Parsons to the Company over the previous four decades. Being a man of "tenacity of purpose and unstinted efforts" enabled Parsons to be promoted through the various stages from apprentice to Fur Trade Commissioner, the highest responsibility in the Fur Trade Department. "This is an achievement, which will serve as an example and an inspiration to all members of our staff, whose esteem and respect you have so well earned."[12] George L. Mercer, another Bay Roberts native, vividly recalled the day Parsons left the Church of England Academy in his hometown and sailed up the Labrador Coast to begin working with the Company. He wrote, "Bay Roberts has reason for pride in many of her sons and daughters who today are occupying important positions throughout Newfoundland, Canada and the United States and particularly is this true in your case." However, Mercer's boundless praise for Parsons had an ulterior motive—he was seeking employment with the Company for his nineteen-year-old son.[13] Archibald L. Fleming, who had first met Parsons in 1911 on Baffin Island, was slightly shocked at the announcement of Parsons' impending retirement. He commented, "It is hard for me to think of the H.B.C. fur trade apart from you," even though Parsons deserved a let up.[14] He especially appreciated Parsons' "extraordinary qualities."[15] George Pendleton of the MacKenzie-Athabasca District, who admitted to experiencing nothing but kindly consideration from Parsons, sincerely regretted his decision to retire.[16] George Watson wrote in an emotion-laden letter: "As Outfit 270 closes and the last King of the Fur Trade retires we come to the end of an epoch. The glory of the Fur Trade dims as 'Commissioner' gives way to 'Manager'." In the St. Lawrence District, Watson noted, Parsons' name was "spoken with affectionate awe."[17] Robert H. Chesshire, who knew that Parsons had been feeling "below par" for the previous year or two, was sorry but not surprised at his retirement. He was convinced that Parsons was "looking forward to a well-earned rest and some real relaxation after being 'on deck' for forty years and actually 'at the helm' during the past ten." Chesshire felt that Parsons could look back with keen satisfaction at the accomplishments of the particularly strenuous years of 1930 to 1935.[18] A. Dudley Copland had "mixed feelings," thinking "that the old ship would have suffered no harm with you at the helm for a few more years."[19] According to Major David L. McKeand, Parsons was about to leave "the home port with all his colours flying."[20] In the opinion of John Milne, Manager of the British Columbia District, Parsons would be remembered for having steered "the Old Fur Trade."[21] Even Philip A. Chester still regarded Parsons as one of his old friends.

The senior men of the Fur Trade Department in Hudson's Bay House decided to hold their own farewell reception for Parsons and make a presentation to him, which was a ship's clock. This reception was held in the Fort Garry Hotel in Winnipeg. The Montreal office was given very little official warning of Parsons' retirement. But soon after the announcement, the senior men of the Fur Trade Department there decided that Parsons' friends in the field should be allowed to subscribe in a voluntary way. A meeting, on behalf of the men of the North — "the Wintering Partners" — was organized in Montreal to honour Parsons. George Watson, in his Presentation Address, stated that Parsons' "achievements in the fur trade will go down in the annals of history with those of other famous fur traders in the past." Watson divided Parsons' Fur Trade career into two parts: first, the opening up of a fur trade empire in the eastern Arctic, and secondly, the decade he spent at the head of the Company's fur trade in the capacity as Fur Trade Commissioner. Watson enthused about the additions Parsons had "made to the historic dates connected with the eastern Arctic." Parsons' "crowning achievement," Watson suggested, had occurred in 1937 when he directed the establishment of Fort Ross on the Bellot Strait, the connecting link in the Northwest Passage, "that Arctic will-o'the wisp which had lured the imaginations of men's minds for over 300 years." The Great Depression of the 1930s.

> ... were dark days for the fur trade but those of us who have been privileged to work with you know with what energy and resolution you grappled with the serious problems of the day and we are proud to know that your leadership, your energy, your courage and your

vision, in a short space of years, carried our grand old Fur Trade back on the paths of prosperity.

Indeed, those who had worked with Parsons called themselves "the Men of the Restoration." Watson found it difficult to verbalize his assessment of Parsons, so he quoted a writer to make his point:

> Give me for a boss the man who has worked hard and accomplished much, who has met the challenge of adversity with a glad smile, who listened to the flattery of success with a doubting ear; who has never belittled the labour that gave him his bread nor fawned on the hand that made up the payroll. Give me this man for a boss, and I'll not work under him, but with him.

As for the form the presentation to Parsons should take, the men of the North were almost unanimously in favour of a model of the famous M.V. *Daryl*, the vessel on which Parsons had had many adventurous voyages during his years in the Arctic. The sixty-seven individuals who contributed to the "very creditable piece of work, which will reflect to the advantage of the silversmiths' art," wished that Parsons would "be spared many happy years of retirement and that their little gift may be a pleasant memento of adventurous days in the fur trade."[22]

Parsons was understandably moved by the presentation. In response to the "great kindness and good wishes" expressed by the men of the North, he promised to "carry the memory of this gathering with me throughout my life." He determined, however, not to believe all the nice things that had been said about him. "For, if I did," he explained, "you would have me worrying how ever you will get along without me." During his forty-year tenure with the Company, he had encountered many grave occasions, but still he felt that his job had "been the most pleasant and interesting one in the world." He would never switch places with anything he could imagine the future might hold for his successors. He readily admitted to being a man on the move. "It has not been an armchair job—neither can it ever be. I could never sit comfortably in an armchair anyway and it is not the armchair part of my life that holds the most interest."

He spoke of the "continuous fight by our men for supremacy against competitors of the most unscrupulous kind." Considering what the Company's men accomplished, more often than not left "alone to work out one's salvation," they could not have been "such slouches after all." Indeed, they were "the most conscientious, hard working, trustworthy group in the world." He paid a glowing tribute to this "silent branch of the service." He then recalled his own service of the Company, joining at seventeen. After five years he was appointed to his first charge, the youngest post manager in the District. In turn he was moved up to the youngest manager of a district, then placed in charge of a combined group of five districts, and finally a decade as Fur Trade Commissioner. One telling comment was later pencilled out of his farewell speech: "It has always been my policy never to out-stay my period of usefulness anywhere—hence part of my reason for retiring now." While proud that he held the Commissioner's job for a longer period than each of his three predecessors, he sorrowfully noted "that the glory of the Fur Trade dims as Commissioner gives way to Manager." A pencilled remark inserted into his speech leaves no doubt about his feelings:

> If I had had another drink or two or if the drinks that I have already had had been Newfoundland Rum I may be inclined to tell the Canadian Committee and the General Manager what I think of them, but this is certainly not the time nor the occasion for such, particularly since we have enjoyed such a splendid meal.

"The Fur Trade has no white shirt jobs," he reminded his audience. "I hope the day will never come when an effort will be made to mechanize the Fur Trade staff and change their mode of living and operating in any way that will undermine their initiative and sense of responsibility." In his conclusion, he issued a challenge to his fellow workers:

> I hope you will have no occasion to regard me as a memory only. Our courses will, I hope, meet on many occasions but wherever you are and I am I shall always count on my best wishes for your continued success. At any rate, I am sure that my spirit will be hovering over Baffinland District long after we all have gone. In the meantime, while my name has been struck from the active service list of the old Company I shall hold myself in readiness to again report for active service should the urgency of these unsettled times require it in the interest of the Company or my country.
> And now, gentlemen, you are still outward bound and I am going ashore with the pilot. Hold to the course I have given you and be careful not to carry too much sail.[23]

Of all the good wishes Parsons received at his retirement, he regarded George Watson's to be the most sincere.[24] On the same day, he also wrote Archibald L. Fleming that he valued his sentiment "much more than any other greeting that I received." While listening to Fleming's telegram being read, Parsons was reminded of an incident regarding the Bishop.

> It was when you invited me into your snowhouse at Etinik and you served up a delicious meal of sealmeat and I compared how much better I enjoyed that meal than the one we were then having at the Manitoba Club.[25]

"A ship has come in for Ralph Parsons," Frank Ryan wrote in his 1940 article, "Forty Years on the Fur Trail."[26] The ship he referred to was the *Fort Amadjuak*, the Company's Atlantic coast inspection vessel, which was no longer required in the Fur Trade Department and which Parsons late in 1939 had asked to purchase.[27] The purchase was not approved, but she became the gift of the Company Governor, and the London and Canadian Committees to the retiring Fur Trade Commissioner. Ryan continued:

The *Fort Amadjuak* near Rigolet, Summer of 1943.

> No other gift could suggest so fittingly the honour the Company thus pays to the man who, in forty years of adventure and achievement, has established twenty-eight new HBC posts, and seen the completion, for commercial purposes, of the long-dreamed-of Northwest Passage.[28]

The folks at Hudson's Bay House in Winnipeg wished Parsons "a grand retirement—and perhaps another visit to Baffinland, in his own boat."[29]

The *Fort Amadjuak* was owned by the firm of Revillon Frères before being bought by the Hudson's Bay Company. The latter then used her essentially as a yacht, for transporting its Fur Trade Commissioner. She made several voyages as far north as Baffin Island, and was named for a trading post on the west coast of the island which Parsons had founded in 1921.[30]

Admittedly, the sturdy ship was not, in Ryan's opinion, a typical tribute to a man of Parsons' stature. Ryan explained the Company's rationale in presenting Parsons with the vessel: "The men who have worked with Ralph Parsons realize that retirement could never mean for him the slippered ease of the fireside nor the garrulous tales of reminiscence." Considering that he was "of that breed of men who love ships and the sea," he would use the *Fort Amadjuak* to "seek new adventure, new horizons." Parsons certainly knew the vessel's "stout heart." "More than once he has been aboard when she breasted the buffeting waves into the quiet shelter of some uncharted cove along the Labrador coast."[31]

Built in Shelbourne, Nova Scotia, by John Etherengton and Sons in 1934, the 10' x 42 1/10' M.V. *Fort Amadjuak* boasted a tonnage of 13.42. She was constructed with hard pine planking and oak ribs, keel, stern and stem, and sheathed with greenheart. The auxiliary sloop, which was extremely well fitted with such things as hardwood panelling and generous amounts of brass, was rigged with one mainsail and two jibs. The four-cycle, three-cylinder diesel engine, with a B. horsepower of 28.5, enabled the vessel to reach a speed of eight knots on one gallon of fuel per hour. Her iron keel weighed 4,000 pounds and she had two anchors and eighty fathoms of chain. Two storage tanks carried 120 gallons of fuel, enough for about 1,000 miles. Two individuals could be accommodated in the cabin and two in the forecastle. The vessel, with electric lighting throughout, was fully equipped with two stoves, sails, running gear, table, cooking utensils, searchlight, siren, four rubber mattresses, code of signals, flags, and linen. She carried a twelve-foot dinghy.[32]

The *Fort Amadjuak*'s later history is as interesting as her earlier career. Harold Horwood, for one, believes that Parsons used the vessel little, if at all.[33] However, David Parsons recalls that his father did use the *Fort Amadjuak* occasionally. After Parsons' retirement, the vessel was under the able command of Captain Sam Parsons, who sailed her for Ralph Parsons to Labrador and on short pleasure trips with his family and friends. The captain had to be both engineer and skipper, and sometimes cook in the small galley up forward.

Horwood remembers that the *Fort Amadjuak* had been lying idly in Bay Roberts for about three years when he bought her in 1949. As late as 1993, he described her as an excellent boat, with a very strong, tight hull, a small diesel engine for auxiliary power, and a suit of sails that would permit her to sail at seven or eight

David R. Parsons with his father, Ralph Parsons, at Bay Roberts, 1939.

knots in a stiff breeze. He took her to Labrador in 1950, and found her quite satisfactory, an exceptional vessel for two or three people to live on board, and a good sailer. On one memorable day, he recalled, when her progress was assisted by a fast tide running out of Groswater Bay, she averaged 9 1/4 knots between Rigolet and Cartwright.

Horwood was forced to sell her in 1952, because he could no longer afford to keep her in seaworthy condition. By then, she needed a new suit of sails, engine and bank of storage batteries (used to run her electric system). However, her hull, topsides, rigging, etc., were as good as ever. He sold the *Fort Amadjuak* to Andrews' Fisheries with great regret, for they subsequently gutted her, her beautiful interior accommodation being scrapped in favour of a fish hold, installed a large gasoline engine, cut down the mast, and used her as a pump boat for herring.

Captain Sam Parsons and Ralph Parsons with fishing guide, Bob Brown, Paradise River, Labrador, 1945. (Brown identified by Charles Lethbridge, Happy Valley, 1995.)

Courtesy of James Y. Parsons

The *Fort Amadjuak* was later bought by Farley Mowat from Andrews Fisheries or another fish firm. He sailed her to St. John's, where she was refitted as a yacht. Unfortunately, he failed to replace her gasoline engine. He sent two men from Burgeo, where he was then living, to the capital city to take his vessel to Messers Cove, Burgeo. The men were running with the engine, which was leaking into the bilges. The engine room hatch was closed. The vapour from the escaping gasoline caught fire, and blew the stern out of the boat. The *Fort Amadjuak* sank stern first quickly about forty miles off the Burin Peninsula. This happened shortly after Farley Mowat had bought her. The men rowed ashore in a dory they had been towing.[34]

Parsons was officially notified on June 1, 1940 that he had been granted a pension of $6,000.00 a year for life. Nine days later, he had delivered in St. John's a new car—a 1940 model LaSalle five-passenger Touring Sedan. The vehicle, with Firestone tires, underseat heater, wheel discs, radio and cowl aerial, fog lights, grill guard, and blue seat covers, cost him $1,636.59.[35] As a further illustration of his love for the Hudson's

Bay Company, he even made sure that the licence plates on his Newfoundland-based automobile always bore the numbers 1670, commemorating the year of the Company's founding.

As he retired, Parsons was still basking in the glow of his many and varied accomplishments. For example, on March 13, 1939, in a letter to Michael R. Lubbock in London, England, he had noted with obvious glee that three of the Company's competitors—Revillon Frères, Northern Traders Limited, and the Canalaska Trading Company—had been forced to close their doors: "without boasting," he continued, "I think that this result is largely a result of our aggressive policy...."[36] He was understandably proud of his achievements which had undoubtedly contributed to the overall success of the Fur Trade.

He was also proud of his relationship with the Inuit, with whom he had traded during the previous four decades. An opportunity to explain his personal convictions came on March 8, 1940, when Archibald L. Fleming informed Parsons that he was writing a book discussing the pros and cons of missionary work among the Inuit. Fleming recalled that when he left Baffin Island, Parsons had written him, speaking positively of the Inuit and of the beneficial results following the Bishop's efforts among them. Fleming then solicited a brief statement from Parsons, showing the impression that had been made upon him in connection with the Anglican Church's missionary work among the Inuit.[37]

Parsons, himself an Anglican, responding on April 2, expressed pleasure at being asked to comment on the effects of Christianity among the Inuit of the Canadian Arctic, fully cognizant that what he was about to write might shock Fleming. He wrote:

> I am of the firm belief that the Eskimo lived very Christian-like lives before ever the missionary or white man went amongst them. They were honest, faithful, unselfish and truthful, and they made a very good job of loving their neighbours as themselves. So, the task of the missionary was to teach the Eskimo our religion, which in substance was very like his own, and, in particular, by example and precept, to counteract the undesirable influences of the white man, with whom the Eskimo came in contact, and I am glad to say that from my own personal observations your missionaries have done a great and noble work for the Eskimo, who are a very lovable people because they live Christian-like lives....[38]

A day later, Parsons realized he may have overlooked exactly what Fleming had requested of him.[39] A more detailed statement followed on

April 16, 1940, in which Parsons discussed the role, not only of the missionary, but that of the trader, as well. The following summarizes Parsons' opinions.

The white or Arctic fox—practically the sole exportable natural resource of the Inuit—was of no interest to the white man until early in this century, when market values advanced sufficiently to make commercial trading profitable.

The white man, who is very aggressive, has slowly extended his activities over the world, exploiting its natural wealth. The trader, by entering the land of the Inuit, confers many of the material benefits of his civilization, provided that undue competition is avoided. The trader, by furnishing the Inuit with improved weapons and a few amenities of civilization, makes their lives less strenuous. However, not all traders have that desirable sense of responsibility.

The responsible trader, Parsons continued, will endeavour to freely give religious guidance and leadership to the Inuit. The white man should convey to the Inuit both the material and spiritual benefits of his civilization.

> It is a well-known fact, to which I can personally testify, that the missionary is a powerful influence for the advancement of the better side of the white man's civilization and he is invariably a factor conducive to decent and honourable living.

Admittedly, the Inuit, before the advent of the white man, possessed many admirable traits, but they lacked the essential spark of spirituality. The role of the missionary, Parsons contended, is to teach the true tenets of Christianity and help the Inuit to avoid the more deleterious features of the white man's lifestyle.

The missionaries' achievements will be great and prosperous if individuals have a broad and generous outlook, live among the Inuit and study their language and problems, and give of themselves in the service of Jesus Christ, the Master. As a result, "the comforts of the Christian religion [will] be made available to brighten the lives of these delightful people—the Eskimo." Furthermore, the missionary usually brings with him hospitals, the true sign of the white man's healing.[40]

A telling newspaper clipping, "The Business of Retirement," is taped to Parsons' "Pensions 1930-1940" file. After four decades of intense activity in the Company, the thought of inactivity must have been anathema to him. The other question for him must have been how he would spend his retirement years—certainly not sitting idly around, merely resting on his laurels of the past, as numerous as they were. The item reads:

> Retirement can be a very happy sequel to working years if it has been planned for. The busy worker who leaves his occupation and suddenly faces a life of aimless idleness may find that the sudden change proves a shock that impairs the health. Hobbies, planned and practised well ahead of the leisure days, provide a way of occupying mind and hands in worthwhile efforts. The hobby may be profitable, useful or amusing but it should adequately fill the gap left by the person's job.[41]

Everybody who knew Parsons realized that retirement to him did not mean inactivity. While Bishop Fleming liked the thought of his friend "in some quiet spot in Newfoundland or the Labrador just camping and fishing far from the 'maddening crowd,'" he also realized it would be virtually impossible to tie him down for any length of time.[42] George Watson wrote Parsons: "Retirement is quite inapplicable to you because that betokens inactivity, and I am very sure that there will be no inaction wherever you are." Indeed, Watson predicted that Parsons would "always be fully occupied and happy, and . . . continue to give much happiness to others."[43] A. Dudley Copland hoped that Parsons would eventually find time to record his many and varied experiences in book form.[44] Nor could S.T. Wood, Commissioner of the Royal Canadian Mounted Police in Ottawa, envision Parsons being inactive.[45] Dorothy Gannon expressed her opinion that Parsons' most recent decision would not "be a retirement of slippered ease," and she hoped he would "enjoy some means of peace & tranquillity." The current state of world affairs offered little of either, she suggested. "But there's nothing to stop each individual working his or her own separate peace!"[46] C.S. Riley of the Canadian Committee could picture Parsons taking on some good-sized administrative job in the country's service. "I think they are missing a good bet in not pressing you into service," he wrote.[47]

On June 4, 1940 Parsons admitted to Philip A. Chester that they had "not always seen eye to eye, but that makes our relationship the more interesting." If, after a holiday, Chester needed Parsons' "services for any purposes whatsoever," he assured him he would "be only too ready and willing."[48] Chester, in his response, admitted to missing Parsons, if for no other reason "because whatever our differences during the past few years you must know that I have always had a very deep regard for you, and the longer I go on in life the more greatly do I value my friends."[49] Chester accepted Parsons' offer to continue to give the Company the benefit of his knowledge and experience.

Parsons went back to live in the old home at Bay Roberts, but he did not break completely with the Company. He kept an office in the Hudson's Bay Company office on Water Street in St. John's, where he spent a portion of time each week. In Bay Roberts, he kept busy. He had a new garage built with an office for himself at the back. He tore down the old barn and had a new shed and carpenter shop built in its place. He added a new veranda to the front of the house and did much of the carpentry work himself on the inside, such as installing a new gyproc ceiling in the dining room and building a large wardrobe closet for himself.

In his leisure time he went trout fishing, for he was an avid and excellent fisherman. David Parsons remembers fishing beside his father by a brook when the senior man would catch several trout to his son's none. Parsons would then take pity on David, and they would swap places, but he would continue to catch trout while David still caught none! Parsons was also an excellent shot with a gun, although David never went hunting with his father.[50]

Another portrait of Parsons in his retirement years is drawn by Jack Hambling in his collection of stories, *The Second Time Around: Growing Up in Bay Roberts*. The author, Parsons' nephew, recalls in vivid detail the year that the Western Union Company started to demolish its staff house on Cable Avenue in the town. Once the dismantling was completed, the business of selling off the material began. Within a fortnight, Hambling's grandfather had bought the billiard table, cues, benches, chalkboard, and overhead lights and become the owner/proprietor of a billiard club. However, he also distinctly remembers that it was his Uncle Ralph who was responsible for bringing the club to fruition, by taking care of the monetary arrangements. In an understatement, Hambling observed, "Uncle Ralph was long used to seeing things through." His career, from apprentice clerk to Fur Trade Commissioner, was deservedly no small feat, especially for a boy from outport Newfoundland. Hambling writes:

> During his retirement, I saw a lot of my uncle Ralph, both at home in his favourite room, surrounded by all kinds of mementoes of his days on the trail, and on those many occasions when he and I travelled the more civilized pathways to a favourite fishing pond. Not once did he even so much as mention his many adventures and

experiences, the likes of which only someone like Jack London could give credence to. There aren't many boys lucky enough to have shared a brookside campfire with a relative who killed a fully grown polar bear with nothing more than a sheath knife in order to save himself and his Inuit guide from certain death. That was the story I heard his brother-in-law, the admirer of athletes, Rev. [Evelyn] Clench, tell Father one night in our living room after their game of chess . . . and Rev. Clench, in keeping with his station, didn't tell lies....

Small wonder that on the opening night of Grandfather's billiard club, the members drank a toast to the health of their absent patron. It was not coincidence that the rum used for the occasion was Hudson's Bay Company dark.[51]

One of the first major projects in which Parsons became involved following his formal retirement was as an invited member of the American Greenland Commission. This project consumed a significant amount of his time from 1940 to 1941, including travelling to and from New York City. It also retained a role for him with the beloved Hudson's Bay Company, with which he had spent the previous four decades. It kept his mind focused during the period of transition from a life of intensive activity to that of a reluctant retiree.

On August 17, 1940, R.A. Gibson, Deputy Commissioner of the Northwest Territories, invited Parsons to sit on the American Greenland Commission. The Commission had been created by Henrik de Kauffmann, Danish ambassador to the United States, on April 25, 1940, shortly after the German occupation of Denmark in April 1940. Subsequent to this, all communication between Greenland and the Mother Country had been cut, leaving the two district Governors of North and South Greenland the responsibility of governing the country, as provided by law in emergency. The Danish Minister in Washington, representing Greenland in the United States, had appointed the Commission to advise in the affairs of Greenland for the duration of the emergency. Headquartered in New York City under the chairmanship of Hans Christian Sonne, the Commission was designed to assist the Governors of Greenland in various ways, among others in facilitating the purchase of necessary supplies for the Greenland people.[52]

The Commission held its first meeting on Friday, May 24, 1940 at the Metropolitan Club in New York City. Members present were Hans Christian Sonne, Leonard T. Beale, Dr. Paul Bentzen, Dr. John Dyneley

Prince, Dr. Henry Goddard Leach, Norvin H. Green, Marie Peary Stafford, Captain Robert A. ("Bob") Bartlett, and Neilson Abeel. One member—Ruth Bryan Rohde—was absent.

Each Commission member spoke briefly. Bartlett, the well-known Newfoundland-born personality, recalled that he had initially visited Greenland with Admiral Robert E. Peary in 1898 and had been there almost every year since. He expressed admiration of the people, hoping they would be protected from unscrupulous traders and fishermen who might bring in disease and infringe on the trading monopoly.

The Commission consisted of two parts: the small business committee, and the larger advisory committee, the latter including all members. The primary concern of the business committee was to ensure that food and supplies were sent to Greenland for the approaching winter, while the main purpose of the Commission itself was to balance Greenland's budget and encourage the people to remain economically self-supporting.[53]

Up to the time an invitation had been extended to Parsons, the Commission had been composed of American citizens. However, a decision was made to enlarge the Commission to include three or four Canadian representatives who could contribute greatly to the fund of knowledge on Greenland's problems and guarantee that Canadian businessmen would have a reasonable opportunity for Greenland business. Parsons was chosen to play an active part for his fund of general knowledge, business acumen, friendly ways, and connection with a reliable trading house, the Hudson's Bay Company.[54]

In August 1940 Parsons' mother had died following a very short illness. Parsons tried to convey his intense feelings of grief to Philip A. Chester. "It has been a shocking blow to me as we meant so much to each other," he wrote to Chester.[55] "While it is easy to say that she had enjoyed a good many years beyond . . . 'the allotted span'," Chester responded, "I know that that makes the unexpected but inevitable all the more hard to bear."[56] Parsons had loved his mother, and she, him. Because he had no wife after 1920, his mother had drawn even closer to him, and he, to her. He may have been her favourite child simply because having lost his wife he had more time to devote to his aging mother. In addition, Parsons' ninety-two-year-old father was quite ill, and he wanted to stand by the elderly man to monitor his condition. After that, he would be glad to serve on the Commission, pending the Company's approval.[57]

Parsons attended his first Commission meeting on September 27,

1940, and in a letter dated October 8, 1940, he expressed appreciation to the Commission chairman, Hans Christian Sonne, for "the very thorough and efficient manner" he was supervising the handling of Greenland's affairs.[58] Parsons, in an undated memorandum regarding the Commission, suggested that as the merchandise requirements of Greenland's population appeared to be very similar to the requirements of communities in Northern Canada, and as Canadian manufacturers had been developing this class of trade for several generations, a considerable quantity of more suitable merchandise could be purchased in Canada more advantageously than in the United States. Therefore, the Canadian market should be investigated by a member of the New York Purchasing Staff who had local knowledge of the kinds of goods most suitable for the Greenland people.[59] In other words, an increase in purchasing from Canada would be of economic benefit to Greenland.

On February 6, 1941, Parsons wrote Hans Christian Sonne, expressing pleasure that definite arrangements would soon be made for the purchase of a portion of Greenland's requirements in Canada.[60] On the same day, he advised Professor Gilbert E. Jackson, a Commission member in Toronto, that the Commission evidently meant to do considerable business with Canada. He had taken it on himself to advise the Hudson's Bay Company of proposed visits by Commission representatives to Canada, believing the Company had the ideal setup for Greenland's requirements.[61]

On April 10, 1941, the Department of State dispatched a press release, announcing the signing on April 9 of an agreement between the Secretary of State, acting on behalf of the American Government, and the Danish Minister, Henrik de Kauffmann, acting on behalf of His Majesty the King of Denmark in his capacity as sovereign of Greenland.

> The agreement recognizes that as a result of the present European war there is danger that Greenland may be converted into a point of aggression against nations of the American continent, and accepts the responsibility on behalf of the United States of assisting Greenland in the maintenance of its present status.
>
> The agreement, after explicitly recognizing the Danish sovereignty over Greenland, proceeds to grant to the United States the right to locate and construct airplane landing fields and facilities for the defense of Greenland and for the defense of the American continent.[62]

In light of this recent development, Hans Christian Sonne recommended to Henrik de Kauffmann that the American Greenland Commission be dissolved. Sonne wrote to Kauffmann:

> I believe that all the Members [of the Commission] will feel as I do, namely, that they will gladly in the future place themselves in an informal manner at the disposal of yourself and/or the Greenland authorities, should you or they desire their advice and help on any specific problems that may arise.[63]

Not long after, Parsons received from Henrik de Kauffmann himself a letter, conveying his most hearty thanks personally for his valuable assistance and generous expenditure of time and efforts in the cause of Greenland. He assured the retired Newfoundlander that his sympathy, understanding and help would always be gratefully remembered.[64]

During the early part of his retirement, Parsons played a key role in negotiating the transference of several Northern Labrador posts to the Newfoundland Commission of Government. The Government was advised that as of May 31, 1942, the Hudson's Bay Company had decided to withdraw from the five Northern Labrador Moravian Mission posts—Makkovik, Hopedale, Nain, Nutak, and Hebron. Parsons wrote Philip A. Chester, "It's more their affair now than it is ours for goodness knows we have contributed our full quota to the welfare of the Moravian natives in the past 16 years."[65] The negotiations, though strenuous, were a source of great pleasure for Parsons who was delighted to be back in harness, doing something constructive on behalf of the Company.[66] By June 13, 1942, there was a final draft agreement regarding the transference of the Moravian posts in place. Parsons later reported: "The Government representative ... was a very agreeable person so that the transfer was made without differences of opinion—at least not much!"[67] The Canadian Committee, pleased with Parsons' performance, offered its commendation and a $1,000.00 cheque.[68]

In a letter from Parsons to Patrick Ashley Cooper, dated late in 1943, the former noted the recent death of his ninety-four-year-old father. More encouraging news was that his son, David, serving with the Royal Canadian Air Force in Europe, had finished his first "tour" with his squadron. The older man himself had recently spent a week in Winnipeg, Manitoba, visiting old friends. The previous summer, he continued, he had again inspected the Labrador posts at Philip A. Chester's request. But he had not spent all his time on business-related activities; he had spent some qualitative time salmon fishing.[69] Indeed, mention of the hobbies of salmon fishing and partridge shooting pepper many of his letters. On March 29, 1944, Parsons complained to Philip A. Chester that Newfoundland's east coast was "not having exactly tropical weather." To the contrary, "we are frozen in and when you mention crocuses, snowdrops and pussywillows in Victoria it makes me envious and inclined to jump the first plane heading in that direction."[70]

Parsons consented again to supervise the operations of the remaining three Labrador posts for the Company. These were Cartwright, Rigolet and Northwest River. This included an inspection in the summer of 1945 and maintaining contact with the St. John's office. He was to use his boat, the *Fort Amadjuak*, for this purpose, and the Company would absorb his expenses. The Company would also continue to pay him the nominal sum of $1,200.00 for his services up to November 30, 1945. The following fall, he was to meet with Company officials in Winnipeg to have the operations assessed.

The portrait of Ralph Parsons which emerges from this chapter is that of the reluctant retiree. Although his retirement had been inevitable, this made it no easier to accept. The most difficult aspect was finding sufficient meaningful activities to keep his mind and hands occupied. Having earlier lost his wife and a son, and by 1943 both his mother and father, he was decidedly a lonely man. The fact that the Fur Trade had been so completely the whole of his life led some people to believe that he would be very unhappy when he found himself with virtually nothing to do. To his credit, he continued to offer himself unreservedly in the service of both the Hudson's Bay Company and his country in any capacity in which he might be utilized. Occasional opportunities arose for him to revert to his former lifestyle of being quite busy, but there must have been the constant realization that these were only sporadic, short-term projects which, when completed, would leave him with agonizing feelings of both emptiness and loneliness.

Ralph Parsons at Bay Roberts, about 1950.

NOTES TO CHAPTER 8: RETIREMENT YEARS

1. "With All Good Wishes," *The House Detective* (II:1), June 1940, unpaginated.
2. Watson, M.D., "Who's Who in Hudson's Bay House: Ralph Parsons," *ibid*. See reprint in *Newfoundland Quarterly* (LXXXVIII:3), April 1994, p. 43.
3. *Loc. cit.*
4. Elwyn Ingrams to Ralph Parsons, November 23, 1939.
5. Ralph Parsons to P.E.H. Sewell, February 7, 1940.
6. Ralph Parsons to Michael R. Lubbock, February 26, 1940.
7. Ralph Parsons to J.S.C. Watt, April 2, 1940.
8. Ralph Parsons to Archibald L. Fleming, May 10, 1940.
9. Ralph Parsons to George Watson, May 29, 1940.
10. Ralph Parsons to Elwyn Ingrams, May 29, 1940. 11. F.A. Hoyles to Ralph Parsons, July 9, 1940.
12. Patrick Ashley Cooper to Ralph Parsons, February 19, 1940.
13. George L. Mercer to Ralph Parsons, February 20, 1940.
14. Archibald L. Fleming to Ralph Parsons, May 15, 1940.
15. Archibald L. Fleming to George W. Allan, May 22, 1940.
16. George Pendleton to Ralph Parsons, May 15, 1940.
17. George Watson to Ralph Parsons, May 16, 1940.
18. Robert H. Chesshire to Ralph Parsons, May 16, 1940.
19. A. Dudley Copland to Ralph Parsons, May 16, 1940.
20. David L. McKeand to R.H.G. Bonnycastle, May 24, 1940.
21. John Milne to Ralph Parsons, May 30, 1940.
22. George Watson, "Presentation Address Delivered to Mr. Ralph Parsons On Behalf of the Men of the North," pp. 1,3.
23. Ralph Parsons, "Farewell Speech," pp. 1-9.
24. Ralph Parsons to George Watson, May 29, 1940.
25. Ralph Parsons to Archibald L. Fleming, May 29, 1940.
26. Frank Ryan, "Forty Years on the Fur Trail," *The Beaver*, June 1940 (Outfit 271), p. 20.
27. George W. Allan to the Governor and Committee, London, England, January 5, 1940.
28. Ryan, "Forty Years," p. 20.
29. Watson, M.D., "Who's Who in Hudson's Bay House: Ralph Parsons," unpaginated.
30. Harold Horwood to John Parsons, November 1, 1993.
31. Ryan, "Forty Years," p. 20.
32. This description of the *Fort Amadjuak* is based on a specifications sheet, and Harold Horwood to John Parsons, November 1, 1993.
33. *Ibid.*
34. Harold Horwood to John Parsons, November 1, 1993, and Farley Mowat to John Parsons, December 10, 1993.
35. W.B. Wardle to Whom it May Concern, June 10, 1940.

36. Ralph Parsons to Michael R. Lubbock, March 13, 1939.
37. Archibald L. Fleming to Ralph Parsons, March 8, 1940.
38. Ralph Parsons to Archibald L. Fleming, April 2, 1940.
39. Ralph Parsons to Archibald L. Fleming, April 3, 1940.
40. Draft of Ralph Parsons' statement to Archibald L. Fleming, April 16, 1940.
41. "The Business of Retirement," undated newspaper (unnamed) clipping in Ralph Parsons' "Pensions 1930-1940" file.
42. Archibald L. Fleming to Ralph Parsons, May 15, 1940.
43. George Watson to Ralph Parsons, May 16, 1940.
44. A. Dudley Copland to Ralph Parsons, May 16, 1940.
45. S.T. Wood to Ralph Parsons, July 5, 1940.
46. Dorothy Gannon to Ralph Parsons, July 10, 1940.
47. C.S. Riley to Ralph Parsons, January 17, 1941.
48. Ralph Parsons to Philip A. Chester, June 4, 1940.
49. Philip A. Chester to Ralph Parsons, June 20, 1940.
50. Information from David R. Parsons.
51. Jack Hambling, *The Second Time Around: Growing Up in Bay Roberts* (St. John's, Newfoundland: Harry Cuff Publications Ltd., 1992), pp. 56-61.
52. See Henrik de Kauffmann to Ralph Parsons, September 11, 1940; and Minutes of American Greenland Commission, May 24, 1940.
53. Minutes of American Greenland Commission, May 24, 1940.
54. R.A. Gibson to Ralph Parsons, August 17, 1940.
55. Ralph Parsons to Philip A. Chester, August 27, 1940.
56. Philip A. Chester to Ralph Parsons, August 24, 1940.
57. Ralph Parsons to Philip A. Chester, August 27, 1940. See also Ralph Parsons to H.L. Keenleyside, August 27, 1940.
58. Ralph Parsons to Hans Christian Sonne, October 8, 1940.
59. Undated memorandum regarding American Greenland Commission, p. 1. See also Ralph Parsons to Hans Christian Sonne, October 12, 1940.
60. Ralph Parsons to Hans Christian Sonne, February 6, 1941.
61. Ralph Parsons to Gilbert E. Jackson, February 6, 1941.
62. Department of State press release #167, April 10, 1941, p. 1.
63. Hans Christian Sonne to Henrik de Kauffmann, September 9, 1941.
64. Henrik de Kauffmann to Ralph Parsons, September 18, 1941.
65. Ralph Parsons to Philip A. Chester, March 18, 1942.
66. Philip A. Chester to Ralph Parsons, May 1, 1942.
67. Ralph Parsons to Philip A. Chester, September 8, 1942.
68. Minutes of Canadian Committee, Winnipeg, Manitoba, December 3, 1942.
69. Ralph Parsons to Patrick Ashley Cooper, December 7, 1943.
70. Ralph Parsons to Philip A. Chester, March 29, 1944.

Chapter 9

A Date With Destiny

"Wherefore I perceive that there is nothing better, than that a man should rejoice in his own works; for that is his portion: for who shall bring him to see what shall be after him?"
—Ecclesiastes 3:22 (KJV)

bout the time of Newfoundland's entry into the Canadian confederation, Ralph Parsons took an apartment in St. John's at No. 3, Allandale Road Apartments, just off Elizabeth Avenue near Churchill Square. There along with his sister, Rachel Fannie Parsons (Miss Datie, to those close to her), he lived during the winter months. During the summer months, Ralph and Miss Datie, the latter being almost four years older than the former, returned to the old family homestead in Bay Roberts, where Ralph kept himself occupied in his carpenter shop, while Miss Datie kept house and did the cooking. They also spent time visiting family members and close friends. During the summer months, Ralph arranged to keep his apartment in St. John's.

Parsons' sister, Florence (Floss, to those close to her) and her husband, John Hambling, Sr., lived in Bay Roberts, as did his niece, Winnifred, and her husband, Howard Moores. His two brothers, Hayward and Gus, and their families lived in St. John's. In fact, Hay-

Hayward Parsons, about 1940.

149

ward and his wife, Sybil, lived at No. 4, Allandale Road Apartments. Living in St. John's during the winter months was more comfortable and convenient for Ralph and his sister but, in the spring, both were anxious to get back "around the Bay" to Bay Roberts.

Hayward Parsons, in a letter to Robert H. Chesshire in Winnipeg, shortly after Ralph Parsons' death, gave some indication of the way they lived during the winter months. Most nights, there were long chats about what they knew best — the long years both had served with the Hudson's Bay Company up North.

> As you know Ralph's apartment here in St. John's was just across the hall to mine and nightly we would alternate our visits, and would often relive our Baffinland and other experiences but promptly at 9:30 p.m. it would be time for our nightcap.[1]

"Nightcap" might simply mean it was time for them to go to bed, but in Newfoundland it refers to a good drink of whisky or rum, likely Hudson's Bay Company dark rum. This was certainly the meaning of "nightcap" in this context, for the two elderly gentlemen — both over seventy — like everyone else in the Parsons family for generations, always enjoyed a drink and a smoke. So the four people at No. 3 and No. 4, Allandale Road Apartments — Ralph and Miss Datie, and Hayward and Sybil — got along well together and enjoyed life by sharing their memories.

Ralph Parsons maintained an account with the Hudson's Bay Company office in St. John's and paid his bills regularly. In the statement of account rendered by the Company in the process of settling his estate, there is listed, among other things, a bill from the Board of Liquor Control in Newfoundland for $24.12. It was dated for July 27, 1956. Presumably, this was the bill for Ralph Parsons' last supply of strong drink.[2]

Hayward and Sybil must have been very lonely during the summer months, when Ralph and Miss Datie were living in the old family home in Bay Roberts. Of course, they too made trips "around the Bay" during the summer, often staying overnight with Ralph and Miss Datie. These trips gave the elderly men a chance to go trouting with their brother-in-law, John Hambling, Sr., who knew most of the prime trouting spots west of Butlerville and North River. For her part, Miss Datie and her sister, Floss, enjoyed all the family visitors during the summer, which often included the well-known lawyer and man of letters, Richard Augustus Parsons,

Q.C., the other brother in the family. The youngest brother, Wilfred, had died suddenly of a heart attack in 1950 at the relatively young age of fifty-one.

In the spring of 1950, Ralph Parsons travelled to Halifax, Nova Scotia, and attended the graduation exercises of his son, David, who received his engineering degree from Nova Scotia Technical College. Two years later, in the summer of 1952, Parsons spent some time with David and his wife, Betty, and their children in Hantsport near Windsor, Nova Scotia.[3] The remainder of his retirement years were divided between St. John's and Bay Roberts.

While in Halifax in 1950, Parsons loaned David $1,500.00, presumably to help his son until he received his first pay cheque from his new job. This was one of many loans that were, for the most part, never repaid. When David saw his way clear and was ready to pay up, his father steadfastly refused to take the money, so a "loan" from Ralph Parsons was ostensibly a gift. David says that whenever he and his family went home to Bay Roberts during the summers of the early 1950s, his father always gave him a few dollars "to help defray the costs," even if the son never asked. David now maintains that his father could "sense" when he was low on funds. "He was always aware of the times I needed money," David wrote.[4]

David and his wife and their three young sons went home to visit in the summer of 1955. They stayed in the old family home in Bay Roberts, but arranged to spend a few days with Betty's mother in St. John's. David remembers that during the visit, Miss Datie, his father and other family members treated them well: "We were treated like royalty. Aunt Floss was a marvellous cook and we sure took full advantage of that fact."[5]

David says that during the summer of 1955, he noticed that his father, now seventy-three years of age, had "really slowed down a bit." He didn't drive his car much but depended on his nephew, Jack Hambling, to drive him around. Parsons told his son that he often had dizzy spells. He had been to the doctor in Bay Roberts, who informed him that he had low blood pressure. That revelation came as a surprise to David because his father "always had a ruddy complexion." When David left his father at the end of his holidays in August 1955, his father for the first time in his life appeared to be an old man. When David said good-bye at Bay Roberts that summer, he did so with a degree of sadness and a strong feeling of apprehension.[6]

During the winter of 1955-56, Ralph Parsons was unwell, and he was very much aware of it, but, being the private and independent-minded person that he was, he kept things to himself and hardly ever complained. His dizzy spells caused him to be fearful of falling, so he always had a tendency to hold on to furniture when indoors and keep close to fences when outdoors. His low blood pressure continued to be a major problem. The summer of 1956, Ralph Parsons and Miss Datie spent only a few weeks in Bay Roberts. He was still unwell, so they returned to St. John's to be near Hayward and Sybil, and especially to be close to the hospital there. By August 1956, his doctor advised him to enter hospital, where he could get better treatment for his various ailments. On August 31, 1956, when Ralph Parsons gave in and agreed to enter the Grace Hospital in St. John's, Miss Datie sent David a message: "Your father not very well and in hospital. Suggest you come home." David phoned his aunt in St. John's to inquire about his father, asking why he had not been made aware of the situation earlier. Her only reply was: "We didn't want to worry you, my son." The "we," of course, referred to herself and David's father. David flew home within a few hours, and went directly to the Grace Hospital in St. John's.[7]

According to a letter, written by David some thirty-eight years after the fact, he found his father to be much worse than he expected. His father was "very ill, in a drowsy state of mind, and sometimes hallucinating."[8] David arranged for private nurses to care for his father, and took payment for these services from his father's account with the Hudson's Bay Company. The doctors informed David that his father's condition was serious and that he required a prostatectomy — prostate gland removal. According to David, Dr. Nigel Rusted felt that his patient's heart was strong enough to handle the surgery and that there was an excellent chance of recovery. David, doing what he felt was best, gave his consent for the operation to go ahead.[9] In an interview on June 20, 1994, Dr. Rusted, then in his eighty-eighth year, verified David's assessment of the situation. Dr. Rusted said the operation was a success, but the patient had a heart attack two days later and could not be stabilized.[10] Ralph Parsons' brothers and sisters were with him in his dying moments; Hayward, Gus, and David were with him to the end. The following is David Parsons' description of the scene:

> The picture blurs around this time as to who was in the hospital room in his last moments. I do remember Uncle Gus was there. My father's

lips were moving. I leaned over the bed to hear him but I could not catch the words.

Just about then I was aware of Uncle Gus pacing back and forth in the room; then he turned to me and said rather angrily, "For God's sake, show him affection! Kiss him!" I immediately kissed my father then on the head and several times after that. I had not kissed him since I was a small boy. The only greeting we exchanged was a handshake, although we both had close feelings for each other but were probably too reserved to be more demonstrative.

My father's breaths were further apart now and I would listen for the next one; finally there were no more. He was gone.[11]

David, along with Uncles Hayward, Gus, and John Hambling, Sr., later went to Carnell's Funeral Parlour in St. John's, where the body had been taken, and selected what they thought was an appropriate coffin: "A magnificent-looking casket of what appeared to be polished bronze covering... I can't remember the cost, but it suited me and seemed to satisfy the family."[12]

On Sunday night, November 25, 1956, the wake for the famed Hudson's Bay Company Chief Factor was held in the old family house "up in the lane" at Bay Roberts. Scores of people arrived to pay their respects and, as was the custom in Newfoundland, some friends and family members stayed up all night. Although tired, David stood by the coffin most of the evening and was greeted by all those who visited. The words of Ralph Parsons' only son are more poignant than the authors' at this point:

> That evening many of his old friends and acquaintances called to see him. I remember especially "Skipper" Abe Parsons, a big raw-boned old "salt" going up to the casket and putting his hand firmly on my father's head and saying loudly, "Ah, my old friend, I will miss you."[13]

Following the funeral and before returning to his family in Nova Scotia, David went back to Bay Roberts for a short visit, where he was told by family members that his father had for several months been ill but would not give in or admit that he was sick: "When we were talking afterwards, I recall Aunt Floss Hambling saying how feeble my father was in the fall of 1955. He would shuffle around like an old man far in excess of his actual years." At the time, David knew nothing of this and did not realize how seriously ill his father was: "I have letters written in July 1956, and although his writing was a bit shaky, I suspected nothing out of the ordinary."[14]

Later while going through some of his father's papers, David found an article on file from *Reader's Digest*, citing clearly the symptoms of prostate gland problems. The article, written by a physician, was dated a couple years before his father's death. So Ralph Parsons obviously had suspicions about his medical condition long before he was admitted to the Grace Hospital in St. John's on August 31, 1956. Parsons was a private person, and nobody, not even his brothers, Gus and Hayward, who were very close to him, were aware of his serious medical problem.

David Parsons ended his letter this way:

> You asked me how I coped with the situation knowing his days were numbered. As I told you, I did not know this until a few days before his death, so it came as a shock to me.
>
> I loved, admired and respected my father, and often also felt pity for him when on occasion my mother's name came up, and he became very quiet and withdrawn.
>
> At Carnell's Funeral Parlour the undertaker asked me if I wanted the ring taken off his finger. It was his wedding ring which he had worn since his marriage. My thoughts at the time, as I remember them, were: "At last he will be beside his wife again." Therefore I felt he should continue to wear the ring, a symbol of his love. I told the undertaker to leave the ring on his finger, and he was buried still wearing his ring.[15]

On July 7, 1956, almost two months before being admitted to the hospital, Ralph Parsons wrote Philip A. Chester in Winnipeg. He told Chester that he enjoyed living in his apartment in St. John's during the winter months, "as we have no stairs to climb and the place is heated which convenience we did not have at the old home in Bay Roberts. Nevertheless, at the first sign of spring we will move back to the old house."[16] Apparently, Chester, in a previous letter, had mentioned a possible trip to Newfoundland and the possibility of meeting Newfoundland's Liberal Premier, Joseph R. Smallwood, the architect of Newfoundland's confederation with Canada. In his letter to Chester, Parsons makes an uncomplimentary and ungracious comment about Smallwood: "You make mention of Joe Smallwood in your letter. Well don't ever get mixed up with him."[17] Ralph Parsons and his family were true Newfoundland patriots who wanted nothing to do with union with Canada. This is rather ironic in light of the fact that Ralph Parsons had spent most of his life in Canada. He had established more than two dozen Hudson's Bay Company trading posts in the North and, by so doing, helped to lay claim for Canada to that vast area of the Arctic. Most Canadian historians acknowledge Parsons' contribution to the Canadian nation in terms of sovereignty in the Arctic.

On the Newfoundland scene, Ralph Parsons' brother, Richard Augustus Parsons, Q.C., ran as a Progressive Conservative candidate in the early 1950s. At the time, the Progressive Conservative Party in Newfoundland was, for the most part, made up of people who previously were the anti-confederates and who were strongly opposed to Smallwood's Liberal Government. Parsons ended his letter to Chester — likely the last one to his old foe — in his typical gentlemanly way: "Here's hoping that you will remain at the helm for a long while yet and enjoy the best of health and happiness."[18]

Less than two months later, David Parsons was at his father's St. John's apartment. The senior man was in the Grace Hospital very ill. On Saturday, September 1, 1956, David sent a message to Robert H. Chesshire, General Manager of the Fur Trade Department of the Hudson's Bay Company, informing him of his father's illness. It was Ralph Parsons' wish that Chesshire be so informed. Chesshire replied a couple days later. An extract from his message to David reads: "Tell him that all his old friends send their warmest regards and good wishes for a rapid and complete recovery."[19] Chesshire followed up with an inquiry to Wilson Cave, of the Hudson's Bay Company office in St. John's, inquiring exactly where in the capital city Parsons was hospitalized. Cave's return message stated that the sick man was in the Grace Hospital.[20]

Wilson Cave, manager, Hudson's Bay Company Store, St. John's, 1956.

On September 5, 1956, Chesshire wrote to Ralph Parsons at the Grace Hospital in St. John's. This letter, which was in reality an attempt to cheer up the former Fur Trade Commissioner, mentioned two of Parsons' old Hudson's Bay Company friends, George Watson and James Cantley. Cantley had once worked closely with Parsons in Montreal and Winnipeg. Chesshire, who was much concerned about his former boss and still trying to lift his spirits, wrote:

> I do hope that by the time you receive this letter you will be well on the road to recovery.... In the meantime, all your old friends here join me in wishing you a speedy recovery, and you may rest assured that our thoughts and prayers will be directed to that end.[21]

The day before, Wilson Cave had written his boss in Winnipeg, informing him of Parsons' condition: "Mr. Parsons is not well by any means. He seems to be very nervous, has low blood pressure and bladder complications. He says he suffers no pain, hopes to be out shortly, but recovery will, I think, be slow."[22] On September 6, 1956, David Parsons sent another message to Chesshire, part of which reads: "My father's condition remains much the same. Outcome still uncertain."[23] On September 7, 1956, Chesshire wrote to Wilson Cave, asking to be informed on a regular basis as to Parsons' condition. The same day, Chesshire wrote David Parsons a letter. Chesshire, a close friend of Ralph Parsons, was genuinely concerned about his friend's condition. The last paragraph of his letter to David reads:

> In the meantime, I gather that your father is being very well taken care of, but I would again ask you to be sure and let us know if there is anything we can do for him, or send him, either from here or at St. John's.[24]

On September 22, 1956, David Parsons, now back in Hantsport, Nova Scotia, wrote Chesshire a long and detailed letter about his father's condition. In this letter to the man who had been Ralph Parsons' assistant during part of the time he was Fur Trade Commissioner, David outlined the full story, complete with medical details, as he understood them from Dr. Nigel Rusted, Ralph Parsons' attending physician. David also told Chesshire that when he was home in the summer of 1955 he had asked his father to continue checking with Dr. Howard Drover in Bay Roberts regarding his low blood pressure. His father promised to do so. In the same breath, David wrote:

> He asked me to promise that I tell no one, especially the family, of his illness because he felt it would cause them undue alarm. This was typical of my father. He always kept his own troubles to himself and

showered the rest of us in the family with unbounded attention whenever we were sick. . . . I did not know anything further about Pop's medical condition until I got word from my Aunt Datie on Labour Day Weekend 1956 saying that he wished to see me and that he was very ill.²⁵

An interesting comment is found in David's letter:

The biggest mistake, the doctors say, is that he had nothing to do this past ten years. If and when he does get back home his time must be filled with well-planned projects every day. He must have a purpose in living and something to keep him occupied. It is too bad he had not written his memoirs of his life with the Hudson's Bay Company, or even done a bit of research for the Company on his own. . . . He was just out of his element ever since retirement.²⁶

David told Chesshire that from all reports he was receiving almost daily from Newfoundland, his father was far from well. Most of his time was spent asleep or in a daze and, when awake, he hallucinated:

In his irrational periods he is always with the Hudson's Bay Company up North—in a ship caught in a storm in Hudson Strait or talking to some old friends. . . . As far as I can see he has the best medical attention, and all we can do is hope and pray.²⁷

All during September and October and up to the time of Parsons' death, Wilson Cave, manager of the St. John's office, kept Chesshire's office in Winnipeg fully informed about Parsons' condition. On September 25, 1956, even Philip A. Chester wrote Parsons a nice letter in an attempt to cheer him up. By this time, however, Parsons was too far gone to relate to what Chester had written:

Knowing you as I do, you are probably a rather difficult patient, but I hope you are at least trying to follow all instructions, and that before very long you will be restored to health again and the full enjoyment of life. . . . This note calls for no reply, as the St. John's office is keeping Bob Chesshire advised about your progress. It is just to send my warmest wishes for your complete recovery.²⁸

Chester's letter was forwarded to Wilson Cave, with another short letter attached from his secretary. Winifred Archer informed Cave that Chester's letter was of no great importance but rather was only an attempt to cheer up Parsons. She wrote:

> If you do not think Mr. Parsons is up to anything in that line, just let it ride—Mr. Chester will quite understand... Just use your discretion about passing on Mr. Chester's letter, although I know if Mr. Parsons is at all himself he will be very pleased to have it.[29]

Undoubtedly, had he been up to it, Parsons would have enjoyed the letter from Chester and would have written an appropriate reply. Parsons was the kind of individual who likely would have long since forgotten the difficult time Chester gave him from 1935 to 1939. It was his disagreements with the Canadian Committee, and particularly with Philip A. Chester regarding the re-organization of the Fur Trade Department, which ultimately led to his retirement in the spring of 1940. Ralph Parsons harboured no malice, feeling that past events in peoples' lives should in no way tarnish future relationships.

Near the end of October 1956, T.D. Lindley, of the Eastern Post Division in Montreal, sent the following memo to Robert H. Chesshire, General Manager of the Fur Trade Department, in Winnipeg:

> Mr. Cave has brought to my attention the fact that he is carrying as a customer's balance an amount for Mr. Ralph Parsons which is now upwards of $2,000 and increasing from week to week. This is for cash advances to his sister, Miss R.F. Parsons, to pay such current expenses as nurses, rent, etc.
>
> Mr. Cave explains that we have always handled such transactions for Mr. Parsons but, during the time that he was able to look after his own affairs, these were settled regularly. As matters now stand, Mr. Parsons is quite incapable of handling his own affairs and Mr. Cave is seeking some guidance in this matter. So far he has acted in this manner because he feels that you would wish him to do everything possible to help out and no doubt R.P. is in good financial circumstances. In view of his present incapacity, however, and the fact that it might continue for some considerable time, he is wondering how far he should proceed.[30]

Chesshire replied to Lindley the next day, October 23, 1956:

> Reference your memo of the 22nd October, re Cave's enquiry about Mr. Parsons' account, I have written Cave direct telling him to continue without any change for the present. I happened to be writing

to him at the time your memo came in, so dealt with this matter at the same time.[31]

The letter to Cave that Chesshire referred to was received in the St. John's office a few days later. This letter, more than any other one, shows the respect and admiration that Robert H. Chesshire had for his former boss, Ralph Parsons. Chesshire informed Cave and the others in the St. John's office to do all within their power to meet Parsons' needs in every way possible and continue to keep Winnipeg informed of his condition. Chesshire also told Cave that he had written to Rachel F. Parsons, but had received no reply.[32]

Cave, for his part, relayed the information in Chesshire's letter to Hayward Parsons. A few days later, Hayward wrote to Chesshire. He said he had had a long conversation with Cave and decided to write on behalf of his brother and sister: "Yes, Mr. Chesshire, I feel sure he received your kind wishes and regards and if he were able to do so would write and thank you, so on his behalf I thank you very sincerely."[33] In a letter to Hayward, dated October 31, 1956, Chesshire acknowledged receiving a letter from Miss Datie. He had been inquiring from Wilson Cave about several letters he had written to Ralph Parsons but had received no answer, wondering if the letters were lost in the mail:

> The last thing I wanted to happen was for Ralph to feel that we had forgotten about him, particularly at such a time as this.... I rather gather that writing further to R.P. at this time would be more burdensome to him than helpful, but I would like you to give him my love and best wishes, and tell him we are all thinking of him and praying for his early recovery.[34]

Miss Datie's letter of October 13, 1956 to Chesshire, which she had delayed mailing for several days, eventually reached the Fur Trade Department office in Winnipeg. In her letter, she acknowledged on behalf of her brother all the letters of good will received from Winnipeg. She told Chesshire that Ralph "loved his friends in the Company and also his work." This gracious lady and the oldest person in the Parsons family of her generation ended her letter to Chesshire with these words: "Thanking you over and over again Mr. Chesshire for your great interest in my brother's recovery."[35] Miss Datie was seventy-eight years of age at the time.

In a letter from Wilson Cave to Chesshire, dated November 1, 1956, it is easy to see that Cave had all but given up hope of Ralph Parsons' recovery: "I visited R.P. during the weekend. At the time he was out of bed and sitting in a chair. Regular routine, rather than a sign of much improvement I would imagine. His condition is very much the same."[36] Another letter from Cave to Chesshire, dated November 20, 1956, ends with this brief paragraph: "We understand that his son David is expected shortly and Mr. Parsons may undergo an operation."[37] Three days later, Cave dispatched the following message to Chesshire: "Mr. Ralph Parsons underwent prostatectomy operation twenty-second. Is doing as well as can be expected, but still on danger list. Will advise further in next day or so."[38] Later in the afternoon of Saturday, November 24, 1956, Cave sent his final message regarding Ralph Parsons to Robert Chesshire: "Mr. Ralph Parsons passed away late afternoon twenty fourth interment St John's twenty sixth stop late address three Allandale Apartments St Johns stop we will attend to floral tribute."[39] David Parsons also sent Chesshire a message informing him of his father's passing: "Deeply grieved to inform you that my father passed away six o'clock this evening. We are ever grateful to you and the Company for your kindness and consideration during his illness."[40]

From all the documentation we have seen and from a few individuals we have talked to, particularly those who were close to Ralph Parsons, and especially his only son, David R. Parsons, it is easy to conclude that Ralph Parsons was an extremely sick man when he entered hospital on August 31, 1956. Whether or not he had lost the "desire to live," as David suggested in his letter of September 22, 1956 to Robert H. Chesshire, is open to question.[41] One thing is certain, however: Parsons, while at the Grace Hospital, received the finest medical care and attention. Dr. Nigel Rusted, in an interview in June 1994, claimed that in his best medical judgement the prostate operation was the only chance of prolonging Ralph Parsons' life. The operation was, in the physician's opinion, a success, but the "pressure and shock" brought on a heart attack and, in Parsons' weakened condition, there was no chance of recovery.[42]

On that fateful, cold, windy Saturday afternoon of November 24, 1956, at precisely 5:50 P.M., Ralph Parsons of Arctic fame crossed the great divide between time and eternity. Another of the great Hudson's Bay Company men of this century now belonged to the ages.

The spring 1957 edition of the *Moccasin Telegraph*, published in

Winnipeg, Manitoba, contained a well-written tribute to William Ralph Parsons entitled, "The Last Fur Trade Commissioner." The first paragraph of the tribute reads:

> Newfoundland has given to the Fur Trade Department many outstanding men. With the death of Ralph Parsons at St. John's on the 24th November 1956, we have witnessed the passing of one of the greatest of these.[43]

The authors of this biography take issue with the above statement, for Ralph Parsons, who had devoted his life to the Hudson's Bay Company and who had served the Fur Trade powerfully and well, was not "one of the greatest" — he was *the* greatest. No Canadian historian or Hudson's Bay Company man alive today would dispute that claim.

NOTES TO CHAPTER 9: A DATE WITH DESTINY

1. Hayward Parsons to Robert Chesshire, December 17, 1956. Ralph Parsons' Personnel File RG2/37/162, Hudson's Bay Company Archives, Winnipeg, Manitoba.
2. Hudson's Bay Company invoice. Estate of the late Ralph Parsons, December 5, 1956. File RG2/37/162, Hudson's Bay Company Archives, Winnipeg, Manitoba.
3. David R. Parsons to John Parsons, February 10, 1995.
4. *Ibid.*
5. *Ibid.*
6. *Ibid.*
7. *Ibid.*
8. *Ibid.*
9. *Ibid.*
10. Personal interview with Dr. Nigel Rusted by John Parsons, June 20, 1994.
11. David R. Parsons to John Parsons, February 10, 1995.
12. *Ibid.*
13. *Ibid.*
14. *Ibid.*
15. *Ibid.*
16. Ralph Parsons to Philip A. Chester, July 7, 1956. Ralph Parsons' Personnel File RG2/37/162, Hudson's Bay Company Archives, Winnipeg, Manitoba.

17. *Ibid.*
18. *Ibid.*
19. Robert H. Chesshire to David R. Parsons (message), September 4, 1956. File RG2/37/162, Hudson's Bay Company Archives, Winnipeg, Manitoba.
20. Wilson Cave to Robert H. Chesshire (message), September 5, 1956.
21. Robert H. Chesshire to Ralph Parsons, September 5, 1956.
22. Wilson Cave to Robert H. Chesshire, September 4, 1956.
23. David R. Parsons to Robert H. Chesshire (message), September 6, 1956.
24. Robert H. Chesshire to David R. Parsons, September 7, 1956.
25. David R. Parsons to Robert H. Chesshire, September 22, 1956.
26. *Ibid.*
27. *Ibid.*
28. Philip A. Chester to Ralph Parsons, September 25, 1956.
29. Winifred Archer to Wilson Cave, September 25, 1956.
30. T.D. Lindley to Robert H. Chesshire (memo), October 22, 1956.
31. Robert H. Chesshire to T.D. Lindley (memo), October 23, 1956.
32. Robert H. Chesshire to Wilson Cave, October 23, 1956.
33. Hayward Parsons to Robert H. Chesshire, October 26, 1956.
34. Robert H. Chesshire to Hayward Parsons, October 31, 1956.
35. Rachel F. Parsons to Robert H. Chesshire, October 13, 1956.
36. Wilson Cave to Robert H. Chesshire, November 1, 1956.
37. Wilson Cave to Robert H. Chesshire, November 20, 1956.
38. Wilson Cave to Robert H. Chesshire (message), November 23, 1956.
39. Wilson Cave to Robert H. Chesshire (message), November 24, 1956.
40. David R. Parsons to Robert H. Chesshire (message), November 24, 1956.
41. David R. Parsons to Robert H. Chesshire, September 22, 1956.
42. Personal interview with Dr. Nigel Rusted by John Parsons, June 20, 1994.
43. *Moccasin Telegraph* (XVI:1, Break-Up, Spring edition, 1957), p. 13.

Chapter 10

The Last Voyage

> *Now the labourer's task is o'er;*
> *Now the battle day is past;*
> *Now upon the farther shore*
> *Lands the voyager at last.*
> —John Ellerton (1826-1893),
>   from *Common Prayer Hymns A & M*.
>   First stanza of Hymn #401.

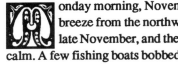onday morning, November 26, 1956, was clear but cold. A light breeze from the northwest had a chill about it that was typical of late November, and the inner waters of Bay Roberts were almost calm. A few fishing boats bobbed gently in the waters of Beachy Cove, not far from the old Parsons homestead.

The funeral service for the late William Ralph Parsons at St. Matthew's Anglican Church was scheduled for 10:30 A.M. The morning service was necessary because afterwards the funeral cortege had to proceed to St. John's, about sixty miles around Conception Bay, where the famed Hudson's Bay Company man was to be interred beside his wife in the Anglican Cemetery on Forest Road, on the south side of Quidi Vidi Lake.[1]

The scene was a sad one. All was quiet as the family gathered around and the undertaker, in the most dignified manner, arranged the shroud around the corpse and gently closed the coffin. In an instant, all that was mortal of this well-known son of Bay Roberts was out of sight of his loved ones and friends forever. Although this was a bitter moment of sadness, there were no tears. The men—David, Hayward, Gus, and John Hambling, Sr. — were dignified in their dark suits, and the women — particularly sisters Florence and Rachel, and niece Winnifred Moores — stood further back, trying to comfort each other.

The funeral cortege then proceeded from the old family homestead "up the lane" to St. Matthew's Church, a short distance away, where the service was conducted by the Reverend Isaac Butler, the rector at the time, assisted by the Reverend Guy Fowlow,[2] the previous rector who had spent seven years in the Bay Roberts Parish before the arrival of the Reverend Butler. Fowlow and Ralph Parsons knew each other well and both had tremendous respect for each other.

Fowlow, who was then serving as the rector at St. Mary's Anglican Church in Heart's Content, had spent the night in Bay Roberts as a guest of Butler. The previous afternoon — Sunday — both men, along with Canon Thomas E. Loder, rector of the Spaniard's Bay Parish, had officiated at the funeral of another great Newfoundlander, the well-known and highly respected Bay Roberts' educator, Dr. Arthur Barnes.[3]

David Parsons recalled thirty-eight years later that most of the family were at his father's funeral, and St. Matthew's Church was almost filled. He also remembered that as he looked upon the coffin in the church that morning, he found it somewhat difficult to accept the finality of death and relate to reality all that was happening. Although a veteran of the Royal Canadian Air Force who had seen action over Europe during World War II, David claims that this was the first time that death affected him so personally.

Hayward, Gus, and John Hambling, Sr., taking everything in stride, comforted the women as the funeral service began. Both Butler and Fowlow, dressed in their white robes, preceded the coffin from the back of the church to the steps leading to the high altar, and both shared the introductory statements or invocation that begins the Order for the Burial of the Dead in the Anglican Church. Jack Hambling's father told him years later that as Butler, in his well-modulated voice, read Job's familiar shout of affirmation, Captain Sam Parsons, one of Ralph Parsons' best friends and one-time skipper of the *Fort Amadjuak*, began to weep openly.[4] "For I know that my redeemer liveth, and that he shall stand at the latter day upon the earth" (Job 19:25).

One of the co-authors, John Parsons, interviewed several people who attended Ralph Parsons' funeral, but none could recall which hymns were sung; neither could David R. Parsons, Isaac Butler or Guy Fowlow, the latter two in their eighties at the time of this writing. In a phone call from his home in Dartmouth, Nova Scotia, Butler replied, "Sorry I can't help you. I can't recall a thing about Ralph Parsons' funeral, other than the fact that I was assisted by the Reverend Mr. Fowlow."[5] John Parsons recalls the day Ralph Parsons was buried. The seventeen-year-old teacher in the sole-charge school at nearby Butlerville, he admits now that the famed Hudson's Bay Company man meant very little to him at the time; in fact, he was more familiar with the late Dr. Arthur Barnes.

John Parsons' father attended Dr. Barnes' funeral on Sunday afternoon and, being self-employed, took time off to attend Ralph Parsons' funeral the following morning, not because he knew Ralph Parsons as a close friend (he knew Hayward and Gus better), but because Parsons was well-known and a second cousin to his father. Hence, George W. Parsons went out of respect for a member of the extended family. He always kept a record of or jotted down a few notes about important events in and around Bay Roberts. According to his notes, the hymns sung at Ralph Parsons' funeral were #'s 662, 621 and 353 in the Anglican hymnal. His journal also contains this terse statement: "Ralph was a top man with the Hudson's Bay Company, but he never lost the common touch."[6]

At funerals, usually some people become emotional during the singing of the first hymn, after which the atmosphere becomes more settled and subdued. Since most family members who attended Ralph Parsons' funeral are now dead, we have no way of knowing the atmosphere for certain, but surely Miss Datie and Floss Hambling must have wept at the singing of the first hymn, realizing that death had taken their beloved brother, mentor and friend away from them forever. But the final stanza of Richard Baxter's touching hymn, "Lord, It Belongs Not To My Care" (1681), must have brought a measure of comfort to the entire congregation.

My knowledge of that life is small,
  The eye of faith is dim;
But 'tis enough that Christ knows all,
  And I shall be with Him.

Psalm 90, the only one in the Psalter attributed to Moses, was read, and the congregation read every second verse in unison. This was followed by the familiar burial lesson from the fifteenth chapter of the First Epistle of St. Paul to the Corinthians:

But now is Christ risen from the dead, and become the firstfruits of them that slept. For since by man came death, by man came also the resurrection of the dead. For as in Adam all die, even so in Christ shall all be made alive. (vss. 20-22)

As the Priest finished the last few sentences of this burial lesson, those in attendance who had known Ralph Parsons must have realized that these words were applicable to him, and memories must have flooded the mourners' minds: "Therefore, my beloved brethren, be ye steadfast, unmoveable, always abounding in the work of the Lord, forasmuch as ye know that your labour is not in vain in the Lord." (vs. 58) Then followed John Ellerton's hymn of true faith, "Now The Labourer's Task Is O'er" (1871), and #621 in the Anglican hymnal: "Father, In Thy Gracious Keeping, Leave Me Now Thy Servant Sleeping." The Reverend Guy Fowlow then stepped to the familiar pulpit and delivered the eulogy, which the local news reporter for the Spaniard's Bay/Bay Roberts area, Edward Harvey Vokey, referred to later in a published tribute as an "excellent panegyric."[7]

The tribute published in *The Daily News* on December 7, 1956 gives a brief biographical sketch of Ralph Parsons and a synopsis of Guy Fowlow's panegyric or eulogy. Fowlow or Butler must have had a copy of Archibald Lang Fleming's book, *Archibald the Arctic* (1956), published only a few months before, because most of the eulogy was evidently based on the kind words that Fleming had said about his old friend, Ralph Parsons. Fowlow's script, if indeed he had one, does not exist, but it is clear that Vokey used the Fleming book when he put together his own tribute a short time later. The following are the only actual statements in the tribute which came from Fowlow's eulogy: "He was a friend without fuss to the poor and needy...he went about doing good."[8] And then Vokey, still referring to Bishop Fleming's book, became somewhat philosophical and, in so doing, demonstrated his unique gifts as a writer. Vokey asked a question, then gave a true but poignant answer to his own question:

Can we, who knew him only in his latter years add greater commendation than this great Bishop of the Church? I think not, except to say that Ralph Parsons continued right to the end, a man of faith and firmness of character seldom witnessed amongst mortals... And so we think of Ralph Parsons whose memory will always be cherished by his friends and relatives—a great and good man yet withal the soul of humility.[9]

Taken together, Fowlow's eulogy and Vokey's tribute may be seen as a gallant attempt to say the right things about the great but humble Ralph Parsons. Nobody today can recall the impact of Fowlow's words, but Vokey's tribute, which reflected in part some of Fowlow's thoughts, undoubtedly did justice to this great Newfoundlander. With the exception of the death notice, Vokey's tribute is the only locally-written — and therefore local historical account — of Ralph Parsons' passing. Members of the family liked and appreciated the tribute in *The Daily News*; many of them clipped it from the newspaper, and some family members and friends still have copies of it in their family Bibles.

The final song of praise sung in honour and in memory of Ralph Parsons at his funeral was Henry Francis Lyte's great hymn, "Praise, My Soul, The King Of Heaven" (1834), which is used at some Anglican funerals as a substitute for a formal death march. As the congregation began singing the final stanza, the pallbearers stepped forward, gently turned the carriage bearing the coffin, and began to move slowly towards the double doors at the back of the church:

Angels, help us to adore Him,
  Ye behold Him face to face;
Sun and moon, bow down before Him;
  Dwellers all in time and space,
Alleluia, Alleluia,
  Praise with us the God of grace.

Ralph Parsons' funeral, which was attended by the brethren of the Masonic Lodge of both Bay Roberts and St. John's, had been a dignified service of praise and thanksgiving for the life and accomplishments of a great man and an exemplary Christian.

If Guy Fowlow had been aware of R.H.H. Macaulay's journal of the voyage north that Parsons had made in 1934 with the Governor of the Hudson's Bay Company, Patrick Ashley Cooper, he could have quoted a dozen passages from the Governor's speeches, all of which praised Ralph Parsons as an individual and for his dedication to his job. That book was easily accessible to Fowlow, because John Hambling, Sr., who lived only a quarter of a mile from the Anglican rectory, had a copy among his collection of books. Nevertheless, Fowlow's grounding of his eulogy in the words of the famed Bishop of the Arctic had the proper effect, and Ralph Parsons deserved every kind word said about him.

For their parts, Isaac Butler and Guy Fowlow were probably not fully aware of the great accomplishments of Ralph Parsons in relation to the oldest and largest trading company in the world, the Hudson's Bay Company. The authors feel that in a way, Fleming's book saved the day and certainly made up for any lack of detailed knowledge on the part of the two priests. Finally, we wonder if Isaac Butler was keeping a separate record of important people at whose funerals he had officiated, for he was the same priest who, twenty-one years earlier, had conducted the funeral service in St. Peter's Anglican Church in Twillingate, Notre Dame Day, for the famed opera singer, Georgina Stirling (1867-1935), the "Nightingale of the North."

Approximately 11:45 A.M., the funeral cortege of family and a few close friends began its sixty-mile journey to St. John's, where the remains of the deceased — William Ralph Parsons — were interred in the family plot, next to his wife and infant son, both of whom had died thirty-six years before. Prior arrangements had been made with the Reverend J.A. Frank Slade, Rector of the Anglican Cathedral in the capital city, who had agreed to perform the committal part of the funeral service.[10]

Some family members appeared a little tired as they followed the coffin among the rows of headstones in the Anglican cemetery on Forest Road to the open grave, next to the big grey stone with the white angel atop, which Ralph Parsons had erected to his beloved wife, Flora May House, a few months after her passing in July 1920. In time, David R. Parsons arranged to erect a brown granite headstone to his father which bears this inscription:

> In Loving Memory
> of
> W. Ralph Parsons
> Born Dec. 1st, 1881
> Died Nov. 24th, 1956
> Servant of God, Well Done

By 2:30 P.M., the wind had veered around to the northeast and the temperature had dropped close to the freezing mark. A light snow fell gently on the mourners. Slowly, the coffin was lowered into the cold ground, so that those standing farther back could no longer see it. Reverend Slade said a brief prayer, committing the body to the ground and returning the soul to God who gave it. The mourners then sang the first and last stanzas of another hymn, written by John Ellerton and a favourite of

Reverend Slade, "The Day Thou Gavest, Lord, Is Ended" (1870).[11] The customary hand-shakes followed, and the Priest spoke briefly with David and Hayward. The mourners then said good-bye and returned to their cars, some to their homes in St. John's, and others "around the Bay" to Bay Roberts. It had been a long, exhausting day.

Ralph Parsons' body was now at rest in the House family plot. Nearby were the remains of Flora's mother, Mary, who died in 1926, and her father, Captain Peter House, a well-known Newfoundland sealing captain originally from Pool's Island, Bonavista Bay, who died in 1923. Ralph Parsons was no more, but the legends and memories of this great man of the North did not die with his physical body, for his story goes on — and this biography is part of it.

As for David, there were a few things to be done before he could return to his family in Hantsport, Nova Scotia, and resume his job as a mechanical engineer. He made brief visits to family and friends, and one more visit to the family homestead. Standing on the front steps of the old house in Bay Roberts in late November 1956, David was very conscious that a significant milestone had been reached and a chapter completed in the saga of the Parsons family of Bay Roberts. His thoughts were flooded with many memories.[12]

David was also briefed regarding legal matters pertaining to the deceased. These matters, for the most part, were the responsibility of Richard Augustus Parsons, Q.C., Ralph's younger brother and a prominent St. John's lawyer and well-known poet.[13] Letters and messages of tribute arrived from individuals in the Arctic and across Canada; letters from officials of the Hudson's Bay Company in Winnipeg were sent to David, Hayward, and Miss Datie. Even Philip A. Chester seemed truly grieved at Ralph Parsons' passing and, in his letters to David, appeared to forget completely the mini-confrontations between himself and Parsons during the years 1935 to 1939, when the two were unable to see eye-to-eye regarding the reorganization of the Fur Trade Department of the Hudson's Bay Company.[14]

Having studied Ralph Parsons' life intensely over several years, the authors can well understand Chester's attitude and sense of grief, for we believe that Ralph Parsons was an individual who bore no ill feelings or animosity towards anyone. He had a way of gaining everyone's respect and admiration, simply because he was incapable of bearing malice, let alone holding a grudge. He was a true lover of people, a man who respected others as much as he respected himself. In the words of E.H. Vokey, he was "a man of faith and firmness of character seldom witnessed amongst mortals."[15]

On December 6, 1956, Philip A. Chester, whose title was now the Managing Director of the Hudson's Bay Company in Winnipeg, sent the following letter to David R. Parsons in Hantsport, Nova Scotia:

> At their meeting this morning the Canadian Committee formally recorded their deep regret at the death of your father and requested that a copy of their Minute be sent to you.
>
> I am enclosing a copy with this letter, and do want to add my personal conviction that your father's achievements in the North have assured him of a permanent and honoured place in the history of our Company.[16]

The Canadian Committee Minute referred to by Chester reads as follows:

> It was thereupon RESOLVED that the members of the Canadian Committee hereby record their deep regret at the death of William Ralph Parsons who for forty years, as Clerk, Post Manager, Chief Factor and Fur Trade Commissioner, served the Company with energy and devotion, opening up new territories in the eastern Arctic and setting a distinguished example to his colleagues and friends in the Fur Trade; and whose retirement deprived the Company of one of its finest servants and marked the end of a great era of expansion by the Company in the Arctic territories.[17]

On November 30, 1956, Wilson Cave, manager of the Hudson's Bay Company office in St. John's, sent a short but informative letter to Robert H. Chesshire, Parsons' successor in the Fur Trade Department in Winnipeg. Chesshire's title, however, was General Manager. Cave informed Chesshire that the funeral had been held on the morning of the twenty-fifth, with interment at St. John's that afternoon. The correct date was, of course, the twenty-sixth of November. In Cave's opinion, "The minister at Bay Roberts paid a very fine tribute to Mr. Parsons."[18]

On December 3, 1956, David Parsons, now back in Hantsport, sent a letter to Wilson Cave in St. John's, expressing his appreciation to him for his kindness to the family during his father's illness and passing:

> My father always showed pride in his connection with the Hudson's Bay Company, and your associates have certainly justified that

feeling. The beautiful wreaths and your attendance at the funeral will ever be appreciated.[19]

A copy of David's letter was sent to Chesshire in Winnipeg. The same day, David also sent a letter to Chesshire, telling the General Manager of the Fur Trade Department about Wilson Cave's kindness during the family's time of trouble. Brief extracts serve to illuminate David's thoughts:

> The Hudson's Bay Company office at St. John's was most attentive and kind at all times, and under your direction they left no stone unturned to do everything for Pop. . . .He died quietly in his sleep. . . . There is consolation in the fact that Pop did not suffer much in his last days, but probably would have had he lived on. . . . In his conversations my father often mentioned your name and always with a kind thought and a word of praise to illustrate his admiration for you.[20]

On December 16, 1956, David R. Parsons replied to Philip A. Chester's letter of December 6, thanking him for forwarding the official Minute of the Canadian Committee. On the top of the original letter in the Hudson's Bay Company Archives in Winnipeg, there is a brief notation in Chester's handwriting, "Seen by Mr. Chester."[21] Whether or not Chester took the time to read and ponder David's letter will never be known; nevertheless, David, obviously still mourning the loss of his father, had reached out to Chester, as if looking for comfort and sympathy, which Chester might have been incapable of giving. Three paragraphs from David's letter serve to illustrate his thoughts at that time:

> As a small boy I was told that my father worked for "The Company," for as such it was known in our family. When I later came to know your organization as the Hudson's Bay Company, I also realized it was still "The Company" to my father, and he thought of it as such to the last.
>
> The licence number of his car was always 1670; however, by a strange coincidence, this was the first year that he could not get these numbers.
>
> After having experienced such wonderful treatment as my family and I have from the Company during my father's illness and death, it is understandable why he was always so proud to be associated with such men.[22]

The last part of this letter is ironic, and if Chester took the time to read it, we wonder if he caught the irony and if his thoughts went back to his ungracious treatment of Ralph Parsons in the few months before Parsons' resignation as Fur Trade Commissioner in 1940. If Chester were capable of a feeling of guilt, then surely David's congenial letter must have brought it on.

On December 17, 1956, Hayward Parsons wrote to Robert H. Chesshire in Winnipeg, thanking him for his kind expression of sympathy:

> We know that your association with Ralph was a great deal more than that of ordinary friendship and that his passing was a sorrow to you that only time can efface... It is nice to know that you have pleasant recollections of your visit with us "around the Bay" some years ago. If it is our good fortune to see you again in Newfoundland we will try our best to repeat the occasion, but alas without the Chief Factor.[23]

On November 28, 1956, only two days after Ralph Parsons' funeral, the matter of Parsons' pension was discussed in the offices of the Hudson's Bay Company in Winnipeg, and a decision was made and sent to the Controller in the Canadian Committee Office: "As the late Mr. Parsons' wife predeceased him, his pension will cease on the date of his death."[24] A handwritten note on this document states: "Advise Mr. Watkins to disregard the above until matter discussed by R.H.C. with Managing Director."[25] Chesshire and Chester were to discuss the matter of whether or not Parsons' pension was to cease at his death. Although David Parsons was unaware of it, at the time, apparently a request had been made by the family in Newfoundland to have the pension, or at least part of it, go to Miss Datie, Ralph's faithful and loving sister, who had cared for him up to the time of his illness and hospitalization.[26] Almost a month later, on December 24, 1956, a note from Chesshire to J. deB. Payne, Executive Assistant in the Canadian Committee Office, rendered the verdict on this matter once and for all.

> I discussed with Mr. Chester the matter of the extension of Parsons' pension to his sister as his sole dependent, and having regard to all the circumstances, Mr. Chester ruled that the pension would cease with Mr. Parsons' death.[27]

On January 9, 1957, Parsons and Morgan of St. John's, solicitors for the Executor of the will of William Ralph Parsons deceased, published a Statutory Notice in the St. John's daily newspapers.[28] On December 18, 1956, Letters of Probate had been granted to the Royal Trust Company of St. John's,[29] and on February 18, 1957, the Exemplification of Letters of Probate were signed by the Registrar of the Supreme Court of Newfoundland, James A. Winter, and the official seal of that court was affixed.[30] In time, all expenses were paid and all assets of the deceased were distributed as per his Last Will and Testament and several Codicils which were later attached. The bulk of the estate went to David, but there were bequests to many other family members, friends, St. Matthew's Church, and to the poor and needy of Bay Roberts. The Last Will and Testament was dated June 28, 1941, and the first Codicil was dated October 21, 1944.[31] Clauses 13 and 14 of that Codicil are worthy of note:

> (13) To the Diocesan Synod of Newfoundland for St. Matthew's Parish Church at Bay Roberts the sum of One thousand dollars ($1,000.00) to be used for such church purposes as the Rector and Church Wardens for the time being may decide.
> (14) To the poor and needy at Bay Roberts in memory of my mother and my wife, the sum of One thousand dollars ($1,000.00) to be distributed over a period of five years by my son David, or in the event of his decease by the Priest in charge of St. Matthew's Church, Bay Roberts.[32]

The documents — the Last Will and Testament and the Codicil — were witnessed by St. John's lawyers, Leslie R. Curtis and Donald W.K. Dawe. A further Codicil of minor significance was added on September 19, 1950 and witnessed by Enid M.D. Clench and Robert Oakley.[33] Still another Codicil was added and dated for October 1, 1952, this too was witnessed by Clench and Oakley. In this document, the following statement is found: "I hereby . . . bequeath the sum of four hundred dollars each to the Church of England Orphanage and the Roman Catholic Orphanage, the International Grenfell Association and the Diocese of the Arctic."[34]

William Ralph Parsons' generosity and good will were clearly evident — even in death.

NOTES TO CHAPTER 10: THE LAST VOYAGE

1. Death and funeral notice, *The Evening Telegram*, St. John's, Newfoundland, November 26, 1956, p. 2.
2. A tribute in *The Daily News*, St. John's, Newfoundland, December 7, 1956, p. 7.
3. Death and funeral notice, *The Evening Telegram*, November 26, 1956, p. 3.

4. Personal interview with Jack Hambling by John Parsons, March 18, 1995.
5. Telephone call to Isaac Butler, Dartmouth, Nova Scotia, by John Parsons, March 13, 1995.
6. Journal Notes, George W. Parsons, Shearstown, Newfoundland, November 26, 1956.
7. *The Daily News*, December 7, 1956, p. 7.
8. *Ibid.*
9. *Ibid.*
10. *Ibid.*
11. Personal interview by telephone by John Parsons with Newton Morgan, St. John's, Newfoundland, March 23, 1995.
12. David R. Parsons to John Parsons, February 10, 1995.
13. See "Statutory Notice," *The Evening Telegram*, January 8, 1957, p. 16.
14. Philip A. Chester to David R. Parsons, December 6, 1956, January 16, 1957, and October 9, 1958. Ralph Parsons' Personnel File RG2/37/162, Hudson's Bay Company Archives, Winnipeg, Manitoba.
15. *The Daily News*, December 7, 1956, p. 7.
16. Philip A. Chester to David R. Parsons, December 6, 1956.
17. Minutes of the Meeting of the Canadian Committee, Winnipeg, Manitoba, December 6, 1956.
18. Wilson Cave to Robert H. Chesshire, November 30, 1956.
19. David R. Parsons to Wilson Cave, December 3, 1956.
20. David R. Parsons to Robert H. Chesshire, December 3, 1956.
21. David R. Parsons to Philip A. Chester, December 16, 1956. See also Ralph Parsons' Personnel File RG2/37/162, Hudson's Bay Company Archives, Winnipeg, Manitoba.
22. *Ibid.*
23. Hayward Parsons to Robert H. Chesshire, December 17, 1956.
24. The Office of the General Manager, Fur Trade Department, Winnipeg, Manitoba, to the Controller, Canadian Committee Office, November 28, 1956.
25. *Ibid.*
26. Ralph Parsons' Personnel File RG2/37/162, Hudson's Bay Company Archives, Winnipeg, Manitoba. Also personal interview by telephone with David R. Parsons by John Parsons, March 22, 1995.
27. Robert H. Chesshire to J. deB. Payne, Executive Assistant, Canadian Committee Office, December 24, 1956.
28. See note 13.
29. Documents, Supreme Court of Newfoundland, St. John's, Newfoundland, dated December 18, 1956.
30. *Ibid.*, dated February 18, 1957.
31. *Ibid.*, Last Will and Testament of William Ralph Parsons and Codicil, dated June 28, 1941 and October 21, 1944.
32. *Ibid.*
33. *Ibid.*, Codicil, Number 3, dated October 1, 1952.
34. *Ibid.*, October 1, 1952.

Epilogue

*"The lights begin to twinkle from the rocks;
The long day wanes; the slow moon climbs; the deep
Moans round with many voices."*
—From *Ulysses* by Alfred Lord Tennyson

Ralph Parsons came from hardy Bay Roberts stock. His forebears had lived in the area for more than 200 years before 1881, the year of his birth. History records that the Parsonses, the Mosdells, the Russells, and the Snows were among the original settlers in and around Bay Roberts. But despite being separated from the Old Country for two or three centuries, many people in Bay Roberts still retain the Devonshire accent. Ralph Parsons, a true Bay Roberts man, was no different and he was well aware of it.[1]

Parsons grew up when the cod and seal fishery formed the basis of the Bay Roberts economy. Since there was little codfish to be caught in Conception Bay in the 1880s and 1890s, most people went to Labrador each summer to fish. Parsons went to Labrador, too, but not to fish; instead, he joined the Hudson's Bay Company. So, unlike most of his contemporaries, he was never involved in the fishery; neither did he become a foreign-going mariner or even a local skipper, as was the case with many of the men in his extended family. Ralph Parsons and his three brothers—Hayward, Wilfred, and Gus—were the first generation to break away from the traditional way of life. Gus became a lawyer, while the other three joined the Hudson's Bay Company.

By the end of the first decade of this century, the whaling industry in the North had all but disappeared. The only thing the Inuit had to trade with the white man was the white or arctic fox, which turned out to be the salvation of the northern people and an important item of trade for the Hudson's Bay Company. In time, Ralph Parsons established more than two dozen trading posts across the Eastern Arctic and into Hudson Bay, all depending mainly on the arctic fox.

His life was not easy. In his work he suffered many hardships and, on more than one occasion, almost lost his life. He got along well with everyone he met—natives, missionaries and traders—an ability of his that lasted a lifetime. In the end, everyone respected him for his courteous and gentle manner.

Frank G. Mercer, who was stationed as a policeman in Northern Labrador in the 1930s, tells of how once when the supply ship arrived, Parsons gave the Post Manager his supplies, then arranged to give Mercer his share as well, even though Mercer had nothing to do with the Hudson's Bay Company. Mercer maintains that Parsons was proud that a young man from his hometown, Bay Roberts, had made it into the police force and was stationed up North.[2]

Undoubtedly, the worst episode in Parsons' life was in 1920 when his wife and second child died. He never fully recovered, and to the best of the family's knowledge, he never developed a close relationship with another woman for the rest of his life. He always wore his wedding ring and was buried still wearing it. Llewellyn Bradbury of Coley's Point, who worked with the Hudson's Bay Company during the last years of Parsons' tenure, says that the Chief Factor always carried a large photo of his wife in his suitcase.[3]

Parsons was devoted to the Hudson's Bay Company. During his years as a District Manager, he always wrote a long section in his annual reports about the competition the Company faced in the North.[4] He was determined to help build up the honourable Company. When he became its Fur Trade Commissioner, he felt his knowledge and experience had prepared him for this senior position in that Department. During his working life, Parsons made a great name for himself as an important official with the Company and was a figure of national importance in terms of the fur trade.

In the 1940s, as a consultant for the Company in the St. John's office, Parsons' life was much easier. His only contacts with those in Winnipeg were by the friendly letters he received and the even friendlier letters he sent out. His inspection trips up to Labrador to Cartwright, Rigolet and North West River during the summers with his old friend and distant relative, Captain Sam Parsons in charge of the *Fort Amadjuak*, were in many ways pleasure trips for which he was paid. Much time was spent salmon fishing and hunting, and sometimes family members went along for the ride, as his nephew, Jack Hambling, did in the summer of 1943.

In the 1950s Parsons divided his time between St. John's and Bay Roberts and occupied himself, in part, by writing letters and visiting friends and relatives. He liked to reminisce about his Arctic experiences and talk about the history of Bay Roberts and area, of which he was very knowledgeable. One of the co-authors recalls a serious discussion about the loss of the sealing ship, the *Huntsman*, between Ralph Parsons and Captain Len Stick, a Newfoundland Member of Parliament at the time. John Parsons eavesdropped in Isaac Churchill's general store in Bay Roberts about 1952 as the two elderly men carried on a friendly argument as to the number of survivors in the disaster which occurred off the Labrador coast. Captain Stick said about half the crew survived, whereas Parsons said there were less than twenty survivors out of the sixth-two men who began the voyage in Bay Roberts on March 5, 1872. Actually, there were nineteen survivors.

During his days as Fur Trade Commissioner in Winnipeg, Parsons advocated that Post Managers should be jacks-of-all-trades.[5] Like many Newfoundlanders of his generation, Parsons could claim to be one himself. During his summers in Bay Roberts he maintained a small, well-organized carpentry shop where he did small jobs, primarily for his own pleasure. His tools, such as his chisels and saws, were always well-sharpened and properly organized on the wall over his workbench. A generous man throughout his life, he nevertheless refused to loan his tools, unless he considered an individual to be as careful and particular about his tools as he himself was. He kept two hunting dogs, and only on rare occasions loaned one of them to another hunter.

During the 1940s and 1950s Parsons, along with John Hambling, Sr., Dr. Arthur Barnes, Magistrate William E. Mercer, and several other prominent Bay Roberts Anglican men, served on the Select Vestry Board of St. Matthew's Anglican Church in Bay Roberts. Eric N. Dawe, years later a Cabinet Minister in the Smallwood administration, the youngest man in the group at the time, and head of the Select Vestry Board, now says that his Select Vestry Board, because of so many prominent men serving on it, was comparable to a present-day university Board of Regents.

On one occasion, the Select Vestry Board asked a local contractor for an estimate to do some repairs on the church and, when given the figure, were ready to borrow the $3,000.00 involved from the bank, but Ralph Parsons promptly offered the money interest free, and settled for a repayment arrangement of $100.00 a month until the loan was paid in full. Dawe recalls that when he eventually gave Parsons the final payment, the latter asked to be informed if and when the church needed another loan.[6]

The bell presently used in St. Matthew's Anglican Church was bought with funds left to the church in Parsons' will.[7] Jack Hambling says, "This final act of benevolence is fully in keeping with one who throughout his lifetime was indeed, as far as humanly possible, his 'brother's keeper.'"[8] Some of the older people in Bay Roberts say that every time they hear the bell ringing, they think of the great Ralph Parsons—a benefactor to the Anglican Church which nurtured his spiritual life; a benefactor to Bay Roberts, a Newfoundland outport that he called home; and a benefactor to the Hudson's Bay Company to which he devoted his working life. His efforts in opening up the North for the Company helped Canada lay claim to a vast area of Arctic territory.

Parsons died peacefully on a windy afternoon in November 1956. His funeral service was held in Bay Roberts, and he was buried in St. John's. He faced much death and suffering during his lifetime but, as Bishop Archibald L. Fleming intimated, he faced every eventuality with a philosophical resignation.[9] Winnifred (Butt) Moores, Parsons' niece, said after the funeral that as he lay in his coffin he looked like a king.[10] Ralph Parsons died as a true Christian, fully fortified by the doctrines and teachings of the Anglican Church of which he was a lifelong member.

What about the individuals—relatives, friends, and business acquaintances—who were closely associated with Ralph Parsons during his lifetime? Len Budgell and Robert H. Chesshire are still living at the time of this writing. Budgell, who lives in St. Boniface, Manitoba and is almost eighty, has a mind as sharp as a university graduate student, while Chesshire, who lives in Kingston, Ontario and is ninety-three, has a mind as keen as a winter breeze down Portage Avenue in Winnipeg. Captain Thomas F. Smellie of the *Nascopie*, who was made an officer of the Order of the British Empire in 1943 for his Arctic work, died in Vancouver in 1963 at the age of eighty-two. Bishop Archibald L. Fleming died in Goderich, Ontario in 1953 at eighty. George W. Allan, longtime Chairman of the Canadian Committee, died in 1940 at eighty. Hugh Mackay Ross died in 1992 at eighty. Ernie Lyall—the Arctic Man—died in Spence Bay, Northwest Territories in 1986 at seventy-six. Chesley Russell, another Bay Roberts man, died in Sidney, British Columbia, in 1994 at eighty-nine. A. Dudley Copland died in Ottawa in 1993 at ninety-two. Archie Hunter died in Vancouver in 1986 at eighty. Michael R. Lubbock died in 1989. Philip A. Chester died in Winnipeg in 1976 at eighty. Wilson Cave died in St. John's in 1994 at eighty-two. Captain Jimmy Dawe died in 1958.[11]

Stephen Dawe, Captain Jimmy Dawe of the *Fort Garry*, Hayward Parsons and Len Budgell, somewhere in the North, c. 1940.

What of Patrick Ashley Cooper, the famed Hudson's Bay Company Governor? The following item from the April 1961 issue of *The Bay News* answers that question: "Sir Patrick Ashley Cooper, thirtieth Governor of the Hudson's Bay Company, died late in March aboard ship on his way back to England from a journey in South Africa, and was buried at sea."[12] He died suddenly on March 22, 1961 at seventy-three.

Captain Sam Parsons, who was skipper of the *Fort Amadjuak*, died at Coley's Point in 1976 at seventy-nine. Stephen Hayward Parsons, who was four years younger than his brother, Ralph, died in 1965. His wife, Sybil, died in 1973 at eighty-three. Richard Augustus Parsons died in 1981 at eighty-eight. John Hambling, Sr., Ralph Parsons' brother-in-law, died in 1980 at eighty-eight, and his wife, Floss, who died in 1985 at ninety-five, outlived everyone in the family in both the nineteenth and twentieth centuries. Rachel Fannie Parsons (Datie) was eighty-eight when she died in 1966. Most of Ralph Parsons' relatives are buried in the Anglican cemetery in Bay Roberts.[13]

And what of the land of the North and the many posts Ralph Parsons established, from Wolstenholme in 1909 to Fort Ross in 1937? Some have grown into fairly sizeable communities, a few have ceased to exist, and others have become significant settlements. Pond Inlet and Pangnirtung on Baffin Island are examples of the latter.

Cyril Goodyear, himself an "Arctic man," writes that Parsons "was a very able man, well ahead of his time. Newfoundland deserves to know more about him."[14] In his 1987 article, "Nunatsuak: Arctic sovereignty," Goodyear points out that although Ralph Parsons was born a Newfoundlander and was only a Canadian during the last seven years of his life, "he made a tremendous contribution to Canada for which political leaders now take credit."[15] This reference is to Canada's claim to that vast expanse of Arctic territory across which Parsons established the presence of the Hudson's Bay Company.

Another individual who is very knowledgeable about Ralph Parsons and his work in the Arctic is George D. Pinkston of Brigus, Conception Bay. In 1973-74 he was manager of the Hudson's Bay Company office in Sugluk, located along the Ivujivik-Wolstenholme-Sugluk coastline. He says that the buildings Parsons erected in 1909 were moved to Ivujivik in the 1950s and used as a camp trading outlet of the Sugluk store. In 1962 those structures were sold, and now serve as a warehouse for the Co-operative which purchased them. In 1934 the Hudson's Bay Company erected a plaque which reads, "Wolstenholme Post—Established by W. Ralph Parsons in 1909." Pinkston says that this plaque, to prevent it from being vandalized, has since been relocated to the municipal office in Ivujivik.[16]

Pinkston also specifically refers Michael Harrington in his "Offbeat History" column in *The Evening Telegram* to a Labrador woman, named Ford and her "poignant, even pathetic story that illustrates the hardships and perils of life in the Far North almost a century ago."[17] The book, *Land of the Good Shadows*, which tells an interesting story about the Labrador woman, was published in New York in 1940. The climax of the story occurred in Wolstenholme on August 18, 1913, when the woman's husband, the Hudson's Bay Company post manager, and his assistant, a young Scot named Shepherd, were drowned only a few yards from shore. Their bodies were never recovered.

Less than a month before, Shepherd's wife had died of consumption several months after giving birth to a girl. A few years later, Ralph Parsons arranged to have a large memorial stone erected at the head of the young woman's grave. The stone is in memory of William R. Ford, Christopher G.T. Shepherd and his wife, Sarah Jane. Underneath the inscription are the words: "Erected by their friends in the Hudson's Bay Company's Service."

The Inuit woman, Anauta (Mrs. Ford) and her children lived for some time in Fogo, Twillingate, and St. John's, but eventually she moved to the United States where she married a former Newfoundlander named Blackmore. In the Postscript to the book there are two letters from Ralph Parsons to Mrs. Blackmore. One of them, dated December 6, 1939, was an answer to a request from Mrs. Blackmore for any information he might be able to provide about her father, George Ford, who had died in St. John's during the Spanish influenza of 1918. George Ford, who was a stepbrother to the father of William R. Ford, who had drowned at Wolstenholme, was the same Labrador man who had accompanied John T. ("Pete") Rowland and Bob English north on the *Daryl* in 1911.[18]

Ralph Parsons has been dead for almost forty years. Only the older people in and around Bay Roberts remember him. In Winnipeg and Montreal and especially in the northern settlements, he is gradually being forgotten. He is now a historical figure. References to him are found in most books dealing with the North and in all books dealing with the fur trade in this century. Arthur J. Ray could not have written his classic study of the fur trade without many references to Ralph Parsons; neither could A. Dudley Copland, J.W. Anderson, Ray Price, and Peter Newman have written their books dealing with the fur trade without references to Parsons. He was a very significant person in the Hudson's Bay Company in the first half of this century. His story needed to be told, and we have done our best to tell it.

Ask an assembly of high school students anywhere in Newfoundland and Labrador to identify Ralph Parsons and chances are very few, if any, will be able to do it. Our hope is that this biography will change that. *Ad captandum vulgus.*[19]

Notes to Epilogue

1. Telephone conversation between John Parsons and Robert H. Chesshire, January 9, 1995.
2. Interview with Frank G. Mercer, March 18, 1995.
3. Interview with Llewellyn Bradbury, February 22, 1995.
4. Outfit Reports 1921-29. Hudson's Bay Company Archives, Winnipeg, Manitoba.
5. Arthur J. Ray, *The Canadian Fur Trade in the Industrial Age* (Toronto, Ontario: University of Toronto Press, 1990), p. 180.
6. Interview with Eric N. Dawe, March 13, 1995.
7. *Codicil to Last Will and Testament* of William Ralph Parsons, dated October 21, 1944, Clause 13.
8. Information from Jack Hambling.
9. Archibald L. Fleming, *Archibald the Arctic* (Toronto, Ontario: Saunders of Toronto Limited, 1957), p. 259.
10. Information from Jack Hambling, February 22, 1995.
11. Obituary File, Hudson's Bay Company personnel, Hudson's Bay Company Archives, Winnipeg.
12. *The Bay News*, April 1961.
13. Church Records, St. John the Evangelist Church, Coley's Point; St. Matthew's, Bay Roberts; Anglican Cathedral, St. John's. Also interview by telephone with James Y. Parsons, May 9, 1995.
14. Cyril Goodyear to John Parsons, May 24, 1995.
15. Cyril Goodyear, "Nunatsuak: Arctic sovereignty," *The Evening Telegram*, October 3, 1987, p. 1A. See also Michael Harrington, "Offbeat History: The Last of the Factors," *The Evening Telegram*, January 29, 1990, p. 5.
16. Michael Harrington, "Offbeat History: Last of the Factors: memories of the early days," *The Evening Telegram*, March 4, 1991, p. 5.
17. *Ibid.*
18. Heluiz Chandler Washburne and Anauta, *Land of the Good Shadows: The Life Story of Anauta, an Eskimo Woman* (New York: The John Day Company, 1940). See Postscript, pp. 323-324. See also John T. Rowland *North to Baffin Land* (New York: Seven Seas Press, 1973), chapers 5 and 6.
19. Latin expression, "To catch the multitude or to make many people aware."

APPENDICES

Appendix 1
The Last Fur Trade Commissioner*

No name was signed to this tribute to Ralph Parsons. It has been suggested that it was written by A. Dudley Copland (1902-1993), but according to Anne Morton of the Hudson's Bay Company Archives in Winnipeg it was very likely written by William Joseph Cobb (1909-1987). Cobb, himself a Newfoundlander, joined the Hudson's Bay Company in 1928 and retired in 1965.

Newfoundland has given to the Fur Trade Department many outstanding men. With the death of Ralph Parsons at St. John's on the 24th November 1956, we have witnessed the passing of one of the greatest of these.

Born at Bay Roberts, Newfoundland, 1st December 1881, Ralph Parsons joined the H[udson's] B[ay] C[ompany] as an apprentice on the Labrador coast in the year 1900. Quite early in his career he must have grasped that "Vision of Empire" which led him to open up "Eskimo-land" to the fur trade. The times were propitious. The whaling industry, the first commercial contact with the natives, was on the way out at the turn of the century, and the white or arctic fox was practically the only commercial commodity the Eskimos could give in exchange for the white man's goods.

It was a bold step forward therefore, to open trading posts in the Arctic where every pound of coal, every stick of lumber, and almost all the food for the staff had to be imported from great distances and at great expense. However, with this "Vision of Empire" Ralph Parsons himself established Wolstenholme in 1909. In 1911 he established Lake Harbour to make it his district headquarters. In 1913 came Cape Dorset followed in 1914 by Stupart's Bay and Frobisher Bay. World War I held up further expansion for a time until in 1921 Pangnirtung and Pond Inlet were established. In 1923 came Clyde and in 1926 Arctic Bay which today remains the "farthest north" post.

---

* *Moccasin Telegraph* (XVI:1, Break-Up, 1957), p. 13.

But a mere recital of this northward march does not adequately convey the farseeing nature of this venture of opening up arctic trading posts when there was no wireless communication, no aircraft, and none of the modern and comfortable steam and motor ships of today. Nor does it mention the numerous incidents of high and dangerous adventure, or the understanding and solicitude Ralph Parsons held for the welfare of his Eskimo customers. No wonder then that he came to be known as the "King of Baffin Land."

With the passing of time and the advance of modern communication and travel, Ralph Parsons moved his headquarters first to St. John's and then to Montreal as he gradually assumed wider responsibilities. In his final years as district manager he was in charge of practically all of the Company's eastern fur trade excepting James Bay. In 1930 he was appointed Fur Trade Commissioner, the last of a long line to be known by that title.

If Ralph Parsons had required courage, determination and great qualities of leadership for the extension of the fur trade to the remote Arctic, such attributes were in even greater demand for the office of Fur Trade Commissioner. For not only did he have the responsibility for the operations of the entire Department, he had to contend also with the crisis brought about by the depression of the thirties. It was a time of great sacrifice and drastic adaptation. But he had the steely courage to see it through so that, in the fortunes of the H B C, he could truly be called one of the outstanding "men of the restoration."

From his earliest days Ralph Parsons had the characteristics of leadership and achievement. He was a disciplinarian who started first with the discipline of himself. He was not easy to know intimately, standing always, as is the way of leaders, just a little apart from the ordinary run of men. But he was above all an outstanding and forceful personality, a man who had served the Fur Trade powerfully and well in his day and generation.

Appendix 2
Nunatsuak: Arctic sovereignty*
Cyril Goodyear

Cyril J. Goodyear (b. 1926) a native of Deer Lake, Newfoundland, has had a distinguished career in the legal field. He served in Labrador as a member of the Newfoundland Rangers and later the RCMP. In later years he became a lawyer and, after serving in several capacities in the legal field, retired in 1989 as Registrar of the Supreme Court of Newfoundland. Over the years he did some part-time work in the field of journalism.

Let's play "Definition."
An interesting game? No? Yes?
Q: Define sovereignty.
A: Possessing supreme power and jurisdiction.
Q: Define jurisdiction.
A: Authority, capacity, power or right to act. District over which authority extends.
Q: Jurisdiction—what is the modern definition?
A: Juris—law or legal; diction—talk. Legal talk, as in offshore and in the Arctic, if you know what I mean.
Okay, we'll vary the game, more seriously this time.
Q: Who is responsible for Arctic sovereignty? Macdonald, Laurier, Pearson, Diefenbaker, Trudeau or Joe Clark?
A: None of the above. It was Ralph Parsons of Bay Roberts, Newfoundland.
Shame on those who write the history books if you didn't know the answer.

If you read and think about history in a shallow way, there will be a lasting impression that kings, queens, princes, conquerors and political leaders are responsible for the acquisition of territory and jurisdiction over it. In actual fact, it was always the adventurers, fishermen, hunters, traders and the generally curious who brought it about.

---

* *The Evening Telegram*, October 3, 1987, p. 1A.

Most of them never made the history books. They often couldn't read or write, had no audience, and couldn't generate their own propaganda. Only when the promoters, the greedy, the egotistical and politically motivated learned of the potential value of the lands and seas discovered by now obscure people did sovereignty or jurisdiction, in the legal sense, come about. They sent out their navies, armies and official representatives to "take possession" while they stayed home in comfort.

So what has changed?

Ralph Parsons was a Newfoundlander. A British subject, not a Canadian. Yet, because of his vision and drive, he made a tremendous contribution to Canada for which political leaders now take credit. He deserves a place in Canadian history and, more particularly, a warm and enduring place in the folklore of succeeding generations of Newfoundlanders and Labradorians.

He was born in Bay Roberts on December 1, 1881: a winter child, made for the Arctic. In 1900, at age 19, he went to Labrador as an apprentice with the Hudson's Bay Company. Nine years later he was a district manager and in 1930 became Fur Trade Commissioner, executive head of the fur trade in Canada for the "Company." He was known as King of Baffin Land. In 1940 he retired.

During his tenure with the Company he changed the course of Arctic history, at last a Canadian by virtue of the Terms of Union and the Canadian Citizenship Act. He was then survived by his brothers, Hayward and R.A. (Gus) Parsons, the latter a well-known lawyer and poet.

MEETING AT NAIN

I met Mr. Parsons at Nain in the summer of 1946. He came with his brother, Hayward, who was then in charge of Newfoundland Government Trading Posts stretching from Hebron to Hopedale. Commission of Government bought these posts from the Hudson's Bay Company in 1942 and operated them through the Department of Natural Resources.

Being the Ranger, I was invited to the home of the manager, Hayward Haynes, for tea. It was interesting to observe the difference between the two brothers—Hayward, outgoing and talkative, and Ralph, commanding and austere with a breadth of knowledge. Hayward Haynes knew them both from his years with the Hudson's Bay Company, and his admiration and respect for both of them was obvious.

That was the beginning of my interest in the story of Ralph Parsons.

A BITING WIT

All who knew him attest to his command of language and his biting wit. I heard a story of that visit to Nain where a missionary, who had known him for years, was taking him around the village. He is reported to have asked, "What do you think of it all, Mr. Parsons?" Ralph Parsons replied, "Well, Reverend, perhaps I can best sum it up in the words of an old hymn, 'Change and decay in all around I see.'"

IN THE SHADOW OF THE POLE

Prior to 1909, trading was "in the bottom of the Bay." In effect, up the Labrador Coast, around Ungava, Hudson and James Bays, largely below the tree line, across the Prairies and into what is now British Columbia. There was some trading with the Eskimo (Inuit) on the fringe of their territory. That trade was mainly in white foxes.

Ralph Parsons saw the potential for trade, but he also had a vision of empire and an effective, rather than heroic, way of making the long-sought "Northwest Passage" a reality. He was a superb organizer, a born leader with iron-willed determination: a Bay Roberts Newfoundlander. His courage and physical stamina were legendary in the Arctic and his personal exploits would—AND SHOULD—fill a book.

MARCHING POSTHASTE

Look at the map; I don't have the time and space to explain. In 1909 he opened Wolstenholme; 1911, Chesterfield Inlet and Lake Harbour; 1913, Cape Dorset; 1914, Wakeham Bay; 1916, Baker Lake and Repulse Bay; and others.

Because of his vision, drive and business ability the march began from west to east: 1915, Herschel Island; 1916, Shingle Point and Baillie Island; 1917, Bernard Harbour; 1923, Cambridge Bay and King William Land; 1937, Fort Ross.

When the Hudson's Bay Company ships, *Nascopie*, from the Atlantic, and *Aklarik*, from the Makenzie River, met in Belot Strait in 1937 to transship furs and supplies, the "Northwest Passage" became a reality. Ralph Parsons had fulfilled his dream and a vast territory had become part of Canada.

THE FOLLOWERS

Behind the Company traders came many people. Among the first were the missionaries, spreading the full Gospel to those who gathered at the full store. After them came the representatives of Canada, the Royal Canadian Mounted Police. Thus the official presence, sovereignty, jurisdiction, was established. The normal pattern of real history had been followed.

WHO WILL WRITE?

This is a story which cries out to be written in full detail. Who will write it? David Parsons of Hantsport, Nova Scotia, his son? Jack Hambling of South River, Newfoundland, his nephew, already an author? Some historian without a "feel" for the man and the times?

A number of his contemporaries are still around, all getting older: Leonard Coates of Pasadena, Hayward Haynes, Frank Mercer of Bay Roberts, to mention a few who can give personal accounts.

Ralph Parsons brought many from Newfoundland and Labrador into the service of the Company. Who will fill this great void in our history and national pride?

WHAT ABOUT CANADA?

Yes, what about you, Canada? We are a major contributing part when our gifts to you are properly credited in history. Will you exercise sovereignty over what Ralph Parsons' vision and effort gave you? Or will you merely exercise Juris (legal) Diction (talk)?

Appendix 3
Be Proud of William Ralph Parsons*
Frank G. Mercer

Frank G. Mercer (b. 1914), a native of Bay Roberts, has the distinction of being the only Newfoundlander to serve in Labrador with three police forces—The Newfoundland Constabulary, The Newfoundland Rangers and the RCMP. Later he worked with the Department of Labrador Affairs from which he retired in 1974. He resides in Bay Roberts.

Ralph [Parsons] was born December 1, 1881, the son of William and Dorcas (Mosdell) Parsons. The father was a well-known foreign-going Captain; the mother, the daughter of one of Newfoundland's foremost fish killers. A brother, R.A. Parsons, was a prominent city lawyer, the author of several books of verse, all locally oriented.

After completing his education, Ralph went to Labrador where he entered the employ of the Hudson's Bay Company. He rose from apprentice clerk to become the Company's Fur Trade Commissioner, an office designated for him in consideration of his invaluable services, and one that, for similar reasons, was to cease with his demise.

During his years of service, forty in all, Ralph Parsons established more trading posts than any other four of his predecessors. He is probably better known among the Innu and Inuit of Canada's Northlands than by his own countrymen, especially by those natives with whom he shared incredible hardships. Arctic travel held no terrors for him for he went where few white people had ventured before his time.

You see, I grew up next door to the Parsons household. As a boy, I was constantly aware of the esteem and respect accorded the family, the son Ralph, in particular. In later years, as a member of the Royal Canadian Mounted Police, I travelled extensively in the North and so got to know Ralph Parsons on a more personal level. I saw him, as well, when he was at the peak of his career. His name was synonymous with integrity; an outstanding personality, one of whom Newfoundland can be justifiably proud.

---

* Excerpt from Letter to the Editor, *The Evening Telegram*, March 21, 1991, p. 10.

Appendix 4

Who's Who in Hudson's Bay House: Ralph Parsons*

"Watson M.D."

Len H. Coulthard (b. 1910) was the editor of The House Detective *in 1940 when Ralph Parsons retired. "Watson M.D." was very likely a nom de plume for Coulthard. In April 1941, Coulthard enlisted in the Royal Canadian Artillery. He did not return to the Hudson's Bay Company.*

Forty years of Arctic experience when the [Hudson's Bay] Company realized more and more the possibilities of the vast trading empire within the Arctic regions; years of increasing responsibility and with it the opportunity to make trading north of Hudson Bay become a profitable reality—such is the record of Mr. Ralph Parsons who retired on May 31st as the last Fur Trade Commissioner. A man of courage and sincerity, Mr. Parsons has left the imprint of his rugged personality on the North of fact and fiction. A rigid disciplinarian, he demanded that all Company employees in the North maintain the high standard of the Company's tradition. His adventures and generosity are legend.

In 1900 Mr. Parsons first exchanged the rugged coasts of Newfoundland for the rugged coast of Labrador when he joined the service of the Company at Cartwright. He was not slow to see the immense possibilities in the white fox trade to the North and in 1909 pioneered the establishment of posts in the Eastern Arctic. Wolstenholme was first. Then followed in quick succession Lake Harbour, Cape Dorset, Stupart's Bay and Frobisher Bay. Here the Great War called a halt. But in 1921 the work was continued with the establishment of Pangnirtung and Pond's Inlet. Further posts came into being in the following years until Fort Ross was established in 1937, at which time the Northwest Passage was finally brought into being as a commercial route across the top of the world.

As soon as Mr. Parsons was able to return to Newfoundland from the

---

* *The House Detective* (II:1), June 1940.

North after the outbreak of the Great War, he volunteered for service. However, the aftermath of two fractured legs which he had suffered previously rendered him unfit for service, and he returned to give the best of his ability to the maintaining of the Company's operations in the North during those difficult years. In 1917 he was made Inspector of the Labrador District. Subsequently he became a district manager and in 1930 he was appointed Fur Trade Commissioner.

There is a real story yet to be written about Ralph Parsons in the North—Ralph Parsons who established more posts in the North than any other man in Hudson's Bay Company history.

There is another side, the side pictured in R.H.H. Macaulay's journal of the 1934 *Nascopie* voyage—Ralph Parsons, the jovial king of Baffinland, knowing his Eskimo "subjects" by name after man years' absence, joining wholeheartedly in the holiday amusements in Lake Harbour, the "capital" of Baffinland. It was seeing the Commissioner in such circumstances which prompted Michael Lubbock to pen the lines,

> *Never yet has history shown*
> *A cleric on a royal throne,*
> *But here we see before us stand*
> *A Parson, King of Baffin Land.*

The Governor and Committee have presented Mr. Parsons with the ship,[*Fort*] *Amadjuak*. We wish him a grand retirement—and perhaps another visit to Baffinland, in his own boat.

Appendix 5

Two Different Attitudes Towards Conservation — the Indian and the white trapper*

Ralph Parsons

William Ralph Parsons (1881-1956) the author of this extract from Rene Fumoleau's book and the subject of this biography, retired in 1940 after forty years service with the Hudson's Bay Company.

Very few white people, taking up trapping as an occupation, give any thought to conservation. The great majority take up trapping in the same way as they would take up any other occupation—to obtain the largest possible return in the shortest possible time....

The Indian may be lazy, improvident and shiftless, but, insofar as the conservation of the wild life is concerned, these failings may be almost regarded as virtues. Hunting is the only occupation for which the majority of Indians are adapted, but, whereas the "White" trapper will go into a territory and not be satisfied until he has cleaned it out, the Indian will only take what he requires to see him through from day to day. He has no incentive to make large hunts. He traps to fill his immediate needs only. It is only when the Indian comes up against the intensive competition of the "White" trapper that he goes to excess in trapping and in killing out wild life. With few exceptions, it will be found that where Indians have been left alone, there is no undue scarcity of animal life in their vicinity. The Indian is unwittingly a good conservationist. When fur is plentiful, he will probably take all he needs to buy his requirements. When they are scarce, he very soon becomes discouraged and does not consider it worthwhile to trap. Thus in years of plenty he is taking animals which, in all probability,

---

* The Indian and the white trapper approached the hunting ground with different attitudes and goals. These were well explained by Ralph Parsons in an article written for the Canadian Press. Quoted in Rene Fumoleau, *As Long As This Land Shall Last: A History of Treaty 8 and Treaty 11—1870-1939* (Toronto, Ontario: McClelland and Stewart Limited, 1973), pp. 239-240.

would die from epidemic later anyway, and in years of scarcity, he leaves breeders which presumably are immune from the disease.

The great difference between the "White" and the Indian trapper is that the White trapper goes into the country with the fixed idea of doing nothing else but trapping and of getting every possible skin he can. The Indian, on the other hand, is settled permanently in the country and all he does is to make a bare living hunting for food and trapping to get the wherewithal to pay for his other few necessities.

The majority of the White trappers are itinerants moving from one place to another and a great number of them are foreigners whose object is to take as much as possible out of the country and to put as little as possible back. The Indian, on the other hand, puts all he makes back into the trade of the locality in which he lives.

It is significant also to note that despite the fact that trade in furs had been carried on in Canada for about three hundred years, it is only within the last thirty years that any real concern has been felt for the preservation of the wild life. While the growing scarcity may be partly due to the expansion of settlement, it must be remembered also that beaver, for which the greatest concern is felt at present, was a much more important article of trade and, consequently, much more sought after, yet it was in no danger of being killed out. Since there were more Indians trapping in those days than there are now, the inference would seem to be that it is only since the White trapper entered the field so extensively that there has been any danger of this animal being killed out.

Appendix 6

Personal Correspondence*

Personal correspondence from Robert H. Chesshire to John Parsons, co-author of this biography. Chesshire (b. 1902) was at one time Assistant Fur Trade Commissioner to Ralph Parsons. See Note at the beginning of Appendix 10.

May 25, 1995

Dear Mr. Parsons:

R.P. was a rather lonely man. He was very independent—a rather private person. He had a stern and well-disciplined mind; his moral code was of the highest. Once he got to know you and felt he could trust you he became a warm and friendly companion.

His differences with Philip Chester and George Allan arose from his refusal to recognize that considerable changes had to be made in the administrative management of the Department. Otherwise, I am sure both Mr. Chester and Mr. Allan liked and admired him as a man.

Sincerely yours,
Robert H. Chesshire

---

* A letter from Robert H. Chesshire to John Parsons, May 25, 1995.

Appendix 7

Letter From Len Budgell*

Len Budgell (b. 1917) who served with the Hudson's Bay Company for forty-seven years retired in 1982. A native of North West River, Labrador, his last position with the company was as General Manager of Moosonee Transport. He resides in St. Boniface, Manitoba.

...[R]egarding Mr. Ralph Parsons' last years with the HBC, I was not in Winnipeg at that time and I saw him only infrequently at Hebron and in the Eastern Arctic usually at "ship time," when everything was in a rush....

Mr. Parsons was a very honest man and a strong HBC man. He would always put the HBC interests ahead of his own, and perhaps he did have some reservations about the new regime—I wouldn't know—but I am sure that as long as he was there he would co-operate fully with Mr. Chester and whoever else was in charge.

From what I saw, Mr. Parsons and Ashley Cooper had a good relationship. Cooper was apparently a stuffy character, but showed none of it when he was visiting around the Posts.

R.P. did a magnificent job as Fur Trade Commissioner. His methods were right for the period and, without a doubt, he saved the Fur Trade, and no one would know better than he when to turn a healthy department over to younger men who would, hopefully, keep it healthy and prosperous during the years of great change that obviously lay ahead.

He served his term in the heat of the day, and when the evening came he had nothing to reproach himself for. He did his work quietly and efficiently. He generated a remarkable loyalty among the Post staff particular for the Company and for himself. If you are looking for a flamboyant, spectacular person you have the wrong man.

I know of only one person who knew R.P. intimately for many, many years. I knew that person, who is now dead, from the time I was a very small boy, and never once did I hear a single word of any confidence that R.P. may have given. There may be diaries that I know nothing of, but I am sure that there would be nothing in them that would give you more information than the brief statements in the Archives have done. R.P. was

---

* Excerpt from Len Budgell's letter of December 13, 1994 to John Parsons.

like many old-time craftsmen: he knew his work, he did it well, and he looked for no other recognition than the one he awarded another faithful servant, "He was a...good man."

Appendix 8

Hudson's Bay Company, Fur Trade Department Organization, 1938*

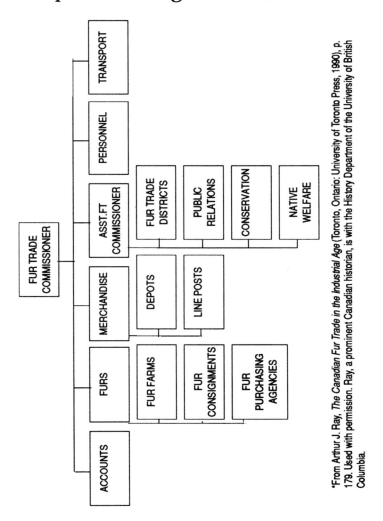

*From Arthur J. Ray, *The Canadian Fur Trade in the Industrial Age* (Toronto, Ontario: University of Toronto Press, 1990), p. 179. Used with permission. Ray, a prominent Canadian historian, is with the History Department of the University of British Columbia.

Appendix 9

Wolstenholme Post Journal 1909-10*

Ralph Parsons

Ralph Parsons (1881-1956) the subject of this biography founded the Wolstenholme Post in 1909.

SEPTEMBER 1910

THURSDAY, 1st. Blowing a gale from N.W. Fine. Parsons at Office Work. Ford stowing away goods in shed.

FRIDAY, 2nd. Beautiful clear day. Wind light from South. Life boat arrived at 7 P.M. They have erected the camp at Loon Cove, and are now ready for the trapping season.

SATURDAY, 3rd. Fine and clear. Wind light from E.S.E. "Pelican" arrived here at 5 A.M. Capt. Smith still refuses to move to the Post, and I will not remain here longer than 6 P.M. today. At 7 P.M. "Pelican" left. It seems very extraordinary to me that Mr. Grahame should give me permission to remove this Post to a more favourable place and that Capt. Smith should not be told about it. However, thank goodness I'm going out of it next year and before I would ever come to a place like this again I'll know what's what from Headquarters.

SUNDAY, 4th. Fine and clear. Wind light from N.E. Capt. Smith has consented to keep a little closer than usual when he gets near Stupart's Bay, so that if there should be any natives around there he would be able to send them this way, but I expect very little from it.

MONDAY, 5th. Fine. Wind light from N.E. Well, here we are for another year and I'm glad to say better fixed with regard to men. Mark Mucko has decided to remain the winter the last minute. So that the crew for this year is Ralph Parsons, Geo. Bird, Mark Mucko, John Edmunds and Jas. Palliser. If there

---

* Excerpt from Ralph Parsons' Wolstenholme Post Journal 1909-10.

are any foxes going we should make a much bigger hunt than last year. We got a porpoise from nets today.

TUESDAY, 6th. Beautiful & bright day. Wind light from West. Caught a "Jar seal" from nets. Servants employed hauling lifeboat to winter quarters and putting felt on shed.

WEDNESDAY, 7th. Fine and clear. Wind west light. All servants employed taking goods from store and restoring it and cleaning out store. Got one larsey from net today.

THURSDAY, 8th. Beautiful bright day, wind light from West. Servants finished piling wood from York and covered and caulked back cornice of house and shed with felt, as the snow drifted in badly last winter.

FRIDAY, 9th. Raining. Blowing a gale from West. Servants employed caulking house, repairing stovepipes and putting linoleum on floor.

SATURDAY, 10th. Snowing fast all day. Wind blowing a hurricane from N.E. About 1

Appendix 10
Retirement Speech*
Robert H. Chesshire

Robert H. Chesshire (b. 1902), one of the most distinguished Hudson's Bay Company officials in this century, was born in Dorset, England. He served thirty-seven years with HBC, twenty-one of which he was associated with the Fur Trade Department. He served as Assistant Fur Trade Commissioner under Ralph Parsons. He became Manager of the Fur Trade Department in 1942 and General Manager in 1945. He retired in 1962 and resides in Kingston, Ontario.

A few of us here tonight will remember the different phases of reorganization through which the Company passed, some of the more painful of which had been completed by the mid-thirties. Subsequently it was my privilege to be very closely associated with the reorganization and rehabilitation of the Fur Trade Department. Like all the other major departments of the Company, it required surgery but here there was more excuse, for over the years the elements of isolation had immunized it against much in the way of critical self-analysis. Thus it was unaware of the changes which were taking place both within and without its boundaries, and was equally unaware of the profound influence which these changes would eventually have on its operations.

Fortunately, Mr. Chester's restless and imaginative mind had come to grips with the many problems involved and his fertile brain had conceived a program for their solution which was as ambitious as it was comprehensive. It involved reorganization and rehabilitation on a massive scale. That, or virtual extinction and there was no room for compromise. It took vision and imagination to draw up this blueprint of revival, and it required courage and persistence on his part to carry it through....

These were men of courage, endurance, independence, and self-reliance. And when I ponder their achievements my thoughts turn to some of the unsung heroes of more modern times. Men like Ralph Parsons, my

---

* Excerpt from Robert H. Chesshire's retirement speech, *Moccasin Telegraph*, Fall 1962, pp. 29-30.

predecessor, whose name will have an honoured place in any history of the fur trade. It was he who established the first Arctic post, and who subsequently went on to pioneer and expand the Arctic trade with such vigour and success. He was an intrepid pioneer, a courageous explorer, a lovable personality and a man who served this Company with selfless devotion. And so it has continued through the centuries—like calling to this—thus creating and perpetuating values which have become traditional, and which have formed the basic fabric of this Company's character. May we always preserve and cherish this great heritage.

Appendix 11

Hudson's Bay Company Fur Trade Commissioner's Office Winnipeg, Manitoba*

This letter was written by Ralph Parsons near the end of his term as Fur Trade Commissioner in Winnipeg. In the book referred to there is also another letter by Ralph Parsons in the Postscript section.

December 6, 1939.

Dear Mrs. Blackmore:

When I first knew of your father he was in charge of Nachvak post, while I was an apprentice clerk at Rigolet. That was in 1900. The District Manager, who was stationed at Rigolet, would arrange to meet your father at Davis Inlet in March of each year, and your father, I believe, brought his annual accounts to Davis Inlet and discussed business matters with the District Manager.

I believe it was in 1905 that Nachvak post was closed out, and it was about that date that your mother must have died.

When Nachvak was closed, your father retired to Newfoundland, and there found employment with Dr. Grenfell, in connection with the herding of his reindeer at St. Anthony. He must have held that position for three or four years. Then he went north in 1911 in a small boat called the "Daryl" owned by the Grenfell Mission, which was purchased from them by the Hudson's Bay Company. The boat was delivered to us at Wolstenholme, and as I was anxious to go out on furlough I arranged with your father to take charge of Wolstenholme during my absence, which was for one year....

He was jovial, pleasant and obliging at all times and to everybody. He was a good trader, very careful and economical with the Company's property, and I believe was a faithful and loyal employee.

Yours sincerely,
Ralph Parsons

---

* Heluiz Chandler Washburne and Anauta, *Land of the Good Shadows: The Life Story of Anauta, an Eskimo Woman* (New York: The John Day Company, 1940), Postscript, p. 324.

Appendix 12
Prairie Trails and Arctic By-Ways*
Henry Toke Munn

Henry Toke Munn (1864-1946) was born in Devon, England and came to Canada in 1886. Involved in a number of enterprises in Western Canada, he founded the Arctic Gold Exploration Syndicate in 1914, and later operated several trading posts on Baffin Island. He sold out to the HBC in 1923 and published his book, an account of his life and work, in 1932.

As [Ralph Parsons] represents most efficiently the policy of the great Company in its dealings with the natives, I will sum up my impressions of him.

A tall, good-looking man, with a pleasant if rather abstracted manner, he is one of the ablest executives I have ever met. His large office in Montreal was run smoothly, efficiently, and very strictly. He has an astonishing grasp of all the varied details of business in his enormous district. I judged that his staff and his traders did not like him, and I got the impression he preferred it to be so. He appeared to me to have no intimates. The only one of his subordinates I ever heard speak enthusiastically about him was Nicholls, the trader in charge of the Cumberland Gulf station ....Like old Dr. McKay of Chipewayan, the great Company is Parsons' god. He thinks of it, and works tirelessly day and night for it.

As we could not discuss it and hardly mentioned it to outsiders like myself, it made him poor company. He has no amusements, and he told me he had no time for them, which I readily believed, for the Company is a hard taskmaster, and Parsons serves it with cold-blooded efficiency. He has been a Company trader at Lake Harbour, on Baffin's Island, for some years, and knows the Eskimos well, but I do not think he has ever understood them. He neither likes nor dislikes them, but regards them merely as instruments to serve the great Company.... For him, their mission is to obtain furs.... His interest is submerged in his service to his

---

* Henry Toke Munn, *Prairie Trails and Arctic By-Ways* (London, England: Hurst and Blackett, Ltd., 1932), pp. 270-272.

Company....He is no visionary..., but a ruthless realist when dealing with their affairs with the great Company.

I have described my impressions of Parsons rather at length, because I consider he exemplifies an ideal servant to the Company from the viewpoint of their profits, for he has to a high degree those qualities a large Company trading with natives would desire their officers to possess to ensure their business being a profitable one....

I found Parsons a hard bargainer, as might be expected....

Appendix 13
"Interesting Years With the HBC"*
W.J. Cobb

William J. Cobb (1909-1987), a native of St. John's, Newfoundland, had a distinguished career with the Hudson's Bay Company. He joined the company in 1928 and retired in 1965. His last posting was as Deputy General Manager of the Northern Stores Department. See Appendix 1.

The great depression of the 30's is still indelibly etched on my mind. It was a struggle to keep operating and the staff in the Labrador Posts, especially the more northerly ones, were placed even more on their own efforts for survival of the natives and themselves. As I look back on this period, I realize to a much greater degree, the tremendous effort made by the late Fur Trade Commissioner Ralph Parsons to save the Department. I am sure that if it had been left to the London Directors, most of the Fur Trade Posts would have been closed, but Mr. Parsons fought with tenacious courage and determination, and by his leadership the Department survived the dirty 30's, battered, with run-down buildings but still standing and with a good basic organization. Ralph Parsons is one of my heroes, and when his period of service comes to be written he will rank with the great men of the Fur Trade.

Towards the end of the 30's when the world started to come out of the depression and the black shadow of war loomed it would have been easy for management to have let the department carry on as it was. In view of the imminent war, most leaders would have concentrated on the development of the large retail stores as many people felt that the Fur Trade was finished. They overlooked Mr. P.A. Chester with his great determination, unrelenting drive and vision of Northern Canada. Mr. Chester chose as his first lieutenant R.H. Chesshire, and they commenced the hard uphill fight to reorganize the Fur Trade Department.

The reorganization and rehabilitation was to be a massive operation and certainly took vision and courage. I could go on and outline some of

---

* Excerpt from W.J. Cobb, "Interesting Years With the HBC," *Moccasin Telegraph*, Winter 1970, p. 27.

the changes, such as living conditions, health, and education policies, in fact basically the Northern Stores Department of today with all its modernization both trading-wise and personnel-wise is the direct result of Messrs. Chester and Chesshire's vision, courage and persistence. They too will go down in the history of the Company as being among the great adventurers.

Appendix 14

"Establishing HBC Baker Lake, N.W.T. Summer, 1925"*

W.O. Douglas

William Osborn Douglas (1895-1978) was born in Bedfordshire, England. He retired from the Hudson's Bay Company in 1957 after thirty-four years service. Before joining the Company he served with the RCMP. He was the first post manager at Baker Lake. During his time with the Company he was involved in experimental fur farming in Cartwright and Winnipeg.

After, Mr. Parsons inspected the post and, I think, was quite pleased with what he saw. His only complaint was about a bunch of junk—old stoves, heaters, etc.—brought up from the old post. It should have been inside, out of sight, not left to disfigure the otherwise pleasant surroundings, he thought.

I replied that, at the moment, I was short of under-cover storage, but that this would soon be taken care of.

Just before Mr. Parsons' departure, I decided to take my Peterhead boat down to Chesterfield to meet the ship, as I thought the quarters on his cruiser might be a bit crowded. Mr. Parsons was not in agreement as he wanted me at the ship before she left and did not think I could make it in time. Given smooth sailing, he was right: I could not make as good time with it as he could with the cruiser. But the glass was falling and if I got a favourable wind, I thought I could stay with him. I had the natives put rock ballast aboard, and both boats got away together. The wind was favourable and freshening—right up my alley.

Baker Lake, some 60 miles long, can churn up quite rough water. The ADMADJUAK had to slow down, and not before she was shipping water. Mr. Parsons' seagoing name was "Stormy Petrel" as he loved rough water.

The outlet from the lake into the inlet is divided into two channels, north and south. Mr. Parsons took the south and I the less-used north

---

* Excerpt from W.O. Douglas, "Establishing HBC Baker Lake, N.W.T. Summer, 1925," *Moccasin Telegraph*, Winter 1970, p. 141.

channel. Before we reached them, the wind was really blowing. The cruiser, travelling down the centre of the lake, had to cut her engine to dead slow. I hugged the shelter of the north shore's high hills and carried on with all sail set and engine running.

On several occasions my old native, a good boatman, suggested we take in a reef, what with the wind blowing so hard. I didn't let on that I heard him. Once or twice, we shipped water but, on the whole, we were making pretty good time. Neither boat could know until we left the channels into the main inlet who had got there first, but it was not until I pulled alongside the NASCOPIE and could see no ADMADJUAK in the water or on board that I knew I was first.

I was under no illusions whatever that my being first would in any way be popular but I must admit it gave me some satisfaction. With the arrival of the cruiser not long after, the NASCOPIE made fast time in getting underway. Chesterfield was not a popular place to hang around in a blow.

I had time to go above to the captain's cabin and drink the usual toast to those wintering in the North—and to have Mr. Parsons ask me if I knew how much a Peterhead boat cost. I told him that I did, and that ours was not written off yet. He replied that if I were left to handle it, it probably would not be long before it was!

With one anchor up and the other chain short, passengers for shore were going down the companionway. Mr. Parsons was on deck, shaking hands and congratulating my natives on their quick trip down. One of my men had been with whalers and was quite proud of his ability to talk jargon.

"Oh yes, makeum very fast trip. Him, Kiuk, crazy....Want get here ahead of you, pretty near drown us all."

I don't know about that, but I doubt I ever sailed in a Peterhead boat as fast again.

For all his queer ways—and they were many—Mr. Parsons was admired by all. A kinder-hearted man, you never met, with a heart the size of an ox and a great sense of dry humour. We parted with the warmest of handshakes and his native Newfoundland blessing, "Long may your big jib draw."

Appendix 15
Parsons, William Ralph (1881-1956)*
John Parsons

John Parsons (b. 1939) and a native of Shearstown, Newfoundland, contributed to all five volumes of the Encyclopedia of Newfoundland and Labrador *between 1981 and 1994. He is co-author of this biography.*

Businessman. Born Bay Roberts, son of William and Dorcas (Mosdell) Parsons. Educated Bay Roberts. Married Flora May House. Ralph Parsons began his career at the age of 19 in Cartwright, as an apprentice clerk with the Hudson's Bay Company. Nine years later he was appointed district manager of the Labrador and Eastern Arctic districts. In 1927 he became chief factor and in 1930 fur trade commissioner, which included responsibility for the Company's extensive transportation system.

Parsons spent the greater part of his life in Northern Labrador and the Canadian Eastern Arctic, particularly Baffin Island. Archibald Lang Fleming, the first Bishop of the Arctic, wrote that "There can be little doubt that the fur trade in Canada owes more to Ralph Parsons than to any other individual during the first half of the twentieth century." Parsons is credited with helping Canada claim sovereignty over the vast northern territory. Important HBC posts established by him in the Eastern Arctic include Wolstenholme (1909), Lake Harbour (1911), Cape Dorset (1913), Repulse Bay (1916), Cambridge Bay (1923) and later Port Harrison on Hudson Bay, Pangnirtung and Pond Inlet on Baffin Island, and in 1937 Fort Ross on Somerset Island. He was known in the Arctic as the King of Baffin Land. He was a legend in his time and in 1992 was probably better known among the people of the north than in Newfoundland. Peter Newman claims that "Parsons ruled over an immense empire with the righteousness of a latter-day Cromwell. The Company was everything to

---

* *Encyclopedia of Newfoundland and Labrador*, Volume 4, Eds., Cyril Poole, Robert H. Cuff (St. John's, Newfoundland: Harry Cuff Publications Ltd., 1993), p. 226.

him, not just his job but his religion." Parsons retired in May 1940 and died in St. John's on November 24, 1956. Frank G. Mercer (letter, Nov. 1991), A.L. Fleming (1956), Cyril Goodyear (*ET* Oct. 3, 1987), Peter Newman (1991), Frank Ryan (*Beaver* June 1940), *DN* (Dec. 7, 1956), *Who's Who in and from Newfoundland 1937* (1937?). John Parsons.

Appendix 16
To "R.P."*

(William Ralph Parsons, at one time Chief Factor and Fur Trade Commissioner of Hudson's Bay Company.)

R. A. Parsons

Richard Augustus Parsons (1893-1981), a native of Bay Roberts and a younger brother to William Ralph Parsons, was a prominent Newfoundland lawyer and man of letters. His last book of poetry is entitled, Curtain Call *(1980).*

The incident, which men call death, we'll strive
To pass, and note his merits which may yet survive
His sojourn here, albeit with concern
For judgment of his worth, for you must learn,
He was a man, who lived long years remote
From crowds in towns or cities who might vote
Upon his attributes or right to hold
High office, by their suffrage duly polled.
And 'tis not meet, that I, his own, grow bold
In praise remembering, or loving hold,
That men should honour him, on being told
He travelled far, at risk, and bought and sold;
But yet old Hudson's Bay men now remain,
Who shared his trek from Baffin Bay to Nain,
And still with kindliness do yet recall,
How he would let his conduct answer all
Its consequence, reluctant to complain
Of other's faults and thus transpose the blame;
How lonely lands and seas, beyond the reach
Of subterfuge, so disciplined his speech
In ways of truth, that men became as fond

---

* R.A Parsons, *Reflections*, Books I and II (Toronto, The Ryerson Press, 1958), pp. 114-117.

Of his own spoken word, as of his bond.
They too, are wont to note he rose to place;
But let no eminence of his efface
The memory of loyalties of those,
Who travelled times agone the Arctic snows;
That igloo, tilt, that lodged an early friend,
Was his to hearten still, to nourish, fend.

I knew him best in his retirement,
When at his leisure, quiet and content,
He voiced his views in whimsical dissent,
Or gave his thoughtfulness a healthy vent
On government, and how the funds were spent;
Appraised the dollar, told how far it went;
Compared our manners, attitudes and ways
Of recent times, with those of other days.

He liked oldtimers yarns, their quiet fun,
Droll wit; indeed a glass of honest rum;
Enjoyed good company, fine books, a pipe,
The gun at autumn 'mongst the partridge, snipe.
The scent of turf in spring, of spruce and pine,
Would gladden him. To song he could incline;
But native birds, the singing reel and line
Sufficed as music, in the summertime.
As one who would indeed again assure
Himself of lands far off; lost scenes restore,
Or look on lov'liness a moment more;
He sailed on seasons to the Labrador.

Of one room favoured, he adorned all sides
With portraits, snaps enlarged, of ancient guides
Interpreters in trade, the Esquimaux
And livyers settled 'long the Labrador,
All clad in robes appropriate, yet borne
Indiff'rently to weather, cold or warm.
About his place, in caches here and there,
Were narwhale tusks and other iv'ry gear,

Kyak and Esquimaux with lifted spear,
Expectant, patient for the seal to rear;
The Komatik, hitched huskies in delight
Restrained, hightailed, from eager headlong flight.

The ships in sail and steam, that spanned the scene
Of venturing, now moored, as he, to dream.
Were pictured here: Ungava, Nascopie,
Old Pelican and square rigged Harmony,
The sev'ral Forts and others yet of name
To rouse a man to derring-do and fame.
As though, he would, their spirits to abide,
And share with him indeed, his eventide,
He kept old snaps, and photographs, beside,
Of those who wrought with him. As soon decide
As she, who loves, the cause against her child,
Could he 'gainst those, who fared with him the wild.

His hand was generous; yet to suffice,
Occasion'ly when asked, he gave advice,
As sound as brief, than fractiously withal,
Assessed its worth, of no account at all.
He was my father's and my mother's son,
To whom, their wishes were as writs that run
In might and majesty of Kings. He fought
For tenets, they in their own lifetime wrought;
And when they passed from earth, he yet sustained
The kindliness, they through their lives maintained.
He kept his faith, though all sorts knew his aid,
And lived in charity and unafraid.

To speak of his achievements, I refrain.
His way of life alone, I but maintain,
And you my masters will not hold me rude,
If I, in circumstance of love, conclude:
He loved his friends, deserved of them their trust,
And feared his God, and was in mercy just.

Appendix 17
Key Man in the Fur Trade*
Archibald Lang Fleming

Archibald Lang Fleming (1883-1953), a native of Scotland, served in the Arctic as an Anglican priest and bishop. Consecrated bishop in St. John's Cathedral, Winnipeg, December 21, 1933, he was the first Anglican bishop of the Arctic and became known as Archibald the Arctic. His autobiography was published posthumously in 1956. Ralph Parsons and Fleming knew each other well.

Of all the men whom I have met in Arctic Canada, the most outstanding personality is Mr. Ralph Parsons, Fur Trade Commissioner of the Hudson's Bay Company.

He began life as a school teacher, but gave that up to enter the service of the Hudson's Bay Company as an apprenticed fur-trader.

For some years he worked at a little trading post on the Labrador coast, sitting at the very desk where the great Donald Smith, afterwards Lord Strathcona, worked in his day.

Truly the mantle of Strathcona fell upon his successor, for step by step, through hard persistent work and sheer ability, Ralph Parsons rose until now he is the key man in the fur trade in Canada.

A man of few words, inclined to avoid the society of other men, he has the reputation of being an extraordinarily keen trader. But that is only part of the story. Mr. Parsons has a tremendous understanding of human nature and knows exactly how to deal with men.

He can be hard when he feels that to be the right line of action and, unless I judge him wrongly, he desires that the world at large shall think of him along these lines. But underneath that hard exterior there is a heart as tender as a woman's and, while he is a fierce enemy, he is a loyal, devoted and generous friend.

And he has this to his credit-that he is often most generous to those who have deliberately opposed him and have been beaten.

---

* From "People I meet in the Arctic," *The Evening News and Evening Mail*, London, England, April 14, 1939; also reprinted in *The Daily News*, St. John's, Newfoundland, May 16, 1939.

Appendix 18
Ralph Parsons was no Ordinary Man*
A. Dudley Copland

Alfred Dudley Copland (1902-1993) was born in Peterhead, Scotland. He joined the Hudson's Bay Company in 1923 and served with the Company until 1939. In 1936 he was appointed as Manager of the Western Arctic District. In 1939 he joined the R.C.A.F. and in 1945 was named a Member of the British Empire (M.B.E.)-Military Division. He spent his retirement years in Ottawa.

Chief Factor Ralph Parsons was no ordinary man. He was a natural leader, a man of vast arctic experience. When he opened the trading post at Wolstenholme in 1909, it was two years before any Inuit appeared to trade. When he had at length convinced the London office that the arctic trade was worth developing, he rapidly organized and expanded his 'kingdom' until the Company was trading with every group of Inuit throughout the Eastern Arctic.

Each of the tiny arctic settlements was a memorial to his vision, for each area had been carefully studied and the location of the post decided upon, so that the maximum amount of produce might be obtained from the hunters. We bought furs, walrus hides and ivory, sealskins, whale and seal oil, salmon and trout, and even mica and garnet crystals.

As we met in conference at Chesterfield Inlet, Ralph Parsons was again reaching out towards the Western Arctic and south to Churchill. Eskimo Point was to be brought into his sprawling St. Lawrence-Labrador District and this he told me, was to be my charge. It was the biggest fur-producing area on the west side of the Bay. It would keep me busy.

---

* A. Dudley Copland, *Coplalook*. (Watson and Dwyer Publishing Ltd., Winnipeg), 1985. Second Edition, 1989. Page, 83.

Fur Trade Commissioner, Ralph Parsons, with Hudson's Bay Company Governor, Patrick Ashley Cooper, in Winnipeg, Manitoba, 1939.

SELECT BIBLIOGRAPHY

GENERAL

Anderson, James Watt. *Fur Trader's Story*. Toronto, Ontario: Ryerson Press, 1961.

Bachrach, Max. *Fur: A Practical Treatise*. London: Prentice-Hall, 1936.

Baker, Peter. *Memoirs of An Arctic Arab: The Story of a Free-trader in Northern Canada*. Yellowknife: Yellowknife Publishing, 1976.

Balickci, Asen. *The Netsilik Eskimo*. Garden City, New York: The Natural History Press, 1970.

Barker, Bertram. *North of '53*. London: Methuen, 1934.

Barr, William. "On to the Bay." *The Beaver*, Autumn 1985.

Bay News, The. April 1961.

Bay Roberts Family Records. Provincial Archives of Newfoundland and Labrador. St. John's, Newfoundland.

Berchem, F.W. "Last Voyage of the *Bayeskimo*." *The Beaver*, August-September 1988.

Binney, George. *The Eskimo Book of Knowledge*. Winnipeg, Manitoba: Hudson's Bay Company, 1931.

Bliss, Michael. *Northern Enterprise: Five Centuries of Canadian Business*. Toronto, Ontario: McClelland and Stewart, 1987.

Bradbury, Cecil E. *Ten Years in the High Canadian Arctic*. St. John's, Newfoundland: RB Books, 1994.

Brown, Richard. *Voyage of the Iceberg*. Toronto, Ontario: James Lorimer, 1983.

Bruemmer, Fred. *Seasons of the Eskimo: A Vanishing Way of Life*. Toronto, Ontario: McClelland and Stewart, 1978 [1971].

Budgel, Richard and Michael Staveley. *The Labrador Boundary*. Happy Valley-Goose Bay, Labrador: Labrador Institute of Northern Studies, Memorial University of Newfoundland, 1987.

"Business of Retirement, The." Undated newspaper (unnamed) clipping in Ralph Parsons' "Pension 1930-1940" file.

Canadian coin catalogues of modern vintage.

Canadian Committee Annual Report for year ending January 31, 1940, dated February 23, 1940.

Certificate of Rejection from the Royal Newfoundland Regiment (Ralph Parsons), November 16, 1916.

Certificate Presented to Flora M. House by the Girls Friendly Society, October 30, 1918.

Chesshire, Robert H. Retirement speech. *Moccasin Telegraph*, Fall 1962.

Church Records, St. John the Evangelist Church, Coley's Point; St. Matthew's Church, Bay Roberts; Anglican Cathedral, St. John's, Newfoundland.

Cobb, W.J. "Interesting Years With the HBC." *Moccasin Telegraph*, Winter 1970.

Copland, A. Dudley. *Coplalook*. Winnipeg, Manitoba: Watson and Dwyer Publishing, 1985.

―――――. "Harvesting the Northern Seas." *The Beaver*, Winter 1974.

―――――. *Livingstone of the Arctic*. Lancaster, Ontario: Canadian Century Publishers, 1967.

Dafoe, Christopher. "Remembering a Man of the North: W.E. (Buster) Brown (1900-89)." *The Beaver*, August-September 1989.

Death and funeral notice (Ralph Parsons). *The Evening Telegram*, November 26, 1956.

Department of State press release #167, April 10, 1941.

Douglas, W.O. "Establishing HBC Baker Lake, N.W. T. Summer, 1925." *Moccasin Telegraph*, Winter 1970.

Draft of Ralph Parsons' statement to Archibald L. Fleming, April 16, 1940.

Family Bible Record (Parsons family).

Ferguson, Chick. *Mink, Mary and Me*. New York: M.S. Mill, 1946.

Finnie, Richard. *Canada Moves North*. New York: Macmillan, 1942.

―――――. "Farewell Voyages Bernier and the 'Arctic.'" *The Beaver*, Summer 1974.

―――――. "Trading into the North-West Passage." *The Beaver*, December 1937.

Fleming, Archibald L. *Archibald the Arctic*. New York: Appleton-Century-Crofts, 1956, and Toronto: Saunders of Toronto Ltd., 1957.

―――――. "People I Meet in the Arctic." *The Evening News and Evening Mail* (London, England), April 14, 1939.

―――――. *Perils of the Polar Pack*. Toronto, Ontario: 1932.

Foster, John E., ed. *The Developing West: Essays in Canadian History in Honor of Lewis H. Thomas*. Edmonton, Alberta: University of Alberta Press, 1983.

Fraser, James. Certificate of Character (Ralph Parsons), dated December 29, 1900.

Garriock, A.C. *The Far and Furry North*. Winnipeg, Manitoba: Douglas-McIntyre, 1925.

Gingras, Larry. "Medals and Tokens of the HBC." *The Beaver*, 1968.

Godsell, Philip H. *Arctic Trader: The Account of Twenty Years with the HBC*. Toronto, Ontario: Macmillan of Canada, 1943 [1932].

―――――. *Red Hunters of the Snow*. Toronto, Ontario: Ryerson, 1938.

―――――. *The Vanishing Frontier*. Toronto, Ontario: Ryerson, 1939.

Goodyear, Cyril. "Nunatsuak: Arctic sovereignty." *The Evening Telegram*, October 3, 1987.

Gordon, Henry. *The Labrador Parson*. Ed., F. Burnham Gill. St. John's, Newfoundland: Provincial Archives of Newfoundland and Labrador, 1972.

―――――. *A Winter in Labrador 1918-1919*.

Grenfell, Wilfred T. In *Among the Deep-Sea Fishers*. XXVI:2, July 1928.

———. "New Developments in Labrador." *Among the Deep-Sea Fishers.* XXV:2, July 1927.

Hambling, Jack. *The Second Time Around: Growing Up in Bay Roberts.* St. John's, Newfoundland: Harry Cuff Publications Ltd., 1992.

———. *Stage Heads and Warm Dandelions.* St. John's, Newfoundland: Harry Cuff Publications Ltd., 1985.

Harrington, Michael. "Captain's daughter remembers." *The Evening Telegram,* August 14, 1993.

———. "Correspondents help fill blanks." *The Evening Telegram,* September 25, 1993.

———. "Offbeat History: The last of the Factors." *The Evening Telegram,* January 29, 1990.

———. "Offbeat History: The last of the Factors: memories of the early days." *The Evening Telegram,* March 4, 1991.

Hibbs, R., ed. *Who's Who in and From Newfoundland 1927.* St. John's, Newfoundland: R. Hibbs, 1927.

"History: Bay Roberts." *Decks Awash.* XX:1, January-February 1991.

Holmes, Douglas. *Northerners: Profiles of People in the Northwest Territories.* Toronto, Ontario: James Lorimer and Co., 1989.

Houston, James. *White Dawn.* Toronto, Ontario: Longmans, 1971.

Hudson's Bay Company, A Brief History. Winnipeg, Manitoba: Hudson's Bay Company, 1934.

Hunter, Archie. *Northern Traders: Caribou Hair in the Stew.* Victoria, British Columbia: Sono Nis Press, 1983.

Innis, Harold Adams. *The Fur Trade in Canada.* Toronto, Ontario: University of Toronto Press, 1970 [1952].

Journal notes (George W. Parsons), November 26, 1956.

Keighley, Sydney Augustus. *Trader, Tripper, Trapper: The Life of a Bay Man.* Winnipeg, Manitoba: Watson and Dwyer Publishing Co. Ltd., 1989.

"Last Fur Trade Commissioner, The." *Moccasin Telegraph.* XVI:1, Break-Up 1957.

Learmonth, L.A. "Sea Gulls and Flag Poles." *Moccasin Telegraph,* Winter 1970.

LeBourdais, D.M. "North West River." *The Beaver,* Spring 1963.

Lyall, Ernie. *An Arctic Man.* Halifax, Nova Scotia: Formac Publishing Co. Ltd., 1983.

Macaulay, R.H.H. *Trading into Hudson's Bay: A narrative of the visit of Patrick Ashley Cooper, Thirtieth Governor of The Hudson's Bay Company, to Labrador, Hudson Strait and Hudson Bay in the Year 1934.* Winnipeg, Manitoba: The Hudson's Bay Company, 1934.

Mack, G. Edmund. "Breaking the Ice for the Allies." *The Beaver,* December 1938.

MacKay, Douglas. *The Honourable Company: A History of the Hudson's Bay Company.* Toronto, Ontario: McClelland and Stewart Ltd., 1966 [1936].

Madden, Dermod C. "Cartwright." In *Encyclopedia of Newfoundland and Labrador*. Volume I, 1981.

Memorandum regarding the American Greenland Commission, June 14, 1942.

Mercer, Frank G. "Be Proud of William Ralph Parsons." Letter to the Editor, *The Evening Telegram*, March 21, 1991.

———. "W. Ralph Parsons (1881-1956): The Last Fur Trade Commissioner of the Hudson's Bay Company." Unpublished article. Synopsis published in *The Compass*, November 9, 1993.

Montague, John, with Isaac Rich. "Fur Traders." In *Them Days*, 1973.

Morrison, William R. *Showing the Flag: The Mounted Police and Canadian Sovereignty in the North 1894-1925*. Vancouver, British Columbia: University of British Columbia Press, 1985.

Morton, W.L. "Donald A. Smith and Governor George Simpson." *The Beaver*, Autumn 1978.

Mowat, Farley. *People of the Deer*. Toronto, Ontario: McClelland and Stewart, 1952.

———. *Tundra*. Toronto, Ontario: McClelland and Stewart, 1973.

Munn, Henry Toke. *Prairie Trails and Arctic By-Ways*. London, England: Hurst and Blackett, Ltd., 1932.

Neatby, H. "Exploration and History of the Canadian Arctic." In *Handbook of the North American Indians*. Volume V, *Arctic*. Washington, D.C.: Smithsonian Institution, 1978.

Newman, Peter C. *Merchant Princes*. Toronto, Ontario: Viking, 1991.

Nichols, P.A.C. "Enter...the Fur Traders." *The Beaver*, Winter 1954.

Obituary File, Hudson's Bay Company personnel, Hudson's Bay Company Archives, Winnipeg, Manitoba.

Oleson, Robert. "The Past Hundred Years." *The Beaver*, Spring 1970.

Outfit Reports 1921-29. Hudson's Bay Company Archives, Winnipeg, Manitoba.

Parsons, David R. Diary 1930. Ralph Parsons' Personal Papers.

Parsons, John. "Huntsman." *Encyclopedia of Newfoundland and Labrador*, Volume III, 1991.

———. *Labrador: Land of the North*. New York: Vantage Press, 1970.

———. "Parsons, William Ralph (1881-1956)." *Encyclopedia of Newfoundland and Labrador*, Volume IV, 1993.

———. "Tigress." *Encyclopedia of Newfoundland and Labrador*. Volume V, 1994.

Parsons, Linda A. "Dr. Arthur Barnes." *Encyclopedia of Newfoundland and Labrador*. Volume I, 1981.

Parsons, R.A. *Curtain Call*. Eds., Harry A. Cuff and Daphne Benson. St. John's, Newfoundland: Harry A. Cuff, 1980.

———. *Reflections*. Toronto, Ontario: The Ryerson Press, 1954.

———————. *The Tale of a Lonesome House*. Don Mills, Ontario: The Ontario Publishing Co. Ltd., 1971.

Parsons, Ralph. "Annual Report—St. Lawrence-Labrador District—Outfit 258." 1928-29.

———————. Article written for the Canadian Press. In Rene Fumoleau, *As Long As This Land Shall Last: A History of Treaty 8 and Treaty 11—1870-1939*. Toronto, Ontario: McClelland and Stewart Ltd., 1973.

———————. "Extracts from Diary of Ralph Parsons on Inspection Trip of Hudson Strait Posts per *Daryl*—Season 1917."

———————. "Farewell Speech," July 7, 1940. Ralph Parsons personal papers.

———————. "Journal. Ralph Parsons, 1917." Ralph Parsons personal papers.

———————. "Wolstenholme Post Journal 1909-1910." Ralph Parsons personal papers.

Phillips, R.A.J. *Canada's North*. Toronto, Ontario: Macmillan of Canada, 1967.

Price, Ray. *The Howling Arctic. The Remarkable People Who Made Canada Sovereign in the Farthest North*. Toronto, Ontario: Peter Martin Associates, 1970.

Ray, Arthur J. *The Canadian Fur Trade in the Industrial Age*. Toronto, Ontario: University of Toronto Press, 1990.

———————. *Indians in the Fur Trade*. Toronto, Ontario: University of Toronto Press, 1974.

Roach, Thomas R. "The Saga of Northern Radio." *The Beaver*, Summer 1984.

Robertson, Heather. *A Gentleman Adventurer: The Arctic Diaries of Richard Bonnycastle*. Toronto, Ontario: Lester and Orpen Dennys Ltd., 1984.

Ross, Hugh Mackay. *The Apprentice's Tale*. Winnipeg, Manitoba: Watson and Dwyer Publishing, 1986.

———————. *The Manager's Tale*. Winnipeg, Manitoba: Watson and Dwyer Publishing, 1989.

Rowe, Frederick W. *A History of Newfoundland and Labrador*. Toronto, Ontario: McGraw-Hill Ryerson Ltd., 1980.

Rowland, John T. *North to Baffin Land*. New York: Seven Seas Press, 1973.

Russell, Chesley. "The Devon Island Post." *The Beaver*, Spring 1978.

Ryan, Frank. "Forty Years on the Fur Trail." *The Beaver*, June 1940 (Outfit 271).

Seary, E.R. with Sheila M.P. Lynch. *Family Names of the Island of Newfoundland*. St. John's, Newfoundland: Memorial University of Newfoundland, 1977.

Smith, Shirlee Anne. "A Desire to Worry Me Out." *The Beaver*, December 1987.

Stevenson, Alex. "Arctic Fur Trade Rivalry." *The Beaver*, Autumn 1975.

Tetso, John. *Trapping Is My Life*. Toronto, Ontario: Peter Martin Associates, 1970.

Them Days. XIX:3, April 1994.

Tolboom, Wanda Neill. "Arctic Bride." *The Beaver*, Spring 1957.

"To the Arctic." *The Beaver*, March 1933.

Tranter, G.J. *Link to the North*. London, England: Hodder and Stoughton, 1946.

Usher, Peter J. *Fur Trade Posts of the N.W.T. 1870-1970*. Ottawa, Ontario: Department of Indian Affairs and Northern Development, 1971.

———. "The Growth and Decay of the Trading and Trapping Frontiers in the Western Canada Arctic." *Canadian Geographer*. Vol. 19, no. 4, 1967.

Vokey, Edward Harvey. "A Tribute to Ralph Parsons." *The Daily News*, December 7, 1956.

Watson, George. "Presentation Address Delivered to Mr. Ralph Parsons On Behalf of the Men of the North." Ralph Parsons' Personal Papers.

"Watson, M.D." "Who's Who in Hudson's Bay House: Ralph Parsons." *The House Detective*. II:1, June 1940. Reprinted in *Newfoundland Quarterly*. LXXXVIII:3, April 1994.

Whalley, George. *The Legend of John Hornby*. Toronto, Ontario: Macmillan, 1923.

Wheeler, Robert C. *A Toast to the Fur Trade*. 1985.

Wild, Roland. *Arctic Command: The Story of Smellie of the Nascopie*. Toronto, Ontario: Ryerson Press, 1955.

Willson, Beckles. *The Life of Lord Strathcona and Mount Royal, G.C.M.G., G.C.V.O., (1820-1914)*. London, England: Cassell, 1915.

Wilson, Keith. *Fur Trade in Canada*. Toronto, Ontario: Grolier Ltd., 1980.

"With All Good Wishes." *The House Detective*. II:1, June 1940.

Wonders, William C., ed. *Canada's Changing North*. Toronto, Ontario: McClelland and Stewart, 1971.

Zaslow, Morris, ed. *A Century of Canada's Arctic Issues, 1880-1980*. Ottawa, Ontario: Royal Society of Canada, 1981.

———. *The Northward Expansion of Canada, 1914-1967*. Canadian Centenary Series, no. 17. Toronto, Ontario: McClelland and Stewart, 1988.

INTERVIEWS (all interviewed by John Parsons)

Bradbury, Llewellyn. February 22, 1995.

Budgell, Len. October 13, 1993.

Butler, Isaac. March 13, 1995.

Chesshire, Robert H. January 9, 1995.

Dawe, Eric N. March 13, 1995.

Fowlow, Guy. March 23, 1994; April 17, 1996.

Hambling, Jack. February 22, 1995; March 18, 1995.

Mercer, Frank G. March 18, 1995.

Morgan, Newton. March 23, 1995.

Parsons, David R. October 13, 1993; March 22, 1995.

Parsons, James Y. May 9, 1995.

Parsons, Jessie. October 22, 1993. Family Archives.

Rusted, Nigel. June 20, 1994.

LETTERS, MESSAGES, MEMOS, TELEGRAMS

Brooks, J. Chadwick, Secretary, on behalf of the Governor and Committee (Board), London, to Canadian Committee, February 20, 1940.

Budgell, Len to John Parsons, November 8, 1993; November 27, 1994; December 13, 1994; undated letter.

Chesshire, Robert H. to John Parsons, January 21, 1995; May 25, 1995.

Chester, Philip A. to David R. Parsons, December 6, 1956; January 16, 1957; October 9, 1958.

Coates, Len to John Parsons, June 9, 1995.

Edwards, W. Stuart to Charles V. Sale, October 9, 1926.

Fleming, Archibald L. to Ralph Parsons, March 8, 1940; May 15, 1940.

Flowers, Augustus H. to John Parsons, June 8, 1995.

Gannon, Dorothy to Ralph Parsons, July 10, 1940. Ralph Parsons' Personal Papers.

Gibson, R.A. to Ralph Parsons, August 17, 1940. Ralph Parsons' Personal Papers.

Goodyear, Cyril to John Parsons, January 21, 1995; May 24, 1995.

Horwood, Harold to John Parsons, November 1, 1993.

House, Arthur to Nathan House, October 21, 1926. Ralph Parsons' personal papers.

Ingrams, Elwyn to Ralph Parsons, November 23, 1939. Ralph Parsons' personal papers.

Kauffmann, Henrik de to Ralph Parsons, September 11, 1940; September 18, 1941.

Lindley, Tom to John Parsons, June 29, 1995.

Lindley, T.D. to Robert H. Chesshire (message), October 22, 1956.

Morton, Anne to John Parsons, February 17, 1995; January 22, 1996.

Mowat, Farley to John Parsons, December 10, 1993.

Newman, Peter C. to John Parsons, January 19, 1995; February 6, 1995.

Nichols, Peter to John Parsons, October 26, 1993.

Parsons, David R. to John Parsons and Burton K. Janes, April 20, 1994; September 26, 1994; June 3, 1995.

Parsons, David R. to John Parsons, November 19, 1994; February 10, 1995.

Parsons, David R. to Robert H. Chesshire, September 22, 1956; December 3, 1956.

Parsons, David R. to Robert H. Chesshire (message), September 6, 1956; November 24, 1956.

Parsons, David R. to Philip A. Chester, December 6, 1956.

Parsons, Flora May to Ralph Parsons, July 10, 1920.

Parsons, Flora May to Ralph Parsons (telegram), July 13, 1920; July 14, 1920.

Parsons, Hayward to Robert H. Chesshire, October 26, 1956; December 17, 1956.

Parsons, Rachel F. to Robert H. Chesshire, October 13, 1956.

Parsons, Ralph to Archibald L. Fleming, April 2, 1940; April 3, 1940; May 10, 1940; May 29, 1940. Ralph Parsons' personal papers.
Parsons, Ralph to Datie Parsons, November 16, 1920; April 2, 1929.
Parsons, Ralph to David Wark, May 16, 1927.
Parsons, Ralph to Elwyn Ingrams, May 29, 1940.
Parsons, Ralph to George Watson, May 29, 1940.
Parsons, Ralph to Gilbert E. Jackson, February 6, 1941.
Parsons, Ralph to Hans Christian Sonne, October 8, 1940; October 12, 1940; February 6, 1941.
Parsons, Ralph to H.L. Keenleyside, August 27, 1940.
Parsons, Ralph to Hudson's Bay Company, November 7, 1922.
Parsons, Ralph to Michael R. Lubbock, March 13, 1939; February 26, 1940.
Parsons, Ralph to Mrs. Blackmore, December 6, 1939. Quoted in Heluiz Chandler Washburne and Anauta. *Land of the Good Shadows: The Life Story of Anauta, an Eskimo Woman.* New York: The John Day Co., 1940.
Parsons, Ralph to Patrick Ashley Cooper, December 7, 1943.
Parsons, Ralph to P.E.H. Sewell, February 7, 1940.
Parsons, Ralph to Philip A. Chester, June 4, 1940; August 27, 1940; March 18, 1942; September 8, 1942; March 29, 1944; July 7, 1956.
Parsons, Ralph to S.J. Stewart and Lorenzo A. Learmonth, October 19, 1926.
Pinkston, George D. to John Parsons, July 25, 1995.
Plaxton, C.P. to Ralph Parsons, November 2, 1922; November 21, 1922; November 28, 1922.
Ploughman, Reuben to John Parsons, February 11, 1994.
Riley, C.S. to Ralph Parsons, January 17, 1941.
Roberts, Will to Ralph Parsons (telegram), July 14, 1920; July 15, 1920.
Sale, Charles V. to S.J. Stewart and L.A. Learmonth, October 19, 1926.
Sale, Charles V. to W. Stuart Edwards, October 11, 1926; October 12, 1926.
Sonne, Hans Christian to Hendrik de Kauffmann, September 9, 1941.
Stewart, S.J. to Ralph Parsons, May 13, 1927.
Watson, George to Ralph Parsons, May 16, 1940.
Wood, S.T. to Ralph Parsons, July 5, 1940.

MINUTES

Minutes of American Greenland Commission, May 24, 1940.
Minutes of Canadian Committee, Winnipeg, Manitoba, December 23, 1937; April 13, 1939; May 25, 1939; December 3, 1942; December 6, 1956.

GOVERNMENT OF CANADA PUBLICATIONS

Dominion Bureau of Statistics, Agricultural Division, *Fur Production of Canada, Annual Reports*. Ottawa 1926-48.

──────. General Statistics Branch, *Recent Economic Tendencies in Canada, 1919-34*. Ottawa 1935

──────. National Accounts and Balances Division, Industry Outport Section, *Indexes of Real Domestic Production by Industry of Origin, 1935-61*. Ottawa 1963.

CONTEMPORARY NEWSPAPERS AND PERIODICALS

British Fur Trade Journal (London), 1923-57.
British Fur Trade Review (London), 1924-33.
Fur Trade Review (New York), 1919-39.
The Northern Fur Trade, 1927.

HUDSON'S BAY COMPANY ARCHIVES, PROVINCIAL ARCHIVES OF MANITOBA

Record Class A. London Headquarters Records:
RG 93 Confidential Files:
Brown, W.E. "Hudson's Bay Company Transportation Including Consideration of Aeroplane Transport." Presented at 1934 Fur Trade Conference, RG 93/43
RG 102, London Secretary's Dossiers:
Accounts Department, 1931-57, RG 102/1-7
Fur Trade Conferences, 1931-37 (see also RG 2 FTC), RG 102/Box 86
Fur Trade Conference Papers, RG 102/Box 86
Personnel Records, Fur Trade Organization, 1936-48, RG 102/Box 86
Fur Trade Organization, 1936-48, RG 104/Boxes 4-86
P.A. Chester's Correspondence and Private Files, 1930-70, RG 2/11/
Record Group 3: Fur Trade Department Files 1912-1942
Library: Hudson's Bay Company Archives
Personnel Files:
    Allan, George W.
    Chesshire, Robert H.
    Chester, Philip A.

OTHER

Bovey, J.A., *The Attitudes and Policies of the Federal Government Towards Canada's Northern Territories 1870-1930*. M.A. Thesis, University of British Columbia, Vancouver, 1967.

Harris, Lynda. "Revillon Freres Trading Company Limited: Fur Traders of the North, 1901-1936." Volume I, Historical Planning and Research Branch, Ministry of Culture and Recreation, Province of Ontario, Toronto 1976.

Tough, Frank. *Native People and the Regional Economy of Northern Manitoba: 1870-1930s*. Ph.D. Dissertation, Geography Department, York University, Toronto, 1987.

BIBLIOGRAPHICAL NOTES

(1.) Most correspondence to Ralph Parsons and from Ralph Parsons cited herein can be found in Ralph Parsons' personal papers, presently in the possession of David R. Parsons, of Hantsport, Nova Scotia.

(2.) An extensive correspondence file for Ralph Parsons can also be found in the National Archives of Canada, Ottawa, Ontario.

(3) All other letters, notes, memorandums, telegrams, messages, references to Canadian Committee Annual Reports and all other documentation relating to Ralph Parsons and his work with the Hudson's Bay Company, including material relating to his death and estate which is cited in the Notes following each chapter and the Prologue and the Epilogue, can be found in Ralph Parsons' Personnel Files RG2/37/161 and RG2/37/162, Hudson's Bay Company Archives, Winnipeg, Manitoba. The period covered in these files is 1907-1956 inclusive.

INDEX

A
Allan, George W., 2, 3, 5, 107, 108, 112-127, 178
Amadjuak, 71
American Greenland Commission, 142-145
Amesso, 30
Amundsen, Roald, 84
Anauta (Mrs. William R. Ford/Mrs. Blackmore), 181
Anderson, J.W., 181
Andrews Fisheries, 137
Archer, Winifred, 157
Archibald the Arctic, 79, 166
Arctic Man, An, 71

B
Bacon, Norman, 1
Badcock, William, 14
Baffin Island, 15, 40, 101, 131, 138, 180
Baffin Land, 49
Baker Lake, 74
Barnes, Arthur, 18, 23, 164, 165, 177
Barnes, Caroline W., 58
Bartlett, Robert A., 142
Battle Harbour, 8
Bay Roberts, 1, 7, 8, 9, 18, 20, 21, 57, 65-67, 86, 97, 131, 136, 141, 149-154, 163-173, 175-181
Bayeskimo, 72
Bay News, 179
Bayrupert, 75
Beachy Cove, 163
Beale, L.T., 142
Bellot Strait, 132
Bentzen, Paul, 142
Bersimis, 50
"Billy London", 10
Bishop, E.M., 14, 15
Blackhall, J.S., 97
Blackhead, 18
Blackmore, S., 181
Bowering, E. and J., 8
Bradbury, Cecil E., 73, 84
Bradbury, Llewellyn, 176
Bradbury, Stephen, 74
Brigus, 20, 180
British Columbia, 132
Brown, Richard, 43-44
Budgell, George, 12
Budgell, Len, 5, 6, 178
Burgeo, 137
Butler, Isaac, 164-167
Butlerville, 10, 15, 150, 165
Butt, Charles, 21
Butt, George, 66
Butt, Ralph, 20
Butt, Winnifred, 17
Button Islands, 99

C
Canada, 131, 153, 155
Canadian Advisory Committee, 111
Canadian Committee, 1, 4, 5, 88, 107, 117-119, 123-126, 135, 140, 145, 170, 172
Canalaska Trading Company, 138
Canso, Nova Scotia, 19
Cantley, James, 77, 155
Cape Chidley, 52, 99
Cape Dorset, 40, 50, 52-54
Cape Fullerton, 45-46
Cape Haven, 44, 45
Cape Smith, 50, 71
Cape St. Charles, 8
Cartwright, 1, 24, 27, 28, 40, 58, 84, 97, 99, 137, 146, 176
Cartwright, George, 97
Cave, Wilson, 155-160, 170, 171, 178
Charlton Island, 103
Chesshire, Robert H., 2, 6, 113, 114, 119, 131, 150, 155-160, 170-172, 178
Chester, Philip A., 2, 3, 4, 5, 107, 108, 112-127, 129, 132, 140-143, 145, 146, 154, 157, 158, 169-172, 178
Chesterfield Inlet, 72, 74
Churchill, Isaac, 177
Churchill, Manitoba, 82, 93
Clarke Companies, 81
Clench, Carrie, 17, 87
Clench, Enid, M.D., 173
Clench, Evelyn, 17, 58
Clyde River, 70, 71
Coley's Point, 8, 10, 11, 176
Conception Bay, 7, 163, 175, 180
Connon, Captain, 44, 48
Coplalook, 74
Copland, A. Dudley, 33, 50, 69, 71, 72, 74, 76, 82, 83, 99, 119, 132, 140, 178, 181
Copley, Thomas, 10
Cooper, Kathleen S., 104, 108
Cooper, Patrick Ashley, 93, 104, 107-114, 119, 123-126, 131, 145, 167, 179
Coral Harbour, 72
Country Road, 8, 10
Crossman, Harriet, 66
Cuff, Harry A., 20
Curtis, Leslie R., 173

D
Daily News, 166, 167
Dartmouth, N.S., 165
Daryl, 45, 46, 47, 51, 52-54, 133, 181
"Davey", 74-77
Davis Strait, 44, 82
Dawe, Azariah, 8
Dawe, C. and A., 8
Dawe, Donald W.K., 173
Dawe, Eric N., 177
Dawe, Henry, 10
Dawe, James (Jimmy) Captain, 99, 178
Dawe, Robert, 23
Dawe, Victor, 11
Dawson, Tom, 97
Deed of Surrender, 78
de Kauffmann, Henrik, 144-146
Denmark, 144
Dickers, William, 30, 31, 32
Doe, Alfred H., 129
Drover, Howard, 156
Dyke, A.P., 27
Dyneley, John, 142

E

Eastern Arctic District, 39, 88
Edwards, W. Stuart, 76
English, Bob, 45-48
Eskimo Point, 74
Erik Cove, 30-33, 43, 45-48, 51
Evening Telegram, 5, 180

F

Fleming, Archibald L., 28, 44, 48, 52, 79, 86, 130-134, 138-141, 166-168, 178
Fogo, 181
Ford (Anauta, Mrs. William R. Ford), 181
Ford, George, 46, 181
Ford, Harry, 99
Ford, John, Sr., 30
Ford, William, R., 181
Forsyth-Grant, O.C., 43, 44, 45, 47, 48, 51
Fort Amadjuak, 75, 76, 126, 135-138, 146, 164, 176, 179
Fort Chesterfield, 82
Fort Chimo, 53, 73
Fort Churchill, 103
Fort Garry, 82, 99, 101
Fort Garry Hotel, 132
Fort James, 84
Fort McKenzie, 53
Fort Rigolet, 82
Fort Ross, 132
Fowlow, Guy, 164-167
Fraser, James, 24, 27, 28
French, Annie, 66
French, Charles H., 1, 113
French, Rachel, 9
French's Cove, 9
Frenchman's Island, 70
Frobisher Bay, 50, 51

G

Gannon, Dorothy, 140
Gibson, R.A., 142
Goodyear, Cyril, 44, 180
Gordon, Henry, 19
Gourley, R.J., 116
Grace Hospital, 152, 154, 160
Grady, 53
Grassy Pond, 9
Great Depression, 88, 132

Greenland, 142-145
Grenfell Mission, 45
Grenfell, Wilfred T., 13, 71, 79
Groswater Bay, 27
Gulf of St. Lawrence, 50, 53, 81, 93

H

Halifax, 99, 151
Hambling, Floss, 149, 153, 165, 179
Hambling, Jack, 16, 17, 52, 141, 151, 164, 176, 178
Hambling, John, Sr., 149, 150, 153, 164, 167, 177, 179
Hantsport, N.S., 18, 169-170
Harrington, Michael, 5, 180
Heart's Content, 164
Hebron, 145
Holy Redeemer Anglican Church, 58
Hopedale, 145
Horwood, Harold, 136-138
House, Arthur, 63, 65, 66
House Detective, 129
House, Flora May, 58, 169
House, Mary, 58, 169
House, Peter, 58, 169
Hoyles, F.A., 130
Hudson Bay, 29, 49, 71
Hudson, Henry, 29
Hudson Strait, 29, 43, 44, 50, 52, 102
Hudson's Bay Company, 1-4, 21-24, 27-29, 39, 54, 57-59, 65, 66, 69, 72, 74, 79, 81, 85, 89, 93, 97, 103-109, 111-113, 122-126, 129-146, 150, 153, 155, 161, 163-165, 169-172, 175-181
Hudson's Bay Company Archives, 4, 125
Hudson's Bay House, 122, 127, 132, 135
Hudson's Bay Railway, 81, 82
Hunt, A.B., 97
Hunter, Archie, 178
Huntsman, 8, 14, 177

I

Ingrams, Elwyn, 130
International Grenfell Association, 67

J

Jackson, G.E., 144
James Bay, 49
Job Brothers, 83

K

Kean, William, 58
Keddie, Kate M., 66
Keddie, Philip, 67
Kelligrew, Rebecca, 10
Ketaushuk, 79
Killinek Island, 99, 100
"Kingmeeghock", 49
Kingston, Ontario, 178
King William Island, 84
Ko-Ok-yauk, 79

L

Labrador, 27, 52, 67, 79, 140, 145, 176
Labrador Coast, 7, 48, 119, 130, 131, 135-137
Labrador Fishery, 7
Lake Harbour, 40, 49, 50-53, 76-79, 101
Lake Melville, 27
Lancaster Sound, 126
Land of the Good Shadows, 180
Leach, H.G., 142
Learmonth, Lorenzo, 74, 77
Lindley, T.D., 158
Livie, Fred, 47
Loder, Thomas E., 164
London, 27, 112, 123, 130, 138
London Board, 1, 125, 126, 135
Lord Strathcona, 27
Lubbock, Mike, 95, 138, 178
Lyall, Ernie, 50, 71, 178
Lyall, Hugh, 116, 125
Lyte, Henry F., 167

M

Macaulay, R.H.H., 93, 97, 101, 105, 167
Makkovik, 145
Martin, Francis, 111, 113
Masonic Lodge, 167

McKeand, David L., 93, 132
McPherson, 84
Mecatina, Quebec, 45
Memorial University of Newfoundland, 21
Mercer, Frank G., 11, 16, 22, 40, 176
Mercer, George, L., 131
Mercer, Henry, 23
Mercer, Samuel A.B., 11
Mercer, Thomas, 9
Mercer, William E., 177
Mercer's Cove, 8
Merchant Princes, 24
Messers Cove, 137
Milne, John, 132
Moccasin Telegraph, 160
Montreal, 27, 29, 35, 53, 60, 62, 67, 80, 127, 130, 132, 181
Moores, Howard, 18, 149
Moores, Winnifred, 178
Moose Factory, 103
Moravian Mission, 80, 145
Mosdell, Harris, 12
Mosdell, Richard, 12
Morton, Anne, 4
Mowat, Farley, 137
Mukke, Mark, 30, 32, 33
Munn, Henry Toke, 53, 66, 78, 105
Murphy, Michael, 97
Murray, Alexander, 125

N
Nain, 145
Nascopie, 71, 86, 93, 96, 99, 101-106, 108, 115, 125, 178
Nelson River District, 85
Newman, Peter C., 24, 104, 108, 112, 114, 119, 181
Newfoundland, 1, 7, 80, 84, 131, 140, 155
Newfoundland and Labrador, 181
New York, 21, 58, 142, 180
Nicholson, F., 99
Norman, Harry, 16
Norman, James, 23
North River, 150
North West River, 27, 28, 146, 176
Northern Trader's Ltd., 138
Northwest Passage, 7, 29, 84

Northwest Territories, 142, 178
Nottingham Island, 44
Nova Scotia, 151, 153
Nova Scotia Technical College, 21, 151
Nutak, 145

O
Oakley, Robert, 173
Oakley, Sybil, 19
Ottawa, 4, 72, 108, 109, 140, 178

P
Paddon, Harry, 97
Palliser, James, 36
Pangnirtung, 70, 71, 180
Paradox, 33
Parsons, Abe, 9
Parsons, David R., 12, 16, 18, 22-24, 67, 136, 141, 152, 156, 160, 164, 169-171
Parsons, Dorcas C., 7, 17, 65
Parsons, Elijah, 97
Parsons, Florence V., 9
Parsons, George W., 13, 165
Parsons, John (1812-1887), 10
Parsons, John (1858-1925), 15
Parsons, John (b. 1939), 164, 165
Parsons, Rachel Fannie ("Miss Datie"), 16, 86, 149, 159, 179
Parsons, Ralph, 1-5, 7, 10, 13-15, 17, 18, 24, 27, 28, 32, 36, 39, 40, 46-48, 54, 57-59, 69, 72-74, 76-81, 83-86, 88, 89, 93, 97, 101, 107-109, 112-127, 129-138, 140-146, 149-161, 163, 165-173, 175-177, 179-181
Parsons, Richard Augustus, 13, 20, 150, 155, 164, 169, 179
Parsons, Samuel (1788-1852), 8
Parsons, Samuel (1897-1976), 10, 136, 164, 176, 179
Parsons, Stephen (1818-1913), 10

Parsons, Stephen Hayward (1885-1965), 19, 97, 149, 150, 159, 164, 172, 179
Parsons, Sybil, 150
Parsons, William, 7, 8, 65
Parsons and Morgan (lawyers), 172
Payne Bay, 70
Payne, J. de B., 172
Peacock, Edward, 125
Pelican, 30, 35, 43, 46, 48, 101
Pendleton, George, 131
Pinkston, George D., 180
Pond Inlet, 21, 70, 71, 180
Pool's Island, Newfoundland, 58, 169
Port Burwell, 52, 53, 71, 99
Port de Grave, 8, 21
Port Harrison, 71, 73, 103
Portland, Maine, 21
Price, Ray, 181
Pudlo, Joseph, 79
Pupik, 75

Q
Quebec, 29, 72, 78, 99, 100
Quidi Vidi Lake, 163

R
Ray, Arthur, 2, 3, 5, 181
Reader's Digest, 154
Revillon Freres, 85, 138
Richards, William, 10
Richardson, J.A., 116
Rigolet, 5, 11, 12, 27, 28, 137, 146, 176
Riley, C.S., 116, 140
Ritz Carlton Hotel, 127
Roberts, Will, 62, 63
Robertson, David, 118
Rompkey, William, 73
Ross, Hugh M., 74, 178
Rowland, John T. ("Pete"), 45-48, 181
Royal Newfoundland Regiment, 52
Royal Canadian Mounted Police (R.C.M.P.), 78, 140
Royal North West Mounted Police (R.N.W.M.P.), 45
Rupert's House, 103
Russell, Chesley, 178
Russell, Rachel, 10

229

Russell, Susannah, 10
Rusted, Nigel, 152, 156, 160
Ryan, Frank, 15, 29, 33, 88, 135

S
Sale, Charles V., 76, 77, 78, 111
Sandwich Bay, 27
Seary, E.R., 8
Second Time Around: Growing Up in Bay Roberts, The, 52, 141
Seduisante, 44-48
Seven Islands, Quebec, 67
Sewell, P.E.H., 130
Shears, W.C., 14, 15
Shearstown, 8, 20, 24
Shelbourne, N.S., 136
Shepherd, Christopher G.T., 181
Shepherd, Sarah Jane, 181
Sidney, British Columbia, 178
Simpson, George, 111
Slade, J.A. Frank, 168
Smallwood, J.R., 20, 154
Smellie, Thomas F., 86, 94, 107, 178
Smith, Donald A., 27, 67
Snow, James, 15
Snowdrop, 44
Somerton, Bessie A., 20
Sonne, Hans Christian, 142-145
Southampton Island, 70
Spaniard's Bay, 17, 58, 166
Spencer, George Henry, 9
Stewart, S.J., 76, 77
Stick, Len, 177
Stirling, Georgina, 168
St. Anthony, 71
St. Augustine, 50
St. Boniface, Manitoba, 5, 178
St. John's, Newfoundland, 5, 20, 53, 59, 83, 84, 99, 141, 149, 167-170, 172, 176, 181
St. Lawrence-Labrador District, 53, 69, 80, 131
St. Lawrence River, 93
St. Mary's Anglican Church (Heart's Content), 164
St. Matthew's Anglican Church (Bay Roberts), 9, 163, 164, 173, 178
St. Peter's Anglican Church (Twillingate), 168
Strait of Belle Isle, 93
Stupart's Bay, 51, 53, 73, 101, 102
Sugluk, 180

T
Taylor, Tom, 103
The Pas, Manitoba, 67
Tigress, 8
Tilton, 10, 17
Toronto, 144
Townsend, Charles, 82
Trading Into Hudson's Bay, 93
Twillingate, 168, 181

U
United States of America, 131, 142
Ungava, 82
Ungava Bay, 99, 100
Ungava District, 48, 52

V
Vancouver, B.C., 178
Veysey, Charles, W., 114, 129
Victoria, B.C., 121, 146
Vokey, E.H., 166, 167
Voyage of the Iceberg, 43

W
Wager Inlet, 82
Wark, David, 76
Watson, George, 130-134, 140, 155
Watt, J.S.G., 130
Western Arctic, 119
Western Canada, 122
Western Union Cable Company, 19, 21, 141
Wild, Roland, 108
Wilson, Arthur, 21
Wilson, James, 67
Winnipeg, Manitoba, 1, 4, 93, 111-115, 118, 119, 126, 127, 130-132, 135, 145-146, 155, 159, 161, 169-172, 178
Winter, James A., 173
Wolstenholme, 48, 71, 73, 96, 102, 180, 181
Women's Patriotic Association, 16
Wood, S.T., 140

ABOUT THE AUTHORS

John Parsons (b. 1939), a native of Shearstown, Conception Bay, taught school in Newfoundland for thirty-two years. A writer and historian with interests in Newfoundland and Labrador history, Arctic studies, military history, and the psychology of religion, he divides his time between St. John's and Shearstown. He is the author of *Labrador: Land of the North* (1970) and the editor of *All the Luck in the World* (1994) by Allan M. Ogilvie. Parsons was the biography consultant for Newfoundland to *The Canadian Encyclopedia* (1988). He did graduate studies at Memorial University of Newfoundland and the Ontario Institute for Studies in Education, and holds a Diploma in Religious Studies from the Anglican General Synod of Canada.

Burton K. Janes (b. 1957) was born in St. John's, Newfoundland. A graduate of Memorial University of Newfoundland (B.A., Religious Studies, 1977; M.A., History, 1991) and Eastern Pentecostal Bible College (1979), he holds ministerial credentials with the Pentecostal Assemblies of Newfoundland. He has written three books and served as Associate Editor of two local religious periodicals, *Good Tidings* and *Reach*. He currently serves as Associate Editor and Book Review Editor of *The Canadian C.S. Lewis Journal* and is owner/operator of EDIT-WRITE, an editing and writing business. He presently resides in Bay Roberts.

"[He] had a way of making the men under him feel that he was not only one whose orders had to be obeyed but also a friend on whom they could rely."
—Archibald L. Fleming

"He loved his friends, deserved of them their trust,
And feared his God, and was in mercy just."
—R.A. Parsons

"And so we think of Ralph Parsons whose memory will always be cherished by his friends and relatives - a great and good man yet withal the soul of humility."
—E.H. Vokey

"[Ralph Parsons'] natural ability and work ethic were twin assets which enabled him to endure in an often inhospitable environment. He never sought an easy life, a fact readily evident from as early as 1909 during the founding of the Wolstenholme post."
—Burton K. Janes

"My father [Ralph Parsons] died in 1956, and although I feel his modesty would not have permitted him to relate many of the incidents included in this biography, I also feel that he would be very pleased...with this...account of his colorful, exciting and fulfilling life."
—David R. Parsons

"[Ralph Parsons] established no less than twenty-eight trading posts on Baffin Island and along the coast of Hudson Bay, every one a lasting memorial to his exceptional vision and determination..."
—Jack Hambling

"Ralph Parsons distinguished himself in the North. In some ways a twentieth century Sir George Simpson, he will always be remembered for opening up the Arctic for the Hudson's Bay Company trade. In addition, the success of his endeavours went a long way towards claiming the northern archipelago for Canada."
—George D. Pinkston

"Ralph was a top man with the Hudson's Bay Company, but he never lost the common touch."
—George W. Parsons

"For many years Mr. Parsons had been the key man in the Arctic for the Hudson's Bay Company."
—Ray Price

"Ralph Parsons was the man responsible for the development of the fur trade with the Eskimos in the Eastern and Central Arctic. He was known at the height of his northern Arctic march as the King of Baffin Land."
—J.W. Anderson